SANTRO

BVR Subbu began his career in Tata Motors where, among other things, he led teams that first conceptualized and then successfully launched the Tata 2213, a truck that metamorphosed the freight industry in India. In 1997, Subbu moved to a freshly minted Hyundai Motor India, joining initially as director, sales and marketing, and later taking on the role of president. Presently, Subbu manages a boutique strategy consulting firm, Beyond Visual Range, advises PE funds and serves on the governing board of the Shriram Institute for Scientific & Industrial Research, New Delhi, as well as various technology and automotive companies.

Praise for *Santro*

'*Santro: The Car That Built a Company* is an insider's take on corporate India, replete with rivalries, conspiracies and corruption.' – *Business Standard*

'Subbu tells the Santro story with great panache… [and] makes it not merely the story of Santro but that of the passenger car business in India, tracing its history in a succinct manner.' – *Times of India*

'[A] former head of Hyundai India pens a riveting account on the humble car's success journey.' – *The Hindu BusinessLine*

'Subbu's prose is exciting and revealing… The book has a refreshing candour and pulls no punches while talking about some of the dubious practices in the industry.' – *Financial Express*

'Vivid anecdotes detail the thrills and challenges of introducing a new product in a new market… Santro has [a] lot [of] firsts to its credit and it makes the book important.' – *The Free Press Journal*

SANTRO

THE CAR THAT BUILT A COMPANY

BVR SUBBU

hachette
INDIA

First published in hardback in India in 2017 by Hachette India
(Registered name: Hachette Book Publishing India Pvt. Ltd)
An Hachette UK company
www.hachetteindia.com

This edition published in 2019

SRD

Hardback edition ISBN 978-93-5195-208-4
Paperback edition ISBN 978-93-5195-283-1
E-book edition ISBN 978-93-5195-209-1

Hachette Book Publishing India Pvt. Ltd
4th & 5th Floors, Corporate Centre,
Plot No. 94, Sector 44, Gurugram 122003, India

Typeset in Minion Pro 11/15.5 by
Manmohan Kumar, New Delhi

Printed and bound in India by
Manipal Technologies Limited, Manipal

MIX
Paper from responsible sources
FSC™ C043100

For M,
dearest friend,
sheet anchor, conscience,
fierce critic, staunch supporter, wife

Contents

A Chronology of Growth

6 May 1996	Hyundai Motor India Ltd (HMI) incorporated
10 December 1996	Ground-breaking ceremony at Irrungattukottai near Chennai
14 January 1998	Global unveiling of Hyundai Santro at Auto Expo in New Delhi
23 September 1998	Global commercial launch of Hyundai Santro in India
31 March 1999	HMI emerges as the second-largest auto manufacturer in India
31 May 1999	Launch of the Hyundai Santro Euro 2 variant
14 October 1999	Launch of the Hyundai Accent
31 January 2000	At the start of the new millennium, Hyundai Santro and Hyundai Accent top their respective segments in January sales
27 April 2000	100,000th car rolls out from the Chennai plant in just 19 months of commencement of operations
8 May 2000	Launch of the Hyundai Santro Zip Drive
12 June 2000	Hyundai Santro car sales cross 100,000
21 July 2000	First major export shipment of 760 Hyundai Accent and Hyundai Santro cars is shipped from the Chennai port for Algeria
November 2000	Both Hyundai Santro and Hyundai Accent bag top honours in the JD Power Asia Pacific 2001 IQS and APEAL studies
29 November 2000	Roll out of the 150,000th car from Chennai plant in just 25 months from the commencement of manufacture
31 December 2000	Hyundai Santro becomes the largest-selling car in its segment for the year for the first time
12 June 2001	HMI rolls out its 200,000th car in 32 months

11 July 2001	Launch of the new-look Hyundai Santro 'Millennium' model
18 July 2001	Launch of luxury sedan Hyundai Sonata
November 2001	Hyundai Santro ranked No. 1 in JD Power Asia Pacific 2001 Initial Quality study
	Both Hyundai Santro and Hyundai Accent ranked No. 1 in JD Power Asia Pacific 2001 APEAL study
31 December 2001	Hyundai Santro remains largest-selling car in its segment for the second year
18 March 2002	Global launch of 1.1-litre E-Epsilon engine in the new Hyundai Santro Zip Plus
26 June 2002	HMI rolls out 300,000th car
16 August 2002	Launch of Hyundai Accent VIVA
6 September 2002	Launch of Hyundai Santro Automatic Transmission
10 October 2002	Launch of Hyundai Accent CRDi
23 October 2002	Launch of Hyundai Sonata 2.7 V6
November 2002	Hyundai Santro bags top honours in JD Power Asia Pacific 2002, tops both IQS and APEAL for the third time in a row; Hyundai Accent ranked No. 1 in APEAL for second time in a row
31 December 2002	Hyundai Santro remains largest-selling car in its segment for the third year
13 March 2003	HMI commences exports to Latin America
8 May 2003	HMI rolls out 400,000th car
22 May 2003	Launch of the Hyundai Santro Xing, the 'Global Small Car'
4 August 2003	Launch of the premium SUV, Hyundai TERRACAN
12 August 2003	Export shipment of 1,500 Hyundai Santro Xing cars leaves for Europe; HMI becomes small cars export hub for HMC
11 December 2003	HMI rolls out 500,000th vehicle in India
31 December 2003	Hyundai Santro remains the largest-selling car in its segment for the fourth year
15 January 2004	Launch of the Hyundai Accent Viva CRDi

31 March 2004	Hyundai Santro crosses the figure of 100,000 sales in terms of annual financial year sales, the first Indian car to do so in its segment
15 April 2004	Launch of the Hyundai Elantra
10 September 2004	Launch of the Hyundai Getz
31 October 2004	HMI crosses the figure of 100,000 vehicle exports and emerges as the largest exporter in the automobile industry
1 December 2004	Hyundai Santro becomes India's largest-selling single brand across all segments with sales of 12,061 units
31 December 2004	Hyundai Santro remains largest-selling car in its segment for the fifth year
6 April 2005	Launch of SUV, Hyundai Tucson
8 June 2005	Launch of the Santro Xing with eRLX technology
17 Aug 2005	Launch of the Hyundai Sonata Embera
18 October 2005	HMI exports its 200,000th car
31 December 2005	Hyundai Santro remains largest-selling car in its segment for the sixth year
13 March 2006	HMI rolls out 1,000,000th car, the fastest in India's automotive history

Prologue

Manufacturing a car is a simple business, really. You take some metal, add three parts of engineering, one part of artistry, stir in a lot of passion, and proceed to craft it with care. You pour in the requisite magic with some deft word-smithy, and for garnish you add a little bit of luck. Then you serve it up with humility (albeit tinged with some flourish) and, if you've done it right, chances are you'll end up with an object of desire that dazzles at first glance and then grows into a longing. It is, however, a double-edged sword; you either end up making a lot of money or losing the shirt on your back. Seemingly, it is all about glitz, glamour and the spotlights, but in reality it entails brutal, backbreaking work and can be exhilarating and frustrating at the same time. It brings with it hypertension and ulcers, grey hair and balding, sleepless nights and the occasional heartache. And, yet, there's no business like the car business.

The story of Hyundai Santro's entry into the Indian market and its subsequent success epitomizes everything that makes the automobile business so special. The excitement of experiencing first-hand an unknown (and rather different-looking) underdog's fight to take on the biggest names in the business, and win – convincingly – was an exhilarating one. As close as you can get to a real-life David and Goliath story in India's car industry. In less than three years, this little car made Hyundai a household name in India, and for a lot of people the company soon became synonymous with the car itself. This then is the story of the Santro, the car that built a company.

Over the years, the story of the Santro and Hyundai Motor India Limited (HMI) has been told in bits and pieces, and yet, as a person closely associated with the company, the car and the brand from the time it was little more than an artist's doodle, through its creation, birth, infancy and growing-up years, I am often asked, even today, to recount those heady years and how a core team went about building something so successful and enduring at a time when no one gave us anything more than a snowball's chance in hell. Whichever way I look at it, the story of the Santro and HMI – the ultimate story of the underdog – remains deserving of recall, even if it runs the risk of being told from a personal point of view.

When, in December 2014, after being in continuous production for just over sixteen years, the sun finally set on HMI's 'Sunshine Car', a completely unprecedented situation presented itself: a long list of unfulfilled customers' orders lay pending across the country. The car that had successfully given India's automobile revolution a new resonance, and brought world-class contemporary technology with global standards of quality to a mass-market product, had in the process rightfully earned for itself the title of 'legend'. Not only had the Santro raised the technology barrier, created a new paradigm in the way India's car consumers were treated by car companies and become the largest product exported by the Indian automobile industry, it had also made a hitherto unknown Korean entity with a near unpronounceable name, Hyundai, into an amazingly successful and profitable company and a household name in India. HMI was the only automobile manufacturer in India to have earned its stripes without the luxury of government protection of the kind that Maruti Udyog Limited (MUL) had for long been a beneficiary or the broad support in terms of vehicle classification and tariffs that was received by Tata Motors Limited (TML).

In the unforgivingly competitive Indian market, where much bigger and better-known global carmakers, and storied Indian names, have sputtered along or come simply to a deafening halt, the Santro helped Hyundai race to its first million-vehicles roll-out within just ninety months of its first production. An unqualified success by any metric, by the time its production stopped, almost 1.9 million units had been produced and sold, with the company holding the category record for the fastest 100,000 cars sold, the fastest to cross the 250,000 units sales mark, and to attain the magic figure of 1,000,000 cars sold in the domestic market. When the decision to pull the plug on its production and sale was finally acted upon, the Santro brand alone was still selling more than half the number of units that the world's largest carmaker General Motors's (GM's) Indian subsidiary, sold across all its brands in a year. It also held the record for the fastest 500,000 cars exported from India with more than one out of every four cars going to markets ranging from Algeria to Zimbabwe, and from the discerning markets of Western Europe to the shores of North America.

Most importantly, the effort was an unqualified financial success – from an unprecedented cash-positive status in the tenth month of commercial operations till the very last car made and sold. In a striking contrast to every other market entrant of the period, the Santro's volume growth helped HMI create financial records for the first ten years of a company's life that have not been surpassed as of today in the Indian auto industry. Incorporated with an equity investment of ₹812 crore in the fiscal year (FY) 1997, in the ten years to FY 2006, HMI returned a cumulative EBITDA (earnings before interest, tax, depreciation and amortization) of over ₹3,600 crore, paid back all its secured borrowings and paid out an additional amount of over ₹400 crore to the parent company as technology and royalty fees. And the remarkable growth story has continued.

The foundation for Hyundai Motor Company's (HMC's) success in India was laid when the company decided to break from the conventional wisdom of its larger, better regarded global peers in its approach to investing in the creation of true capabilities in India. Although it did initially consider the very same product segments as the other entrants of the time, and proposed to make and sell both the Accent and the Sonata models – the Accent to take on the Esteem, and the Sonata because consumers were expected to logically take the next step up thereafter – it decided to avoid the assembly route and set up a full-fledged manufacturing operation.

Hyundai committed large capital investments to manufacturing its products – rather than merely setting up facilities to paint and assemble cars. This move gave HMI the game-changing flexibility in product strategy when, months after it formalized its investment pattern and location, it decided on entering the Indian market with the Santro rather than the Accent as its calling card. Large upfront capital investments enabled the company to achieve a high level of localization, and thereby price competitiveness, which ultimately became a major differentiator and the determinant of its success in the marketplace.

It was perhaps the critical step of choosing the Chennai location, that helped set the tone for Hyundai. An amazingly decisive chief minister who wanted to speed up industrial development, then recently unshackled from the location diktats of New Delhi; an exceptionally supportive state cadre bureaucracy at the Centre; a truly responsive bureaucracy in the state itself; abundant availability of a skilled, productivity-driven workforce; an established auto component manufacturing base; guaranteed availability of power and unmatched logistics infrastructure combined to ensure that the much-feared 'unknown unknowns' of establishing manufacturing operations in India were taken care of, enabling the team to focus on the real task at hand.

Recognizing early on that competing profitably against MUL in any segment would necessitate attaining a cost structure that would be broadly comparable to that of the industry leader, Hyundai put together all the required building blocks. Attaining a localization level of well over 80 per cent within the first year of operations was seen as an absolute imperative. This meant that all sheet-metal panels like the body, doors, bonnet and fenders, the engine and gearbox, the drive axles, the interior trim panels and dashboard, and the suspension components like shock absorbers and struts would have to be 'manufactured' locally in addition to the usual batteries, tyres, paint and assembly that less committed or less driven companies have regularly passed off as 'localization' in India.

HMI undoubtedly started with somewhat of an advantage. After a prolonged indifferent run, Hyundai Motor Company (HMC) had just decided to halt manufacturing operations from its modern plant in Canada, which produced cars for the North American market. A substantial part of the most expensive initial investments required for a highly localized manufacturing operation – the stamping press line, for instance – were simply moved from Canada and reinstalled in India, thereby sharply reducing initial capital investment outlays. The lumpy investment in the press shop accounted for, Hyundai went ahead with a major vote of confidence in the project by deciding on another significant investment exclusively for the India project – a full set of press dies for both the outer and inner sheet-metal panels for two products, first the Santro and then the Accent that HMI had by then decided to introduce. Hyundai's production engineering group went further to build an innovatively designed welding line (where inner and outer sheet-metal panels are welded together to make, say, a door or a bonnet,) and large cubing and integration jigs and fixtures (which are used to put the side body structure, roof and floor of the car together, for instance) that could effectively be used for both the proposed products.

Focused on ensuring cost-efficient procurement from component manufacturers, Hyundai eschewed the typical Japanese approach of *keiretsu* – a structure in which companies have cross-holdings of ownership particularly in supplier companies in a manner that enables informal 'cooperation' between them; Toyota and Nippon Denso, for instance. The *keiretsu* connection could often be seen as creating a preference for a particular linked supplier under the plea of 'quality' being the determinant of selection, but has sometimes been questioned for its opacity. The Korean chaebol too operate a variant, but HMI chose instead to work as far as possible with existing Indian component manufacturers reputed for the quality of their products and preferably those located within easy reach of the plant. The logic was unbeatable: since these manufacturers were already well established with substantial sales to other original equipment manufacturers (OEMs), the apportioning of overheads to the supplies they made to Hyundai would be significantly lower, the logistics costs would reduce, a just-in-time (JIT) manufacturing system could be established from the inception of the plant and left few chances of time over-runs due to delays that could come about if a new component manufacturing project was to be initiated. In the case of some components, Hyundai's vendor partners in Korea were encouraged to enter into technology joint ventures with chosen Indian component manufacturers in order to enable a seamless transfer of quality processes and working methods so critical to establishing a high-quality, high-productivity and low-cost component-supply ecosystem.

The next logical step was to set up from scratch the distribution network for this relatively unknown brand. The literally high-decibel show with which Hyundai introduced itself to India, with Korean janggu drummers and hanbok-clad ladies who walked through the

Auto Expo held at the Pragati Maidan in New Delhi in 1996, did draw a lot of attention to the brand. The Hyundai cars on display – the Sonata, the Elantra and the Accent – too attracted some notice and helped marginally to create a semblance of brand salience, but this was largely restricted to the areas in and around Delhi and what is today the National Capital Region (NCR), and a few car enthusiasts and component manufacturers from other parts of the country. But even this had largely dissipated by 1997 when the process of setting up the distribution network actually began. The bigger and better-known global names were all the rage, and the antics of Daewoo, which had, to the chagrin of its consumers, repriced the Cielo at an unbelievable discount, had not helped the image of Korean companies whatsoever. Recognizing that the introduction of a small car would necessitate the building of a widespread post-sale support system, not just in the large urban agglomerations but in the Tier 2 and Tier 3 cities as well, HMI however decided to match MUL in terms of operational dealership locations to cover at least 90 per cent of the potential market by volume. This would mean setting up at least 75 dealerships at a time when GM, Ford and Honda together probably had just over 30. The sheer audacity of the intent caused raised eyebrows and much impolite commentary from the industry as well, but HMI remained unfazed as it held its chief competitor, MUL, clearly locked in its sights.

Since TML's Indica and the Daewoo Matiz were unveiled at the same time as the Santro in 1998, the impact on MUL was multiplied manifold. Fortunately for HMI, the long waiting lists for the Maruti Zen had seemingly lulled the company into a false sense of complacency. Even as sales of the Maruti 800 showed signs of fatigue, the Maruti Zen continued its strong showing in terms of consistent sales volume growth, and thanks to MUL's distribution strategies, apparently managed to attract a sizeable unofficial premium above the company price. It essentially enabled HMI to attain remunerative product pricing very soon in its India journey, something I had always believed ought to be a major pillar of the strategic focus. MUL then inadvertently did HMI a good turn by focusing most of its energies on what it saw as staving off the threat of the Tata Indica. And something that appeared to have started as a tiff between the two helped push a new environment debate in India – and by mid-1999 HMI grabbed the initiative, sensing a never-before opportunity for leadership. From there on HMI attacked MUL relentlessly with technology and product quality reinforced by exceptional customer-care efforts.

The constant 'pushing the envelope' in terms of technology, quality and communication that started with the Santro was given a further fillip with the introduction of the Hyundai Accent late in 1999. And in January 2000, the very first month of the new millennium, Hyundai overtook MUL in both the segments in which it competed with the market behemoth. The *Economic Times* immortalized the event with a headline that said it all: 'Hyundai Tall Boy's Accent robs Maruti's Zen of its Esteem'! With market leadership now clearly established in consumers' minds, the task ahead for HMI became even more clearly defined – retaining and expanding the lead.

Within months thereafter, what had started late in 1999 as an export of in-house manufactured components to the parent company grew into a full-fledged export effort. Cars manufactured in India were exported initially to Southeast Asia and North Africa, then within two years back to Korea, and ultimately to Western Europe and North America – all within five years of starting commercial production. The consistent domestic sales volume growth of the Santro that came along with profitability enabled HMI to substantially improve on global standards of the cost of production, even as it attained and sometimes bettered the quality standards achieved by the parent organization. Significantly, HMI's export success wasn't merely based on importing overpriced completely knocked down (CKD) kits and exporting them after under-valuing assembly costs, often with a view to sidestep entry barriers to the parent company's home production or to take advantage of countertrade requirements in Eastern Europe. In fact, it was the styling of the Indian version of a model produced in India (based on the original model made for South Korea) that actually garnered a much healthier consumer acceptance across the world. Since HMI's products were so heavily localized, it was truly representative of a 'Make in India' effort with neither hoopla nor hype surrounding it. Soon enough, Hyundai's exports from India crossed 100,000 units. Then, in a very deliberate move to cock a snook at competition, something that HMI had become known and reviled for by its competitors, but loved for by its many supporters, HMI invited Dr V. Krishnamurthy, chairman of the National Manufacturing Competitiveness Council and a former chairman of MUL, to flag off Hyundai car number 200,000 to be exported from India.

Not that any of this brought any recognition from the Government of India, beyond the customary plaques commending export performance, though. When in 2005 the government constituted the working group to create the Automotive Mission Plan 2006–2016, ostensibly to focus on, among a host of other things, 'upgrading the infrastructure of production, induction of technology exports and finally environmental and safety concerns', the mandarins at Udyog Bhavan did not even see it fit to invite the company that had set standards far ahead of the rest of industry on each of the issues mentioned. But then HMI was focused purely on winning the hearts of India's consumers – not those of its policy-makers.

The credit for all that HMI managed to do goes to a wonderful team of professionals, both Korean and Indian, that created a never-before amalgam of Korean industriousness and single-minded focus with Indian creativity and ingenuity in the pursuit of a common goal. Led by Yang Soo Kim (Y.S. Kim), a man whose hermit-like calm cloaked a steely resolve, the team of 'pioneers', as I like to call them, regularly worked eighteen-hour days almost without a break for eighteen months – from the laying of the foundation stone of HMI's manufacturing plant near Chennai in December 1996 till the first pre-production prototype rolled out in early 1998 – setting thereby the first of many, often global records that no automobile manufacturing company in India has since broken. Every aspect of project planning and implementation – the construction of the plant, the installation of the equipment, developing vendors, human- resource training, covering legal aspects and coordination with the government, development of distribution networks, training the sales, marketing and service teams – came together as in a symphony led by a maestro conductor, and in a record twenty-one months from ground-breaking, the Santro had been prototyped, tested, manufactured and commercially launched.

With a foundation of rarely seen strength, breadth and depth, HMI launched itself on a growth trajectory with few parallels, and globally too Hyundai started to soar, soon being counted among the world's top five automakers.

The relentless push by Hyundai's chairman Mong Koo Chung (M.K. Chung) for cost efficiencies, his exceptional foresight that saw the takeover of Kia which in turn changed the market dynamics and profitability of Korean car exports and thus HMC finances literally overnight, a near-missionary zeal in the quest for the highest global quality standards and his commitment to a styling flourish that spoke a bold new design language of a confident global company, are what legends are made of. When that was superimposed on a launch pad built around the Santro, the 'Tall Boy' design helped ensure that HMI forever earned for itself a place in the Indian sun.

I have been a part of this amazing journey, the formative first decade of HMI, and have since looked back often and reminisced fondly of my days there, and how I came to be at HMI.

*

My entry into the automobile industry was not something I'd planned on. I acquired a Masters degree in Economics from Jawaharlal Nehru

University (JNU) in New Delhi, which was, even then, as it is today, at the forefront of student activism, with a definite left-of-centre ideology providing the theoretical underpinnings for its social science curricula. Not quite the conventional nursery for those considering a corporate career, JNU was better known as the ultimate finishing school for aspirants to the civil services, but what it did provide me was the training to analyse situations in many ways rather differently from the well-structured case-study-led academic rigour that many of my colleagues in the corporate world had gone through in their Masters of Business Administration (MBA) courses. More comfortable, perhaps, with discussions on primitive capital accumulation, or the transformation problem, or the-snake-and-the-tunnel characteristics of the European monetary system, or Marxian dialectics or strategies of war as enunciated by Mao, than with balance-sheet analysis, I entered the Tata Administrative Service (TAS) in 1977 – probably one of the few places in the private-corporate sector then that openly welcomed and accommodated different streams of thought and academic training amongst its covenanted management cadre.

From there, a series of what might best be termed as 'historical accidents' led me into the Tata Engineering and Locomotive Company Limited, better known now as Tata Motors Limited, rather than the three other group companies that I had interned at and which had also indicated their willingness to tolerate me. TML was then the ultimate 'engineers' company, constantly focused on the belief that 'the best is yet to come' and creating competencies in manufacturing, design, machine-building and information technology leagues ahead of the rest of India's industry. Thanks primarily to its legendary chairman, Sumant Moolgaokar (or SM, as he was reverentially referred to), TML, for most of us then, was not merely a job; it was a mission. In an era of mile-long customer waiting lists, TML constantly innovated, improving products, bringing in new technologies and remaining consumer oriented.

Other than engineering, till the day Moolgaokar demitted office, quality and the service function effectively reported to him. So just one simple customer complaint or suggestion often received directly by him from single-owner operators at highway truck stops during his weekend trips between Bombay, now Mumbai, and Pune, could galvanize the entire organization to move in response. Even in days of a seemingly unending shortage of trucks, Moolgaokar remained not just one of the most accomplished engineer-managers in the country – the man behind the cement giant ACC, the man who created Tata Steel's capability to rebuild itself, the architect of India's automobile industry and the creator of TML – but also, and more importantly, the very conscience of the organization and the chief representative of the customer in the company.

One of the most enduring lessons from his unwavering consumer focus that has remained with me came when, as a young profit-centre head in my early thirties, I committed the ultimate sacrilege of raising the prices of spare parts for the newly introduced Tata 407 seemingly unilaterally. When questioned about why I had done that, I spoke of the need to improve profitability. Moolgaokar looked straight at me and told me in no uncertain terms that what was good for the consumer was ultimately good for the company, and that my job was to look after the consumer's interest – and it was he, not I, who needed to be concerned about shareholders' interests. The scheduled hour-long meeting with the marketing and sales division concluded after just ten minutes, and my then boss Pushpendra Sinh (fondly and simply called 'Push') later told me, perhaps just half in jest, that the only reason I had not been sacked that day – for focusing on profits rather than on the customer – was my age! Even during those days of an unofficial premium on almost anything that the company manufactured and sold, it was always more difficult to convince Moolgaokar of the need for a price increase than it was to convince the Bureau of Industrial Costs and Prices (BICP), the government watchdog on industrial prices, about the same. The process of convincing him of the need for a price increase involved detailed discussions on what (if any) productivity improvements had been attained through the adoption of new materials, machine technology or improved operating practices, before he sometimes agreed and, even then, invariably very reluctantly.

TML gave me a deep sense of belonging and taught me all I know. My years there ingrained in me the humility to realize that I know very little and constantly need to learn as the world changes around me every day. While there I worked across functions to gain a holistic understanding of the automotive business. I got the opportunity to work alongside and learn from two other exceptional world-class companies, Mercedes-Benz (MB) and Honda. The crowning glory of all that learning was when the team that I led conceptualized, tested, configured and, with the consistent support of colleagues in the production division – like Yogendra Nath in particular, who helped create it in a skunk works effort at TML's Pune plant – introduced the Tata 2213, a 22-tonne GVW multi-axle heavy commercial vehicle, still acknowledged in India's road transport industry as a watershed development for the market.

The World Bank, in an internal study in the early 1990s, observed that the 2213, was one of 'the two most innovative approaches to the market taken by TML in the last twenty years.' The appropriately designed 2213 brought a structural transformation in the country's road freight industry that has not only endured but has since grown from strength to strength. What we simply did with the 2213 was to juggle the guts of the two-axle vehicles then being produced in large numbers (which customers were already familiar with), beefing them up marginally in terms of engine power, altering the transmission ratios and tyre sizes ever so slightly to achieve mandated gradeability among other things and presenting them in a three-axle configuration to enable them to legally carry payloads of 15 tonnes. That customers used these modifications to push overloading the trucks to even higher levels was, of course, another matter. India's road freight sector hasn't looked back since.

Considering that all the foundations and much of the superstructure of whatever I have learnt about the automotive business were laid in TML, leaving it was a difficult choice. Every time the idea crossed my mind, I reminded myself of what I had once been told – 'companies are permanent, bosses are not'. But the inevitability of the move finally came home to me in early 1996. In February that year, on the side-lines of the Auto Expo, I met Y.S. Kim in the first of what was to be a series of interactions before he invited me in August to visit the Hyundai headquarters in Seoul to meet Se Yung Chung (S.Y. Chung) and B.J. Park then chairman and president, respectively, of HMC.

On the return flight to Mumbai, an investment-banker friend, surprised to see me on a flight from Seoul, buttonholed me and, despite all my attempts at obfuscating and changing the subject, told me that if I was considering moving to a Korean company, I should choose carefully. He then went on to tell me a joke about Korean business executives which, to my recollection, went something like this:

> What would executives of the Korean chaebols do if they accidentally ran into a bear while walking in a forest?
>
> The Hyundai executives would, without hesitation, pick up the nearest club and attack the bear; the Daewoo guys would immediately call their chairman for instructions; the Samsung chaps would convene a meeting to consider next steps in front of the bear; and the LG group would wait for Samsung's response, and then do the same.

In their own ways, he said, each one of them was a great company, and a world-beater, but, he remarked very perceptively, for me, Hyundai would be the best fit. I did not comment, but I filed away that piece of advice. I finally left TML in October 1996, after uncharacteristically dithering for close to two months, and accepted Y.S. Kim's offer to join HMI as director, sales and marketing.

When I walked away from TML, I left behind many friends – and an office with an amazing view of the Arabian Sea. But I took with me some wonderful memories and nearly two decades of unparalleled cross-functional learning in what was then, I've always believed, India's most exceptional company. Along with this came some genuine, long-lasting relationships with the media, automotive dealers across manufacturers and vehicle types, the financial services sector and component manufacturers. I also took with me one of my favourite quotations from the speeches of Mao made at the Conference of the Communist Party of China in March 1957: '*He who is not afraid of death by a thousand cuts, dares to unhorse the Emperor – this is the indomitable spirit needed in our struggle.*' It was written on a sheet of my TML letterhead and stayed in the top drawer of every desk I'd had in TML.

That sheet of paper moved with me to the rather spartan start-up style open plan office of Hyundai in Chennai. With the air conditioning unable to keep up with the fluctuations in the rather erratic power supply, the office invariably alternated between freezer and sauna bath throughout the day, with the muggy Chennai weather only making things more uncomfortable. I realized to my extreme horror that not only were my Korean colleagues always dressed in formal business suits, but they also never considered draping their jackets on the back of their chairs even in such extenuating circumstances. For me, coming as I did from the informal, open-collar, no-neck-tie culture of TML, this was perhaps the first of many a culture shock.

But very soon Hyundai adapted to India – and as practicality edged out sartorial stuffiness in the company's India headquarters, the foundation was laid for the achievement of a spate of Indian and global records – all made possible by a heart-warming if somewhat unattractively styled little car with a big heart – the Santro! Which is why I believe its story is one worth recounting.

1

The World As It Was Then

'It is well known that when you do anything, unless you understand its actual circumstances, its nature and its relations to other things, you will not know the laws governing it, or know how to do it, or be able to do it well.'

– Problems of Strategy in China's Revolutionary War,
Mao Tse-Tung

Since a company's growth is determined significantly by the environment it operates in, the starting point of a book such as this ought to be an examination and analysis of the market landscape.

In an industry not particularly affected by disruptive technology, factors like the stage of economic growth, the regulatory regime, the fallibilities or arrogance of some competitors and the incompetence of others, are among the various factors that often have as much of a role in creating a company's successes as does its own efforts. Even as I recognize that my own understanding or analyses of all these could be debated by those better qualified than me, I believe there were probably three potential inflection points which had great bearing on the growth and structure of India's passenger-car industry.

The first was in 1965, when TML stepped back from the opportunity offered by the government of India to produce a 'small car' along with trucks, while both Hindustan Motors Ltd (HM) and Premier Automobiles Ltd (PAL) continued to do so, during the highly constricting regulatory regime of the period. The second was in 1986, when TML was denied permission by the government to create a true 'manufacturing' – as distinct from 'assembly' – operation, with internationally recognized standards of technology and product sophistication in a joint venture with Honda. And the third came about in 1996, when Mercedes-Benz AG (now Daimler AG) decided not to pursue a compact car project with TML after a series of discussions that started at the same time as the discussions on setting up a joint venture for the production of the Mercedes range of luxury cars. TML eventually quit the venture, after setting out alone to bring in the Indica.

Though it is nothing more than a matter of conjecture today, I've always wondered what the face of the Indian automobile industry would have been if each of the above events had played out differently. But if I were to hazard a guess, had TML entered the small car market in the mid-1960s, given its exceptional leadership, professional competence, approach to industrialization and technology development, it may well have helped ensure a more technologically competent and price-competitive, truly 'national' passenger car industry comprised of TML, HM and PAL, thus obviating the need for Suzuki Motor Corporation (SMC) to make an entrance through MUL. By not permitting TML to enter the passenger car segment in the mid-1980s, the government effectively helped ensure that the exploitative 'oligopolistic pricing policies as well as technologically conservative behaviour' of MUL were not tempered by a highly competent and focused 'national' competitor. That in turn would have made India an even more difficult, if not impossible, market for companies like Hyundai to enter and prosper in. Lastly, but for the decision taken by MB in the mid-1990s, Hyundai may never ever have put down roots or grown as rapidly as it did in India, faced as it was by a truly global-quality product from the stables of a national champion. Though history is replete with such ifs and buts, an appreciation of what might have been always serves to ensure that any sense of achievement of a company or individual is infused with a dose of much-needed realism – and humility.

The foundation of India's automotive manufacturing industry was effectively laid down in 1949 when the Government of India banned the import of vehicles completely built outside the country, and was further cemented in 1953 when the Tariff Commission ruled that Indian manufacturers would not be permitted to assemble imported vehicles without increasing local content. Unwilling to invest in India in order to set up the facilities that the mandated increase in local content would have required, both GM and Ford shut down their Indian assembly operations. HM, promoted by the Birla family (which had started life by producing Studebaker trucks) got into car production with technology from Morris of the UK, and PAL, promoted by the Walchand Group (which had started its life by producing Dodge/Fargo trucks), entered the car race with technology from Chrysler of the USA. The two became India's only passenger-car manufacturers. PAL, which then inked a joint venture with Fiat in 1951 to produce the Fiat Cinqcento, also went on to offer the Fiat Millicento by 1954. The much smaller Standard Motors Products Ltd (SMPL) commenced manufacturing variants of car models made by UK-based Standard Triumph and light trucks as well.

In 1956, the government established the second Tariff Commission tasked with looking at costs and prices of cars produced in the country and, more importantly, defining the kind of car that was to be manufactured in the country. Even as it advocated that pricing decisions ought to remain within the domain of the manufacturers, the commission referred to the need to have four ranges of cars: baby, light, medium and big – and went on to emphasize the suitability of a 'baby car' for the country. The commission noted that sub-optimal utilization of resources by manufacturers could result from multiple projects and in turn could impact the ability of the industry to attain economic scale. Effectively, it advocated the need to restrict competition and created a further anomaly by deciding to protect a whole product rather than its components by favouring what appeared to be an arbitrary phasing of the manufacturing programme. In hindsight, this seems to have been more a reflection of the present incumbents' production capabilities than an objective analysis of the most appropriate technical and engineering approach for the industry.

In response to the opportunities that seemed to be opening up, TML, in its very first attempt to enter the passenger car business informally started discussions with the government for the licensed manufacture of a DKW 900 series car. DKW was a part of the Auto Union, then owned by MB, which had already partnered with the Tata group to establish a very successful truck-manufacturing joint venture at what was originally a locomotive manufacturing facility in Jamshedpur. (Which is why TML was originally called the Tata Engineering and Locomotive Company Ltd – or, simply, TELCO). The tremendous strides made by the TMB (Tata Mercedes-Benz)-branded truck produced as a result of the joint venture stood in sharp contrast to the Bedford and Dodge efforts of HM and PAL. The TMB truck was a modern product based on global state-of-the-art technology manufactured at a vertically integrated manufacturing facility, which first produced castings and forgings, then machined them into components, assembled the components into aggregates like engines, transmissions, front and rear axles, suspensions and steering, and finally put all the aggregates together to make trucks and buses. The company then created an exceptional nationwide product support network, and by December 1964 TML had delivered truck number 100,000 and effectively pushed both the Bedford and Dodge trucks into total oblivion in India. Given the company's track record, TML's proposal of the DKW model car might well have had somewhat of a similar impact. The proposed 4.3-metre long car, came with a three-cylinder 896 cubic centimetre (cc) engine, weighed in at 970 kilograms, and boasted a fuel efficiency of just under 10 kilometres per litre, which was considered to be class-leading at the time.

But it was not to be.

In his statement to the shareholders in the Annual Report of TML in 1965, the company's then chairman J.R.D. Tata noted, 'In May this year, having ascertained that the Government of India might be willing to consider such a possibility, we held discussions in Germany with our partners, Messrs Daimler-Benz, to ascertain the feasibility of producing in India a suitable model of the DKW car manufactured by Messrs Auto Union which has been for some time a 100 per cent subsidiary of Daimler-Benz. As a result of recent developments, however, Daimler-Benz no longer hold a controlling interest in Auto Union. Our discussions revealed that, as a result of the altered circumstances, and for other reasons, it would be neither desirable nor feasible for your company to undertake the production of any model of the DKW. We have therefore had reluctantly to inform government that we are not in a position to put forward a scheme for the manufacture of a small passenger car.'

Thus, despite its merely poor to middling showing with cars and trucks, it ultimately fell on HM to manufacture the 'baby' cars. That HM then appeared to squat on the approval and not get around to producing one, reportedly the Morris Minor, is another matter. Capacity pre-emption, where industrial houses often applied for large licensed capacities, obtained licences for a substantial part of the government-ordained capacity, seldom fully established the licensed capacity on the grounds of insufficient demand, then kept supplies low and prices high, was a common affliction in Indian industry at the time. The 'small' Standard Herald from SMPL, was produced in such small numbers that it remained a fringe player, even in consumer perceptions. Interestingly, both HM and PAL continued to produce both cars and trucks – as did SMPL which for a short while was probably the market leader in light commercial vehicles and India's first exporter of automotive engines to Western markets. This move by TML to forgo the opportunity of manufacturing a car in the 1960s may well have been the only misstep in its amazing history of staying at the vanguard of the automotive industry in India. (Incidentally, Auto Union, of which DKW was a part, was sold to Volkswagen, and from 1967 DKW models came to be sold under the Audi brand.)

Over the years, committees were appointed by the government to study the manufacture of a small, economical 'people's car', but the passenger car industry remained tightly regulated by the government, to the extent even of price control. In 1966, with the economy facing severe resource constraints and starved of foreign exchange, the third Tariff Commission recommended to the government that in order to attain scale efficiency it was necessary to minimize the number of models produced and control prices as well. Statutory control of car prices eventually came in 1969, better known as the year of the nationalization of banks and the passing of the Monopolistic and Restrictive Trade Practice (MRTP) Act. The MRTP Act, the forerunner of the Competition Act of 2002 provided a host of things for the use of industrial licensing to prevent the concentration of economic power in the hands of large industrial conglomerates (then defined as those with assets in excess of ₹25 crore.) It effectively led to the unbridled growth of an inefficient (and worse) public sector on the one hand, and a rent-seeking, technologically obsolete and inefficient private sector on the other. The combination helped keep India in the backwaters of industrial growth and technology development over the next two decades – and, I believe, contributed greatly to robbing successive generations of Indians of their rightful place in the sun.

It wasn't till the early 1970s that the idea of mass-producing a small car was taken up again in India. Prime Minister Indira Gandhi's son Sanjay Gandhi put together a proposal for the indigenous design and development of an affordable, fuel-efficient car for India's rapidly growing middle class. Following Sanjay Gandhi's initiative, the Union Cabinet proposed the production of a 'people's car' and passed a unanimous resolution for its development and production. Despite a lack of real experience in automobile mass-production or a proven design concept, Sanjay Gandhi's company Maruti Limited, incorporated in 1971, received land, substantial bank funding and a favourable tax treatment from the government. And when, despite all the support, the company failed to produce a single marketable car and instead went into assembling road-rollers, many state governments provided the company with a ready and willing market.

Meanwhile, the Indian car industry represented by HM, PAL and SMPL lurched along in a vicious cycle of low technology, low production and abysmal financial performance due to the erroneous evaluation of costs and dictation of selling prices by the government. Ultimately, in 1975, the Supreme Court, ruling on a petition by car manufacturers, held the government method of calculating costs as incorrect and pushed it to lift price controls on cars. The government soon followed up with the Industrial Policy Statements of 1977 and 1980, which marked the beginning of the liberalization process, but the damage to the passenger car industry had already been done. However, unfortunately, neither HM nor PAL appeared to display the technical competence, managerial ability or the desire to build their respective Bedford and Dodge truck businesses, which might have helped them escape the debilitating effect of price control on the cars they made and the restrictions they faced on capital equipment imports that were necessary for upgrading both product and manufacturing technology. With little effort invested in improving product technology or even quality, both the Bedford and Dodge brands soon became a rarity on Indian roads. The quality and reliability of the Bedford was generally seen as so far below the expectations and requirements of customers that a HM truck dealer in Maharashtra who also ran one of India's best trucking organizations was known to routinely induct Bedford vehicles into his trucking fleet because of his dealership, and then, as soon as the warranty had lapsed, promptly replace most of the aggregates of the truck with those procured as spare parts from TML!

It was only after 1982, when the passenger car industry was added to Appendix 1 of the Industries Development and Regulation Act of 1951 (IDRA 1951) – the core list that gave it a strategic status in terms of the Indian economy's industrial base – that things really started to move. The implication of this inclusion was that the government would then treat the industry's expansion and modernization needs more favourably – at least akin to what the two-wheeler and commercial vehicle industries received. By 1975, for instance, capital equipment imports for replacement were allowed for the commercial vehicle industry as long as the net foreign exchange outflow was zero, thus bringing in an early version of an export commitment. TML, which had already moved successfully into global markets ranging from South East Asia to West Asia to Africa and even into parts of Eastern Europe was an automatic and deserving beneficiary. As a general industrial policy, the government had then also permitted commercial vehicle makers, as an exception, to automatically expand their manufacturing capacity by 25 per cent every five years, despite the normally limiting provisions of the MRTP Act, over and above the 25 per cent that was already allowed under the provisions of the IDRA.

Meanwhile, in 1977, Maruti Limited went into liquidation. Eventually taken over by the Government of India and incorporated in 1981 by an Act of Parliament as a public limited company, it was rechristened Maruti Udyog Limited. Its first chairman, Sumant Moolgaokar, the legendary creator of TML, believed that MUL would be treated with respect by global automakers when it went scouting for partners, and that it would be able to ensure better financial and technology terms for a small car manufacturing project from the world's biggest and best if it could first prove its automotive credentials. He reportedly proposed that TML would supply MUL with the technology required to produce light commercial vehicles for a start. But primarily, it would appear as a tribute to Sanjay Gandhi's memory, the idea of producing a 'fuel-efficient small car' prevailed. After Moolgaokar's resignation to continue his professional focus on TML, MUL's board of directors, constituted mainly from Delhi's rarefied heights of power, and obviously with a keener appreciation and better understanding of the mandate, decided that the company would manufacture a small car and proceeded to scour global markets for a technology partner. A few months later, its project report for the manufacture of passenger cars and light utility vehicles spoke of the production of a fuel-efficient 'people's car' suited to Indian driving and climatic conditions, with foreign technology and equity participation, creating the potential for earning foreign exchange through exports and generating employment through the establishment of ancillary industries.

As Moolgaokar had apparently feared, MUL tried in vain to attract the attention of global automotive technology leaders in Europe and big Japanese names. It settled, ultimately, for the low-ranked Japanese company, SMC, best-known at the time for its relatively high-revving motorcycle engines, as its technology and financial partner. Much was made in the news reports of the day of the ability to attract Suzuki, which was widely touted as the single-largest exporter of cars with an engine capacity below 550 cc, without enlightening anybody about what proportion of these cars constituted Japan's total car exports, at what prices they were exported and to which countries they went. For SMC, unable to compete on technology or financial prowess with the biggies in Japan – Toyota, Nissan, Honda and Mitsubishi – the move to enter into business with MUL was perhaps born out of sheer desperation, but that hardly showed in the terms it ultimately managed to extract from the people and the Government of India. Referring to the move to enter India, Osamu Suzuki, then president of SMC, is quoted by Kazayuki Motohashi in his book *Global Business Strategy* as saying, 'No one else is going to India, so we have an opportunity. We were the lowest-ranked among domestic manufacturers, and wanted to be at the first place somewhere.' To Osamu Suzuki's credit, he had read the tea leaves well and recognized the true potential of the Indian market – and offered to it all SMC's wares at an apparently lower project and product cost. In addition, it was claimed in news reports and in replies to questions at Parliament by the government of the day that Suzuki committed to provide highly acclaimed Japanese manufacturing and management practices through a process of knowledge transfer that would enable a localization of 95 per cent by 1988–89. Suzuki's equity participation offer was also considered higher than that of all the other potential partners MUL was in discussions with.

There is little doubt that the market demand for an affordable car for India's emerging middle class was present since the early 1960s. By 1980, two decades of industrial growth, even if patchy at times, had been accompanied by a significant spurt in the contribution of the services sector to a growth in the Gross Domestic Product (GDP) with interesting implications for income distribution and an unprecedented wave of urbanization. Rising incomes and aspirations of India's new urban middle class, combined with early indications of a perverse wealth effect creeping in, created a mass of consumers that looked at upgrading from two-wheelers, which were until then ubiquitous. With the average life of a vehicle being stretched thanks to a scarcity of new cars, a steady growth of demand for replacement of personal vehicles was also anticipated. The continued strain on the country's balance of payment and its high dependence on oil imports, which in turn led to rising fuel prices, meant that fuel-efficiency of cars remained a priority, thereby automatically tilting the consumers' preference towards smaller cars. It was at this point that SMC entered the market, and the Indian consumer saw the arrival of the Maruti 800. Though it was essentially this combination of economic growth, rapid urbanization and the imperative of fuel-efficient cars that created the necessary conditions for the emergence of India's small car focus and the resultant unprecedented growth for MUL, its success as a company was inextricably linked with the government and the consistent political support that enabled the use of the taxation and licensing regime, often quite adroitly, to effectively neutralize all opposition to its emergence and rapid growth.

The personal interest that Prime Minister Indira Gandhi took in the creation and building of MUL and the widely rumoured close involvement of her nephew Arun Nehru in the organization's day-to-day planning activities – including dealer and vendor selection – ensured that any possible bureaucratic interference was entirely neutralized. The Indian auto industry stood witness to a speed in government decision-making that it had probably never ever seen before. This, in an era when automobile manufacturers importing machines had to convince the people at the Directorate General of Technical Development (DGTD) why they were bringing in a particular make of machine rather than another.

More was to come. By a special notification, the government decreed that cars with fuel-efficient engines below 1,000 cc displacement were eligible for a customs duty levy of only 40 per cent while others paid effective duties ranging from 140 per cent to 160 per cent. This effectively meant only MUL would benefit, because the small Bangalore-based start-up Sipani Automobiles Ltd (SAL), which was also bidding to make a low-cost car with engine and other technology sourced from Reliant Motor Co. of the UK, was in any case bound in so much red tape and worse, that it would have been a miracle for it to take off.

The extent of the support that MUL got was unprecedented. For instance, MUL was allowed to import steel blanks (cut-to-size steel sheets used for stamping skin panels) as components, paying a customs duty of just 40 per cent even as the rest of the industry, which had invested in expensive capital equipment, employed people and added value in India through activities like shearing, blanking and stamping had to import the steel coils at a customs duty of 130 per cent. (Japanese companies seem to have an amazing ability to convince the government of India to see their viewpoint on such matters. Exactly the same thing, though at different rates, was sought under the India–Thailand Free Trade Agreement in 2003. Amongst the biggest potential beneficiaries, if it had not been challenged and eventually changed, would have been Toyota and Honda.) Even to the uninformed observer, the excise rates appeared to have been deliberately adjusted to favour the aesthetically superior, albeit smaller and therefore logically more fuel-efficient MUL products. While existing manufacturers paid an excise duty of 25 per cent, MUL products were charged just 15 per cent. But for these benefits it is highly unlikely that MUL would ever have been able to attain the 'people's car' pricing of ₹47,500 that it started off with, in keeping with the government's promise. But there was an interesting side-effect. With demand for the car surging far ahead of production capacity, both MUL and its suppliers struggled to absorb the technology they had acquired with relative ease, and necessarily ended up with varying degrees of import intensity in their respective products. The definition of indigenization that evolved from the Phased Manufacturing Programme (PMP) that the auto industry had to comply with basically meant that component manufacturers who supplied to MUL, for instance, could import 70 per cent of the component by value, add 30 per cent value in terms of labour cost of final assembly and local logistics, and when they supplied it to MUL, it would be treated as domestic procurement – not imported. This, of course, also enabled a reporting of a more impressive indigenization effort, than may have been factually or technically correct. Beyond what this did to the existing automakers, the approach also ended up discriminating against the large indigenous auto-component industry that OEMs had helped create and nurture in the early years of India's industrialization, with all its constraints and tribulations. Meanwhile, a huge unofficial market-price premium on MUL cars became the order of the day. As Karol Bagh in Delhi (the hub of unofficial intermediaries in the automobile business) became the informal centre of the national car retail market, what essentially happened was that potential public-sector savings invariably ended up as unregulated and untaxed private household savings that eventually went into consumption expenditure which, by its composition and nature, probably helped create even further strains on the country's balance of payments. Some part also became private corporate-sector profits in Indian Non-Banking Financial Companies (NBFCs). But, worse still, the management of the export prices of components and kits by Japanese companies ensured that some part of what could have been potential tax revenues in India during that period effectively got converted into private corporate profits in Japan. A simple comparison of price realization on the export of small cars by SMC to Western markets and those of component exports to India would have been revealing. But India's policy-makers seemed content to ignore national interest – and there is no record of the government having conducted any such analysis or allowing its dissemination.

As MUL not only offered relatively higher standards (though not necessarily global state-of-the-art product technology) but also sold its products at a substantially lower price than the other car manufacturers, its main competitors, HM and PAL, with what was then considered little managerial or technological competence, and even less financial muscle, rapidly ceded ground. Amidst growing clamour against the partisanship of the government, the self-appointed guardians of MUL allowed a relaxing of import regulations and provided fiscal support in order to enable the incumbents HM, PAL and SMPL to upgrade their product technology as well as improve their fuel efficiency. While PAL brought in the already phased out Fiat 124 and shoehorned a fuel-efficient Nissan engine, HM opted for a phased-out Vauxhall Victor and re-engineered it with an Isuzu engine. Both manufacturers soon released diesel variants as well. With great foresight, HM (which produced a rather low-spec vehicle called the Trekker, basically using the proven and widely maintainable engine, transmission, axles, steering and suspension of the Ambassador) also tied up with Isuzu to manufacture the Trooper, a move that could have ended the extremely profitable near-monopoly of Mahindra & Mahindra in the utility vehicle space. Yet, inexplicably, HM did not proceed with the introduction. Taking a different route, SMPL waded into uncharted territory and brought in what was generally touted as India's first luxury car – the Standard 2000, a variant of the Rover SD from UK – but came a cropper when the poor performance of the car on most counts led to a slew of lawsuits and the ultimate demise of the company in 1988.

In 1985, within days of Rajiv Gandhi assuming office as prime minister, industrial license 'broadbanding' was introduced and even companies that came under the purview of the MRTP Act were permitted capacity expansion, whether as greenfield or brownfield projects. Broadbanding did away with production licenses for a specific commodity and, instead, encouraged the production of a range of related products. Thus, a manufacturer 'licensed' to make only trucks, like TML for instance, could begin to manufacture passenger cars as well, thus bringing tremendous flexibility to a range of lumpy investments such as metal forming, or even machining, and helping greater optimization in capital utilization. Yet, in reality, the passenger car sector remained subject to a very tight regulatory regime and witness to the government's continued support for MUL. By the end of 1986, it was back to the same old story of using tariff and other levers to promote the interests of MUL, as the government suddenly withdrew all concessions for fuel-efficient vehicles with engine capacities greater than 1,000 cc, leading to an overnight increase in the vicinity of 30 per cent of the prices of vehicles made by HM and PAL. To most industry observers the timing looked rather suspect. MUL had just about completed an expansion of its production capacity and needed to ensure high utilization. Even its new mid-size offering now came with a 1,000 cc engine in keeping with the new tariff provisions, leaving observers wondering which came first.

It was in such an environment that TML went to the government with a proposal to manufacture – not assemble – cars, starting with the Honda Accord in a proposed joint venture with Honda. Earlier, another fervent suitor, Fiat, had offered TML technology to produce the Regata 175, with a diesel option, at exceptionally lucrative terms and backed by some very strong 'recommendations'. TML, however, chose Honda, impressed by its huge strides in technology and the amazing volume growth it had achieved in the US market, probably one of the most difficult to enter. The joint venture envisaged, among other things, an equity investment by Honda in TML, rapid localization to achieve an indigenous content which, even at the commencement of production, would be above 60 per cent in terms of localization, much higher than the 47 per cent local content (or the 'real' level of 30 per cent that most industry insiders reckoned) that MUL publicly laid claim to in the fourth year of its operations and a clearly committed substantial offsetting of imports by exports. The partners had informally started talking about a possible joint development of a diesel engine pickup truck for the US markets. With TML's proven ability at building production scale, developing localization, and keeping both costs and prices well under check, the TML–Honda Accord with air conditioning was to be launched at a price in the region of ₹1.65 lakhs in 1987, when an air-conditioned Maruti 800 sold at about ₹75,000.

While alarm bells would definitely have rung at both HM and PAL, I have no doubt that they pealed the loudest at MUL. After all, if the Honda Accord came in from TML, it would automatically ensure that the head room both in terms of pricing and profits of MUL would definitely be constrained and held in check to a level more in keeping with the kind of product and technology that it purveyed. Honda too had a range of products, including smaller products like the Honda City, then a runabout with a 600 cc engine that could pull the small car rug from under MUL's feet. A lot of questions were soon swirling in circles that mattered in Delhi on the need for manufacturing a 'luxury car' like the Honda Accord using up scarce foreign exchange resources which, according to what the then finance minister V.P. Singh said on a television show, ought ideally to have been going into the import of edible oils for India's masses. With secrecy shrouding every decision made by the government, it would have been difficult for the public to know the true foreign exchange cost of MUL's so-called 'people's car', or, for that matter, any truly informed debate. As it turned out, permission for the TML–Honda joint venture was simply not granted!

Many conspiracy theories, some of substance and some of doubtful veracity, did the rounds in those days about the TML–Honda joint venture not being approved by the government, even after the then prime minister, Rajiv Gandhi, had expressly indicated his support for the project in private conversations. I remain convinced that, had the proposed joint venture been allowed, MUL would probably never have grown to the dominant position that it did, with the government support it received effectively ensuring that it faced no real competition for the first fifteen years of its existence as a carmaker. In an attempt to project MUL as a shining beacon of public-sector competence, India's policy-makers of the day ended up fostering the worst kind of state monopoly. Under the guise of a joint venture, effective control was thus ceded to a foreign manufacturer which in turn managed the cost levers in such a way as to ensure that the real surplus accumulation arising from unfettered market control probably took place outside India – and the then main shareholders, the government and people of India, received a paltry ₹13 crore to ₹20 crore annually as dividend. Amusingly, when in May 2002, the government of India inked its revised joint venture agreement with SMC, this meagre dividend payout and the fact that 'in the year 2000–01, MUL did not declare any dividend' were put forth by the Ministry of Divestment as part of the rationalization for the ultimate divestment and sale of controlling interest in MUL to SMC. (In the same document, the ministry reported MUL's profit in 2001–2002 as ₹55 crore. Just by way of comparison HMI's profits after tax in the same year were ₹274 crore! Readers are free to draw their own inferences after juxtaposing this fact against the earlier statements in this paragraph.)

Independent studies have made various estimates of the 'hidden subsidy' that MUL allegedly received over the first five years of its existence. But, if I recall correctly, never did India's policy-makers ask the Bureau of Industrial Costs and Pricing (BICP) to study MUL's costing and pricing practices. I have always wondered how a twisting and bending of the rules would have been perceived if the beneficiary of the largesse thus bestowed was a regular Indian private-sector company, rather than one in which the government held considerable stake. It was also conveniently overlooked that the other significant stakeholder in the beneficiary company was a Japanese private-sector corporation. Beyond what this did to the incumbent auto manufacturers, the government's extensive support to MUL helped rob Indian car consumers of technologically better product choices and the introduction of global-standard technology, while at the same time leaving them open to the risk of super-normal profits accruing to a single seller of not really cutting-edge or world-class automobile technology. Not to forget, the loss to the people of India from the virtual gifting away of shares to SMC first in 1989 and then again in 1992.

In 1989, after MUL had been in commercial production for well over five extremely profitable years, and been the recipient of unprecedented government support and largesse, Suzuki was allowed to raise its stake via a rights issue from 26 per cent to 40 per cent – at par. More was to follow. In 1992, MUL issued a further 2.2 million shares to Suzuki for a total consideration of ₹592 million, at an unbelievable price of ₹269 for a ₹100 par value share, and the then majority shareholders – the government and the people of India – did not even earn a control premium for handing over effective control of the company. (Incidentally, just for a comparison, in June 1992, HM had a market share of 13.4 per cent, and PAL of 9.4 per cent against MUL's market share of 74.8 per cent. Small wonder then that the pricing of the MUL shares raised eyebrows in industry and financial circles so high that they merged with hairlines. The government of India ultimately admitted the poor pricing decision of 1992 when it pointed out in 2002 that it had then attained a price that was 219 per cent higher than it would have if it had stuck to the share pricing formula used in 1992.)

In its 1987 review of the automotive products industry, even the World Bank spoke of the need for measures to discipline organizational behaviour and push firms to innovate. It observed that '...the combination of a concentrated industry structure (scale considerations aside) and high levels of trade protection are likely to continue to foster oligopolistic pricing policies as well as technologically conservative behaviour in domestic firms. In addition, even if dynamic domestic competition was to occur, improving managerial efficiency, unit costs would still be significantly higher than international norms because of suboptimal production scales. To expose firms in passenger cars…to competition, the government should announce a move toward greater competition.' But the policy-makers, normally very quick to see merit in recommendations from the World Bank, remained unmoved. It was ultimately post the macro-economic crisis of the early 1990s, and the liberalization that followed, that India's passenger car industry was truly thrown open to competition.

Notwithstanding the setback with the Honda joint venture, using learnings from its involvement with Honda, TML took a stab at developing a small car in-house in 1986. In what might today seem a little more than an enthusiastic skunkworks effort, TML acquired two Honda Acty pickups at a State Trading Corporation (STC) auction, then procured the entire lot of engine components and other spare parts lying in stock from The International Crops Research Institute for the Semi-Arid Tropics (ICRISAT), the original owners of the pickups, got off-the-shelf steering, suspension and brake components of the Maruti 800, used drawings of the overall dimensions of the Honda City out of Britain's *Autocar* magazine, and built a mule for testing. At a time when getting an approval for importing an engine for research and development could take anything up to six months, this simple expedient, had the effort rolling out in just two months. According to Puspendra Sinh, then director of sales at TML, the 'enthusiasts' were made to see reason after Moolgaokar made the observation that TML would need to build a lot more capability, particularly in the design and manufacture of body dies, before it could match Suzuki's aesthetics. He also made a rather pithy noting that it was 'better to be known as a good truckmaker than a bad carmaker', or words to that effect. Ultimately, TML shelved the well-guarded secret project to make a micro car that it intended to pit against the Maruti 800. But much of the engineering and design knowledge that TML gained from its extremely close involvement with Honda (amazing as it may sound, Honda had even handed over to TML key drawings to help speed up the Honda Accord product development and manufacturing process, which TML later returned) came in handy when TML started work on the 207 Tatamobile, an ambitious attempt at going global on the advice of the consulting firm Arthur D. Little. Sinh and the domestic sales team, however, remained unconvinced about a pickup truck and rooted instead for a utility vehicle to take on the monopoly incumbent in the category, Mahindra & Mahindra. Not surprisingly, the 207 Tatamobile bombed, and TML's sales team had to wait five more years before they could bring to the market what they considered to be appropriate for it.

Clearly, India did not see value in the pickup concept in the late 1980s, and in an attempt to make the best of a bad bargain TML used the platform to build first the Tata Sierra (inspired by the Chevy Blazer) and then the Tata Estate. Though, as Ratan Tata acknowledged in an interview to *Time* magazine late in 1998, the two vehicles were a 'cut-and-paste job on the same platform ... bridge vehicles: rough and tough, not so well finished' and probably a tad crude in global terms. Yet, the two vehicles were India's first, true home-grown passenger cars. They also brought in their wake some exceedingly interesting car advertising and marketing innovations, including the first attempt at relationship marketing (with the Sierra Vista) and at customer relationship management (CRM) in the Indian automobile industry. The Tata Estate was also the government's vehicle of choice to ferry around dignitaries for the G15 summit in Delhi – specially remade off-line by an after-sales service team for the event, and maintained with dedication and a prayer! The experience of making and selling the Sierra and the Estate helped TML launch the blockbuster hit vehicle, the Sumo, which raced to a 50 per cent marketshare (in the markets in which it was launched) against Mahindra & Mahindra, in just over a year from launch, and became the first choice among private owners of utility vehicles in both urban and rural India. For its marketing approach, the Tata Sumo won the first Business Standard Brand Derby, and notched up the fastest sale of 100,000 units – a record that remained intact till the advent of the Hyundai Santro.

But TML remained constantly on the lookout for the opportunity to launch the ideal car, and was soon to be closely involved with the other product development process that had the potential to rewrite the history of India's passenger car industry – the Project Globus initiative of MB. Started during 1994, Project Globus sought to create, I believe, among other things, a global supermini designed to be produced in a cost-efficient manner across the world. Despite their undisputed knowledge of cars, the Globus team went about the process of understanding the Indian consumer with a humility and focus that was truly exceptional. They spoke with industry experts like Gautam Sen – an industry insider given his early career at MUL, globally recognized as the pioneer in automobile journalism in India and then editor of *Auto India* – a host of automobile dealers and the ordinary consumer too. Consumers spoke of crowded roads, lack of parking – things they still gripe about today – and often of the relevance of a 'big enough small car' for India that did not sacrifice passenger safety. Clearly, Indian consumers adored the Maruti 800, but they also wanted the roominess that they loved about HM's Ambassador.

There is no doubt that the HM Ambassador has been the ultimate reference point for practically every automobile manufacturer desirous of entering India. Even in 1985, as part of its 'benchmarking' activities in the proposed joint venture with Honda to manufacture the Accord, TML airlifted an HM Ambassador vehicle to Japan to be used as a reference for a teardown analysis. When the car was unloaded at Tokyo's Narita Airport, its 'retro' look apparently led to a near stampede of curious onlookers. Of course, value-seekers that

Indian consumers typically are, practically all of the respondents of the Globus study referred to the ideal price point as that of the Maruti 800. Characteristically, too, the list of must-have features seemed never-ending. The only thing they didn't ask for was a car that ran on water! For me, it was a learning to iterate with the MB team on the approaches to resolving such apparent contradictions. They clearly believed that the role of technology was to provide greater value to customers through better performance and safety standards in a cost-efficient manner.

In January 1995, MB sent its product proposal on the 'small car' to TML. The concept drawing revealed a car with an overall length that was about 10 centimetres (4 inches) longer, 20 centimetres (8 inches) wider and 15 centimetres (6 inches) taller than the Maruti Zen. By increasing the seating height of the front and rear seats and reducing the height of the seat reference point (SRP) (the intersection of the compressed seat back and cushion) from the street surface, the designers managed to increase the standard interior volume quite substantially. Quite exceptionally, despite all of this, they had managed to end up with an aerodynamic design with a low coefficient of drag to help improve both speed and fuel efficiency.

The proposed car was to have four engine options: two petrol and two diesel. Besides pushing for maximum fuel economy, the engine concepts were created to meet challenges of the present and the future. Pitching for an 'unpretentious, robust, easy-to-produce and reliable engine' and marrying it with what they had observed of Indian traffic conditions, the MB design team recommended in its note, a gasoline engine 'because the low-end torque layout of the gasoline engine permits a good driving performance with strong torque even with low engine speed'. What's more, the designers recommended a 'monocoque, double-floor – straight member – concept with a great potential for optimization of the safety qualities, the torsional rigidity and the bending deflection'. Using steel sheets of optimized thickness and quality, the MB designers had managed to achieve torsional rigidity to improve handling and vibration in Indian road conditions, and a bending deflection at the tunnel with appropriate strength to absorb the energy in the event of a crash, without transmitting it to the passengers, thus creating for India what would have been a truly world-class car in terms of ride and handling, and safety standards too. The proposal spoke of using one platform to build seven variants, including a three-box car, a passenger van, two cargo van versions, a pickup version and a dual-cab pickup version. In the proposal note the model was named 'Indica'!

The ability of the Globus team to bring technology to serve the consumers' stated and unstated requirements while ensuring a product that was relatively future-proof and imbuing it with an emotional connect via the name was an exceptional learning, and one that would stand me in great stead when I started to work with the product development team on the Santro. Where, unfortunately, the Globus team fell short was in its appreciation of the true size and potential of the Indian car market. Within weeks of the January 1995 proposal note, teams at MB and TML had started work on better defining what then came to be called the Compact Car India (CCI) project. TML believed that it would be necessary to develop two models, one addressing the lower end of the market then controlled by the Maruti 800 and another addressing a higher end that could potentially compete either with existing cars or proposed new entrants in the ₹4.5 lakh to ₹5 lakh price category. At the heart of TML's analysis of the market was the insight that with the Maruti 800 then priced around ₹2.2 lakh and a clutch of models priced above ₹4.4 lakhs, there existed a great opportunity to straddle both segments and position a new product offering right in the middle. TML believed that Indian consumers would move in incremental steps rather than in large leaps while looking for their first upgrade from the Maruti 800. The Maruti Zen had clearly shown that such a slot did exist. Sales of the Maruti Zen a whisker short of 15,000 units in 1994–1995, were projected by the company at vendor meets, to grow by 100 per cent in the next year and by a further 50 per cent in the year after.

Meanwhile, PAL was all set to begin assembling the Fiat Uno at an expected initial selling price of ₹3 lakh. With its rich experience and knowledge of the Indian consumer, PAL was the only other company that had strategically positioned itself to take on MUL by attempting a model introduction strategy – a largish hatchback, and a smallish sedan. Both the Fiat Uno and the Peugeot 309 were – in terms of size, and a host of other attributes – very close to what the market wanted. Unfortunately for PAL, its move to tie up with both Fiat and Peugeot to address the segments (best identified then with the Maruti Zen and the Maruti 1000/Esteem) separately resulted in serious organizational complications. Years of labour unrest combined with internal management issues and the near-debilitating effects of the discrimination the company faced from government vis-à-vis MUL since 1983 only added to its woes, and a once highly regarded automobile industry pioneer lurched from one crisis to another till its existence effectively ceased to matter.

By the summer of 1995, Fiat as part of its global strategy, had reportedly decided to start production of its model 178 world car – later to be known as the Fiat Palio – in India, in collaboration with PAL. Daewoo Motors, too, had started hinting about its Tico being India-bound. However, even as MB appeared to accept the reasoning and analysis of TML on the direction the market would take, it did not necessarily seem to regard as feasible the volume growth trajectory that TML thought possible.

What caused this huge divergence between the way TML and MB looked at the Indian market? With little structured data to work with, projections of market size varied greatly. Even the report of the Sub-Group on Traffic Forecasts and Fleet Requirement in the

Ninth Plan set up by the Ministry of Surface Transport – on which I had served as a nominee of the Association of Indian Automobile Manufacturers (AIAM), as SIAM was known before its reconstitution – while admitting that 'the data on road transport is extremely scanty in the country', chose to build one set of projections on the basis of an extrapolation of the historical trend of sales during the period 1966 to 1996 with an assumed annual growth rate of 8.1 per cent for cars. For an alternative approach, it assumed an income elasticity of demand for cars of 1.8, which it superimposed on varying growth rates in the Gross National Product (GNP) ranging from 6 per cent to 7 per cent. Its estimates of cumulative car sales for the five-year period 1998 to 2002 thus ranged from 2.23 million to 3.84 million. Other approaches came up with similar overall numbers.

Inarguably, these approaches could best serve as mere indicators, because they overlooked the fact that the supply of cars had generally been constrained, practically since the early 1950s, by 'licensed' (and therefore, invariably, installed) production capacities. Most forecasting methods seemed content to project yesterday's scarcities into tomorrow, a typical problem with the majority of studies of demand estimation, be it for power, steel or cement. This worsened things by getting reflected in the creation and invariably the pre-emption of 'licensed' capacity, which further led to constrained availability, perennial shortages, rent seeking, supernormal profits, and ensured a vested interest in projecting an underestimation of real demand – and even deliberately constraining production. For instance, most cement demand estimation studies probably did not factor in existing shortages, the reality of permits and alleged black-marketing through the entire value chain, and used the data of production minus year-end stocks to determine annual consumption, which in turn became the base for estimating the following year's demand. Never one to accept the license raj way of thinking, TML tried to work with unstructured data arising out of sources like the All

India Income Tax Statistics to look for demand indicator surrogates to understand the true potential of the Indian market. Starting with the number of income tax assesses across income brackets to arrive at a distribution curve, TML 'adjusted' the curve of taxpayers at various income levels for estimates of avoidance and evasion and, taking a guess on the effects of perverse wealth effect that was so obviously in evidence with the stock-market and real-estate spurt, it arrived at what it believed could be the true potential of the market.

By the year 2000, it estimated that the size of the market below the ₹5 lakh price level would range between 750,000 units and 1,100,000 units. By contrast, MB used the DRI McGraw-Hill study which estimated the market size to be 281,000 units and Globus arrived at the figure of 290,000 units. Most importantly, while TML looked at a sales volume in the ₹2.5 lakh to ₹5 lakh price range of between 300,000 units and 500,000 units by year 2000, DRI McGraw-Hill estimated 80,000 units and Globus pegged it even lower at 77,000 units for the same span of time. Considering that MUL, as indicated to its vendors, expected the Maruti Zen to account for 45,000 units by 1996–1997, MB probably reasoned (as it turned out, quite wrongly) that there was little headroom for growth for a new brand. The first indicator that TML's approach was clearly the practical way of looking at market potential came with the overwhelming response to the call for bookings for Fiat Uno in January 1996. Over 290,000 units were 'pre-ordered' by consumers. Incidentally, the sales in the ₹2.5 lakh to ₹5 lakh price category in 2000 totalled a shade under 300,000 units and then went on to grow to over 700,000 units in 2005.

Notwithstanding Globus's inability to look beyond conventional metrics and methods in demand estimation, Ratan Tata's introduction of TML's car concept to both Indian and international media, defining it as 'the size of the Zen, interior space of the Ambassador, price of the Maruti 800 and the advantage of diesel', reflected the exceptional work of the product development team at MB. It had clearly received an unmistakable stamp of acceptance from a CEO whose understanding of automobile technology and appreciation of the true potential of India has had very few parallels in Indian industry.

With MB choosing the low-risk option, and effectively preferring to sit out the chance to own a substantial chunk of the opportunity of entering an emerging India, TML chose the path of its own 'assisted development' – with separate, independent entities contributing to specific subsystems – rather than a joint vehicle development with an unquestioned global leader in automotive technology. This was the second time in three years that TML had had to choose the assisted development route and had to strike a different path from MB. Earlier, in 1992, TML chose to buy diesel engine technology from Cummins rather than further build upon complete-vehicle technology for its truck range that could have come from MB along with engine know-how.

TML's decision to go it alone for mass-market cars led it towards I.DE.A for body styling and vehicle engineering, marginal external support for engines and a host of global subsystem manufacturers to help build the Tata Indica. The transmission, however, was done entirely in-house. The managed development and integration of the Tata Indica was a commendable effort, no doubt, and one that undoubtedly left the gates open for the entry of more established global car-manufacturing competitors.

The resultant oligopolistic, or in fact near-monopolistic, market structure ensured that the technology available in the Indian market was not world-class while car prices were completely out of line with those in developed markets. The combination of MB's inability to comprehend the real potential of the Indian market and TML's resultantly not being able to bring into the Indian market proven passenger-car manufacturing capabilities was, to my mind, one of the luckiest breaks for other prospective entrants, and just the opening that Hyundai needed. I firmly believe that a great deal of Hyundai's success in putting down roots in India, can be traced to the event of TML and MB agreeing to go different ways on the CCI. A couple of years later, MB bought a 10 per cent stake in HMI's parent in Korea, one of its most profitable investments, but sold out well before HMI became a hugely successful player in India and Hyundai achieved stratospheric global growth.

2

Hyundai Readies for Battle

The involvement of Korea Inc. and Hyundai with India effectively started with the visit of India's Prime Minister P.V. Narasimha Rao to South Korea in 1993. India was by then a regular buyer of Korean steel, ships and offshore drilling vessels and yet remained nowhere on the investment horizon of the chaebol. The prime minister's summit meeting with the Korean President, and his discussions with Korean industry leaders on a wide range of measures for promoting economic cooperation and the Korean private sector's investment in India, changed all that. Within months of that path-breaking interaction, the Daewoo, LG and Samsung groups moved into India to establish a presence in the automotive and consumer electronics sectors.

However, it was not until November 1995, that HMC made its intentions known, and its then chairman, S.Y. Chung, announced plans to set up a joint venture to manufacture cars, at an outlay of $600 million, with an initial annual production capacity of 1,00,000 units. According to media reports at the time, work on the proposed plant was expected to commence in 1996 and manufacture of the Hyundai Accent and the Hyundai Sonata was to start in 1998. Hyundai also spoke of its intention to expand the capacity to 2,00,000 units by the year 2000 at an additional outlay of $400 million.

Most auto industry insiders and observers in India took these expressions of intent with a lot more than the proverbial pinch of salt. Hyundai's global track record was not exactly awe-inspiring. After a fairy-tale start in the early 1980s, it had a rather unremarkable, even disastrous, showing both in the United States and Canada, as serious quality problems led to the brand becoming the butt of some very uncharitable jokes on American television and it consequently saw a continuous decline in sales. Its plant in Bromont, Canada, set up in 1989 at a cost of $400 million, operated far below its capacity rated at 100,000 units. Production at this unit peaked in 1991 at a tad above 28,000 units and then fell away sharply to just over 14,000 cars in 1993, the year that production was stopped at the location. In 1995, the plant was finally shuttered.

The Bromont disaster brought in its wake one important learning for Hyundai other than the need for consistent quality. While on the one hand, a weak Canadian dollar made imported parts expensive, on the other, the lack of a plant where engines and transmission could be manufactured (ostensibly because the company's capacity didn't warrant building one) severely impacted both product cost structures and the company's balance sheet. All three issues – consistent quality, a high degree of localization as a risk-mitigation imperative and the setting up of integrated production capability with powertrain production – became central to the development and planning processes in Hyundai thereafter, with India becoming its first laboratory for creating the building blocks for sustainable global expansion. An equally important learning from Bromont about ensuring better communication with the workforce was also not forgotten when the Hyundai team set about building their edifice in India.

In February 1996, Hyundai first made its presence felt in India with a colourful display at the Auto Expo at Pragati Maidan in New

Delhi. But the bigger global names were the ones that garnered both media and peer-group attention. Just weeks earlier, Y.S. Kim and a crack team, most of whom had worked together in Bromont, had set up Hyundai's beach-head operation in Chennai and started a search for a suitable local partner. But potential Indian joint-venture partners, including two large conglomerates with significant automotive interests, remained largely unconvinced about Hyundai's technological competence, having also possibly taken into account the word in the market on the way Hyundai's compatriot Daewoo operated and the general behaviour and attitude of its people. On its part, Hyundai was also less than convinced it needed an industrial partner other than the two it showed some interest in, and thought a wholly owned operation would bring both speed and flexibility if it managed to understand the legal environment and the market with the involvement of Indian professionals.

Eventually, in an eyebrow-raising departure from what was then considered conventional wisdom, Hyundai chose not to partner with an existing Indian business group while entering a country of which it knew very little. This decision to go it alone was perhaps one of the contributory factors that enabled the keen focus and speedy decision-making that became the hallmark of Hyundai in India. Discussing this approach years later, Jong Il Kim (J.I. Kim), who succeeded Y.S. Kim as managing director of HMI, recalled that the decision arose from the thought that with the exception of two Indian business groups no one else could bring anything of substance to the table in a joint venture. J.I. Kim had himself worked closely with an Indian business group in another Hyundai venture which had very soon stumbled its way into extinction. Hyundai knew it was bringing with it technology, production know-how and processes, and finance, and thus needed no hand-holding on the internal-facing activities. In order to build a robust and profitable business, it was on the external-facing matters that it needed to clearly understand the Indian reality. Most Indian business groups at that stage could not have matched Hyundai on any of the technology and process parameters and during joint-venture discussions they presented as their critical strengths and possible contribution their 'connections and relationships' with governments, their perception of their brand value and their ability to provide an established local distribution network.

Noting that, by 1995, the government itself was speaking of allowing 100 per cent foreign-owned ventures in the automobile industry and a more normative approach to doing business, Hyundai strategists reasoned that it first needed professionals who understood India's legal and regulatory systems intimately, and could translate Indian legal and bureaucratic jargon into a simpler work-oriented and rule-driven operating system. They rightly concluded that this approach would be preferable to exposing the company to a different set of risks brought on by entering into a business partnership with people whose claim to fame and fortune had more to do with proximity to the powers-that-be and an ability to prosper from manipulating the license raj than technology achievements or managerial competence. With this in mind, Y.S. Kim first zeroed in on T.M. Kumar, then a young lawyer with a Chennai law firm which was already working with Hyundai on company incorporation and related paperwork. He found that the youngster could think outside the box and take a more international business perspective rather than most of his litigation-led colleagues were wont to. T.M. Kumar came on board the Hyundai team as general counsel and, except for a brief period when he agreed to be a member of the company's management, has remained so, till date.

The other, bigger challenges that Hyundai realized it would face was that it did not truly understand the hearts and minds of Indian consumers, had absolutely no brand recognition and nothing by way of relationships with any of the other stakeholders in the business, be they dealers, vendors or financial-services partners. But, as J.I. Kim put it, Hyundai believed that both the understanding of the consumer and the establishment of such relationships lay more with professionals in Indian companies than they did with the promoters of business groups, and therefore decided it was better off co-opting such capabilities into the management of the company in India rather than entering into a co-ownership structure which would be fraught with its own complications and potential for stress – not to speak of the avoidable sharing of profits. Which is why, apparently, Y.S. Kim and Jong Dae Bae (J.D. Bae), who was to be my Korean counterpart when I joined HMI a few months later, had in unison insisted they would get me on board, as Bae once said, 'irrespective of the cost' and in the face of opposition from the human resources (HR) team, which was afraid my employment terms could potentially disturb the overall corporate salary structure that they had put in place by then. I discovered later that after meeting with me both Y.S. Kim and Bae had apparently reasoned with their colleagues that it appeared that the thought of competing against and beating Japanese competition did not seem to scare me at all. That, I realized many months later, was the ultimate music to Korean ears!

By the time HMI was incorporated in India in May 1996, the market for cars had already started looking crowded. MUL, the state-sponsored joint venture with Japan's small-car specialist SMC had assiduously built, albeit with unprecedented government support, what appeared to be an impregnable fortress with a market share of 80 per cent plus, leaving a gaggle of players, including HM, PAL, GM, Ford, Peugeot, Honda, Fiat and Daewoo scrapping for leftovers. Significantly, India's most respected and trusted brand name, TML, the commercial vehicle behemoth hitherto largely restricted to the utility vehicle market where it competed with Mahindra & Mahindra, had also decided to enter the mass market for cars. TML hoped to bring to bear its substantial expertise in the automotive business to benefit from what it correctly perceived as a big opportunity brought about by broad-spectrum economic growth coming in the wake of the economic reforms of the early 1990s and the subsequent rise of an aspirational Indian middle class.

GM, Ford and Honda, however, chose to stick with strategy prescriptions possibly based on observed trends in other global markets that were typically doled out by consulting companies, and seemed to believe (completely wrongly as it would later turn out) that Indian consumers too would move rapidly from the Maruti 800 to large three-box sedans. They built their product strategies for market entry accordingly, and Ford came in with the Escort, GM with the Opel Astra, and Honda with the City. Consumers, on the other hand, were obviously very hesitant to move up at the pace consultants believed they would, and the three big names found sales volumes lagging for the product segments they chose. Already unable to conclusively establish the economic rationale of setting up integrated manufacturing plants to meet the low-volume forecasts, they soon ended up reconciling themselves to staying stuck in a vicious circle of non-performance. The low volumes meant that the companies could only set up screwdriver facilities which imported Semi Knocked Down (SKD) or CKD kits from their plants in UK, or Germany, or even Thailand, paid relatively high customs duties on the imports of the kits, and then assembled cars from them. In turn, the focus on assembling rather than manufacturing meant other things, poor localization, except for perhaps things like batteries and tyres, leading to uncompetitive product costing and therefore uncompetitive pricing compared with say the Maruti 1000/Esteem, which was the first step for consumers upgrading from the Maruti 800. Low indigenization also meant high prices of spare parts and unaffordable service-related maintenance expenses. Small volumes also resulted in a poor distribution spread, only making service more difficult to access. With each negative having an inevitable multiplier effect on the other, these companies seemed destined to remain in a state of low-level equilibrium for a long time.

Earlier, over the months leading to the Auto Expo of 1996, Y.S. Kim met with all the policy-makers in Delhi from the prime minister downwards to try and convince them of the need to allow 100 per cent foreign-equity ownership in the automotive industry, a thought that had already been exercising the minds at Udyog Bhavan. They listened closely to Y.S. Kim – as they did during the same period, incidentally, to Volvo Trucks.

Along the way, HMC made some very important commitments to the government of India. First, that it would build a facility with an annual capacity of 100,000 units and attain an indigenization level of over 70 per cent by the fourth year of its operations. This it would achieve by creating an integrated manufacturing facility that would contain an engine and transmission machining, assembly and testing operation. One part of this commitment, a large chunk, really, was relatively simple to meet, because it entailed the movement of the sheet metal decoiling, blanking and press line, among the single-largest equipment investments in a car plant, from Hyundai's plant in Canada, which had been mothballed a few months earlier. The line had barely been used, thanks to the circumstances surrounding the Canada operations, and it would essentially create an annual body panel-manufacturing capacity of 125,000 units. For the finishing, it would have to be mated with a paint shop of a matching capacity. With a significant portion of the cost of paint and pre-treatment facilities consisting of fabrication work, which when localized would bring down costs substantially, Hyundai reckoned that it would definitely be feasible to offer a locally done global-quality paint shop for its India project. These would then become determining capacities for the proposed plant. The high-volume engine line machining investments were also not going to be complicated, though they are typically designed for a specific model to be produced, because in any case the original decision was for the plant to mainly manufacture the Hyundai Accent. The second, more important, commitment made was that it would develop the India operation as an export base.

The choice of plant location was the next big hurdle for the HMI team. Early in 1996, *Business Today* magazine had published a survey on the best states for locating new investments among manufacturing and service companies already operating in India. The objectives of the survey included identifying, in order of importance, the parameters used by industry to determine which state to locate projects in, obtaining a rating of all the states and union territories on each of those parameters and combining the ratings to create a composite rank for each state to identify its position in the hierarchy. The parameters were grouped into four categories – infrastructure, government, labour and social factors. The respondents to the survey placed the highest importance on physical infrastructure; the availability and cost of power; support from the state government; law and order; the quality of administration; and the quality of work culture. The survey concluded – just like another survey published by *World Link*, the World Economic Forum's magazine, three years earlier – that Maharashtra, Gujarat, Tamil Nadu and Karnataka were the best locations for industrial investment. The HMI team shortlisted all four of these locations and one state in northern India.

Of these, Tamil Nadu ticked all the boxes. With the chief minister providing executive leadership (while it was J. Jayalalitha who got the deal all stitched up, her arch-rival M. Karunanidhi ultimately oversaw the implementation – and yet that caused no hiccups), the bureaucracy in the state and its cadre members on deputation at the centre worked to put together, in record time, a clear policy formulation on all aspects of the support that Hyundai sought. They then went ahead and proposed a location – Irungatukottai – that was quite simply everything that HMI wanted, perhaps more. The exceptionally located land was just 35 kilometres from Chennai airport, situated on a major national highway, with unmatched access via road connectivity to a major port and rail connectivity to the rest of the country. The area had adequate water supply, with a large fresh water source within touching distance, and came with high-tension lines already in place for continuous availability of clean, low-cost power. Besides, being close to Chennai meant a reliable supply of highly skilled, relatively low-cost labour with an enviable work culture. Topping it all was a flexible and highly supportive state government with a well-defined policy framework for tax relief, subsidies and other incentives for industry and a no-nonsense approach to law-and-order issues. The infinite patience of Y.S. Kim, dovetailed perfectly with the hard-as-nails and cold-as-ice negotiation tactics of T.M. Kumar and E.H. Jin and backed by meticulous and structured legal documentation capabilities, ensured the finalization of a tailor-made and 'future-proofed' incentive package that left no room for either subsequent reinterpretation or malafide legal challenge by any entity interested in doing so. Effectively, it laid the first brick of the foundation for HMI's profitable growth.

Right through the exercise of getting the incentives package cleared and approved by the state government to the subsequent implementation of the project, there was a clearly demonstrated willingness on the part of the HMI executive team to ideate and implement entirely in consonance with the letter of the law, working to build consensus from the ground up and drawing the attention of senior policy-makers to acknowledge and recognize the spirit of the law when and where required. This stood in sharp contrast to the approach of other large foreign investors in the state, who never seemed to hesitate to call in the senior members of their countries' diplomatic corps to personally call on the highest echelons in the government to push the case for solving so-called 'minor issues', most of which would in reality be so complex that sorting them out would entail significant alterations in either administrative or legal processes. HMI's approach helped create immense goodwill and win the company friends and well-wishers in the corridors of power in Fort St. George (the seventeenth-century complex that houses the Tamil Nadu government secretariat), placing Irungatukottai firmly on India's automobile-manufacturing map.

On 18 July 1996, the government of Tamil Nadu and HMI signed a memorandum of understanding (MoU) in which Hyundai confirmed the setting up of the project. It committed that 'the investment in fixed assets to be made by HMI will be more than ₹1,500 crore and a total investment including the above will be up to ₹2,400 crore in the first phase within five years from the date of MoU and another ₹1,300 crore in the next five years in the second phase, both subject to all government approvals being given in time.' On its part, the state government confirmed Hyundai India's eligibility to receive the incentives announced for super-mega projects for manufacturing cars and/or trucks, and components thereof, for a period of fourteen years. It also clarified that all investments made for substantial expansion or diversification would also qualify for all the incentives promised to the company. The approach of the government towards enabling investments was most significantly highlighted by its commitment to provide possession of at least half of the land identified for setting up HMI's plant within 100 days of the MoU being signed and the balance within 90 days thereafter. The MoU document also clearly stipulated deliverables from the government on matters of power and water supply, effluent treatment and the provision of training facilities.

But the sweetest part of the deal came in the form of fiscal incentives. The MoU fully exempted HMI from sales tax leviable on all inputs and capital equipment purchases, and any duty or tax that could be applicable on the purchase of energy from an independent power producer or on captive production. The government confirmed that the company would be eligible for either sales tax deferral or sales tax waiver for a period of fourteen years from the date of commencement of commercial production, subject to a limit of 100 per cent of the value of investments in fixed assets – an incentive which would prove to have great significance for the future financial performance of the company – perhaps far greater than ever envisaged by the government. Considering the initial indications by the company of its intent to produce the Hyundai Accent and Sonata, and its expectation that the choice of model itself would result in relatively low sales, the Tamil Nadu government may well have anticipated a much lower deferred accrual of tax revenues on account of the sales tax incentive. The change in the product portfolio that was formalized a few months later, however, meant that the company would now enter the mass market in direct competition with MUL and TML, bringing in its wake a significant increase in volumes and therefore in potential deferred revenues and revenue loss on account of input tax exemptions. The MoU being model agnostic, this had clearly not quite been factored in by the government. In any case, during private conversations, many bureaucrats of the day confided that they did not expect that the 'different looking' (as they politely referred to it) Santro would really see significant sales volumes in a market that was widely expected to remain dominated by MUL and TML – with everyone else reduced to the status of bystanders.

Just days after the signing of the MoU, I went to the Hyundai headquarters in Seoul on Y.S. Kim's invitation. With the acquisition of land for the plant out of the way, HMI had now moved on to the part of the job that was even tougher. All my conversations in Seoul seemed to revolve around the right model for the initial market entry – and then came the revelation that Korea's largest carmaker might well have a surprise for India. I can't say I was blown away by the forerunner of the Santro – the MX, to be later badged the Atoz. Quite to the contrary. My gut feeling, which I unhesitatingly stated, was that it could work in India but with some – more like, a lot of –

tweaking to reflect the needs, both stated and unstated, of the Indian consumer. Then there was the challenge to making and selling a global technology and global quality car at an appropriate price – and attain profitability at the end of the process. Since the entry price was critical it also became imperative to attain cost competitiveness through cost- and time-efficient project implementation and effective vendor development to ensure a high level of indigenization.

On 10 December 1996, less than five months after signing the MoU and in the midst of a torrential downpour, HMI held the ground-breaking ceremony for its plant. The Indians in the crowd were upbeat because they saw the rains as a good omen, while the Koreans were downcast because in their culture rain apparently signified exactly the opposite. But the latter's misgivings were unfounded. The project implementation at HMI set new records, not just nationally but globally as well. In a mere seventeen months, the project went from ground-breaking to prototype manufacture – not merely assembly – with strict cost budgeting and time management firmly in place.

Hyundai Engineering & Construction Ltd (HECL), the group company entrusted with the construction activity of the plant was already making its presence felt at the site and the first signs of land development were visible even during ground-breaking. Within days thereafter a full-fledged site office came up on an incline in the south-west corner of the plot and, even more significantly, a complex of residential barracks consisting of two buildings was also constructed. These were to be the homes of a remarkable group of plant construction engineers led by Moon Hee Lee, HMI's first deputy managing director, who chose to live on the site in order to ensure that the work was monitored literally 24x7, and the construction schedule, more aggressive than any India had ever known, was met while maintaining global standards of quality at Indian costs. Making this possible was a very committed group of Korean and Indian construction engineers led by S.P. Kwon and the site management group at HECL's main contracting partner, Larsen & Toubro Construction (L&T Construction, then known as ECC). Already a byword for quality and time performance in construction in India, L&T Construction, had won a competitive bidding process against the likes of Shapoorji Pallonji and Hindustan Construction Company after the Hyundai team had seen their work at the Nehru Stadium in Chennai. They did not disappoint. After laying the roads and completing drainage-related work, excavation for the main buildings began and their construction was completed on the scheduled date to the high standards set by Hyundai's global experience.

The process of installation of equipment adhered to similarly exacting schedules. The press shop which was to produce the sheet metal parts that make up the body of the car was designed to be a fully integrated operation. Cold-rolled steel sheets, typically with very low carbon content, and using titanium to give high tensile strength and formability, were to be brought in the form of rolls direct from steel manufacturers. The steel would then be decoiled and, in a flat form, cut in a blanking press into specific shapes for each component in such a way as to minimize the resulting scrap. The blanks would then go through either of two large-bed transfer presses, which automatically carried out a multi-stage forming process using multiple dies where each die in the system added more form to the blank steel sheet until it attained its final desired form.

Simple, common-sense-driven layouts ensured highly efficient workflows, starting from the decoiling station to the stacking of pressed panels, from the main buck assembly to the body-finishing and inspection line. The robotization of the body weld line was seen as an absolute imperative to ensure superior quality with maximum productivity, since it had become clear that HMI would enter the volume market. This made the plant one of the most highly automated manufacturing units among those newly established by new entrants in the Indian automobile market at that point. (Some months later, when reduced pitch for car body spot-weld became a significant element of product design for India, thereby ensuring more welds per metre on the Indian product as compared to the global product, to compensate for the stresses the car body would have to contend with on Indian roads, the focus on robotization from inception and the large capital outlay that it entailed was more than compensated for in terms of quality and productivity.)

The layout of the engine plant was, similarly, both simple and efficient. From the first unit of production, all the 5 Cs – the cylinder block, cylinder head, crankshaft, connecting rod and camshaft – were machined in-house, making HMI quite exceptional; only MUL and TML could compare favourably in terms of overall manufacturing plant technology. Simple and appropriate automation of quality-related processes on the machining line and an intelligently designed assembly line for different engine combinations, leading to a well laid-out engine test facility, ensured capital efficiency of a very high order and provided a perfect fit for a financially beleaguered first-time market entrant into a high-capital-cost economy. The layout culminated in a simple and efficient assembly line where the fully painted body was mated with the mechanical aggregates – the engines, gear boxes, axles, steering – and the suspension, tyres, interiors and electricals to complete the manufacturing process.

If one were to point out, albeit in retrospect, the misses here, one of them would be the paint shop design that seemed not to take into account the weather in Chennai. A layout design where the ovens are placed at the highest level in order to ensure better heat extraction and thereby improve the working environment, yet lowering the cost of climate control in the spray booths, might have been more appropriate. The high temperature and arduous working environment of the paint shop ended up making it a labour hotspot for the company. The second was an area that could have done with greater automation from inception –

the door hemming and welding stations. These involved highly fatiguing manual-labour operations and again led to labour issues that could have been avoided. These two layout and installation issues aside, the Hyundai India plant was a truly exceptional effort even by Hyundai's exacting standards and compared with what had been achieved at its earlier Canadian venture. Interestingly, in anticipation of the expansion to phase two of the plant, all the pillars and the flooring for the expansion had been cast at the time of the first phase of construction itself, and then used primarily as a large stockyard for incoming material. With this advance foundation construction out of the way, all that HMI's civil engineering team had to do when the expansion was required, was to put in place the steel structure and cladding. This meant that the enhanced capacity assembly line with additional stations were completed and ready for equipment installation literally in a matter of days when finally needed – with no disruptions to regular production. This kind of simple common-sense approach characterized the entire plant construction activity.

While Hyundai engineers pushed the envelope in terms of construction schedules, the state government displayed both commitment and resolve in equal measure. In keeping with the commitments made in the MoU, both power supply and its requisite infrastructure reached the project site ahead of schedule, and the main water pipeline was probably just a couple of weeks off from the promised date. Some months later, keeping to another MoU condition on not locating any other environmentally hazardous plants within a 15-kilometre radius of the Hyundai plant, the state government shifted the site allotted to a Saint Gobain glass plant much further from the location initially offered to them in order to prevent damage to the paint quality of newly finished cars parked in the Hyundai plant prior to despatch from possible particle emissions from the glass-manufacturing process. HMI too did not lag in ensuring that the plant was built in conformity to then prevalent global environmental standards, and to exactly the same standards as HMC applied in other parts of the world. During this period, T.M. Kumar helped bring global environmental best practices to the attention of policy-makers in Tamil Nadu, and played a pivotal role in getting the state to mandate some of the most progressive environment protection norms for industry – even as larger, better-known global investors kept up a constant chorus for a relaxation or worse, seriously diluting the proposed standards. It appeared that they expected everyone else in the industry to adopt similar double standards, one for their home country and another for India, as a result of which, their callousness would go unnoticed. Fortunately for its people, the government of Tamil Nadu thought and behaved otherwise. The global standards of environmental compliance that HMI implemented at its plant, became the norm for industry in the state. Unfortunately, more often than not, it is the laxity of India's law-makers and law-enforcers that encourages environmentally unscrupulous and deviant behaviour among profit-hungry corporates – or their 'performance' oriented executives. (Many years later, GM got hauled over the coals when its executives in India allegedly fudged environmental compliance tests on its Tavera. GM ultimately got away by changing some components on the non-conforming vehicles, and paying a per unit 'penalty' totalling less than what its dealers may have charged for washing the vehicles. Unfortunately, companies, not their executives, take a larger part of the reputational risk in such cases, and GM struggled thereafter, till it finally announced the downing of shutters on its sales operations in the Indian domestic market in mid-2017.)

Just a few weeks after the ground-breaking ceremony, I ultimately joined HMI in February 1997. Within a few more weeks, the decision to enter the ultra-competitive subcompact segment of the Indian market with a newly developed variant of the model MX, which I had first seen in the Hyundai design studios in Korea in August 1996, was formalized. This was the variant that ultimately became the Santro. It was then decided that the Santro would be the first car to be launched by HMI, to be followed as soon as rationally possible, by the new-generation Accent that was being worked on in the Namyang research and development centre for a global launch in 1999. The Sonata, was thus effectively pushed down to third place in the list of priorities. Despite a clear decision on model phasing having been made, purely as a strategy to keep the competition guessing, the vendor team commenced simultaneous development of components for both the Santro and the Accent, knowing full well that every one of our product moves would be relayed to TML and MUL by executives at some of our vendor partners. Y.S. Kim and I went one step further to add to the confusion, and when speaking with the media deliberately differed on which model – the competitor to the Maruti Zen or the Maruti Esteem – ought to be, and would be, launched first. Of course, neither had a brand name tagged on at that stage. They were simply MXI and LCI.

It was abundantly clear to all of us at that stage that in order to survive, let alone succeed, in those segments against either model, particularly with the dominant position of MUL and the imminent entry of TML, it was imperative that HMI would have to attain a cost structure at least close to that of the dominant player. If the construction, equipment installation and production commencement effort helped lay the foundation of HMI's future by ensuring manufacturing overheads at least comparable with those of TML, it was the second pillar of the edifice – the vendor development and localization effort – that helped give HMI a fighting chance against MUL. The architect of HMI's exceptional but generally not widely written about localization effort was the brilliant Min Ho Lee, HMI's first director of procurement). What people saw most often of this diminutive, extremely focused man was his rather acerbic no-nonsense approach to and his merciless demolition of any mediocrity or a lackadaisical work ethic that came to his notice. His sheer genius in engineering terms and in the implementation of product development programmes to strict cost and time budgets has had few parallels in India's automotive industry. Softening Min Ho Lee's often brutal frankness was his perfect foil, another critical member of the pioneering team, J.B. Lee, who eventually succeeded him.

But for Min Ho Lee's detailed engineering knowledge and the punishing schedule he maintained (and personally ensured that every vendor partner maintained alongside), getting two global-quality products developed and delivered from scratch, with a localization level exceeding 70 per cent even on the first car, the first in 21 months and the next within a period of 12 months thereafter, to exacting cost targets, would have been inconceivable. No automotive company in India has managed anything comparable as yet. For the first few months of the vendor development process, in line with our 'confuse and confound' strategy, Min Ho Lee and his team kept the selected vendor partners guessing which of the two models they were simultaneously working on would come first to market. Though Lee wanted greater openness in dealing with vendor partners, this was a deliberate attempt to keep marketing and product strategy confidential because vendors could potentially be the first source of information for competitors. I recall mentioning at an internal meeting at HMI how, while I was at TML, in response to a simple verbal request to a certain vendor for an opinion on how MUL was looking at market growth over the coming years, we received a fax of the presentation of proposed market volumes for the Maruti Zen et al given at an MUL vendor conference held in Chennai literally minutes after it concluded. In an attempt to ingratiate themselves with OEM managements, it is no secret that some elements of the Indian auto component industry have even been guilty of providing confidential competitor information, including model-wise weekly and even daily roll-out plans of competing OEMs, which they are, as suppliers, privy to.

The emergence of MUL and the modernization of the Indian auto-component industry that followed in its wake was just the kind of enabler that was needed for the aggressive localization that HMI planned and implemented to perfection. A variety of factors had led to a situation where MUL had built a base of about 400 suppliers and subcontractors. An estimated 50 per cent of these were small enterprises, with the majority of them dependent solely on MUL for their business. The cost implications of such a structure probably did not cause too much concern for MUL in the near-monopolistic market that it enjoyed for the first fifteen years of its existence, because demand was in any case far ahead of supply and cost increases even due to manufacturing or procurement inefficiencies could be passed on by way of price increases to consumers. TML had an even more unwieldy procurement structure with an estimated 1,500 variously tiered suppliers bringing in components every day to meet the production-line requirements. Notwithstanding some attempts by TML at creating a more streamlined inbound logistics system, it remained an area of significant weakness both from the quality and cost perspectives, and was often allegedly riven by mismanagement and worse.

Recognizing that HMI could not afford either situation, Min Ho Lee based his vendor development strategy on two specific planks – first, to commit single-source procurement in order to provide economies of scale to the vendor and, second, to use existing Indian suppliers as far as possible. Conventional wisdom in India's automotive industry in those days typically looked at multisource procurement for most items primarily as a risk mitigation requirement – be it on account of labour issues, or power availability, or logistics concerns – or then a combination of all three. Bosch, primarily because of its global control of diesel fuel injection technology, and some auto-component manufacturers based in southern India, initially because of their adept management of the licensing regime at a particular stage in India's industrial history and subsequently thanks to their consistent focus on quality, had generally remained relatively less impacted by this rule. After the emergence of MUL, however, even this had somewhat changed. But the broad consensus remained in favour of having multiple vendors for each component to prevent the operational problems at any one vendor from impacting the vehicle manufacturing operations of the OEM. But this approach brought on its own share of problems. For one, the inefficiency of the marginal producer often served to set the level of component costs, as the dominant player in an oligopolistic situation invariably adjusted reported costs upwards over a period of time to obtain the same pricing and, invariably, higher profitability. Differential quality and performance issues between component manufacturers also had an impact on the OEM brand but the more serious long-term problems arose due to internal management issues that often surfaced within the OEMs that followed the multiple vendor policy. With quality ratings of components potentially subject to manipulation both at the time of receipt and thereafter, decisions on the share of business allotted to competing component manufacturers often faced the risk of unethical distortion. Even more critical from the point of view of the OEMs was the fact that component manufacturers have typically had little real commitment to a brand, and generally as mere riders on the OEM gravy train have often used the 'OE-approved supplier' status primarily as a license to enter the replacement parts market, and then walked off with a disproportionate share of a vehicle's life-cycle profit opportunities, to the long-term detriment of the OEMs. But, in a market for vehicles that was also oligopolistic, this seemed to be less of a priority for the OEMs themselves, though this effectively hurt the interests of two sets of stakeholders, the shareholders of the OEM and the customers.

Given that the primary concerns of HMI were to ensure quality and cost-competitiveness with MUL, and recognizing that this was highly unlikely with procurement being fragmented, Min Ho Lee implemented a single-source procurement policy for the first time in India by a mass-production automotive operation. HMI, therefore, effectively told component manufacturers that once they were selected as vendor partners, their management needed to be solely focused on ensuring that quality cost-and-delivery parameters were met as per commitment, without having to constantly worry about share-of-wallet and looking over their shoulder for potential competitors. This commitment was essentially made till the company obtained a predetermined production and sales volume. In return, HMI wanted the component manufacturers to start supplies at a cost assuming the absorption of overheads at a specific annual production run rate, with an implicit commitment that if the vehicle production run rate, and consequently the component off takes, fell below that level HMI would compensate overhead absorption appropriately and contrariwise if HMI exceeded the run rate. Few could have complained about this innately fair treatment. As a logical extension of this approach, Min Ho Lee then sought out Indian and multinational component manufacturers already operating in India and known for attaining and maintaining global standards of quality as his first-choice vendor partners. This was most effective because established component manufacturers would ensure lower overheads than a new entrant. This marked a significant difference to the *keiretsu*-based approach of Japan Inc., which essentially – often on the specious plea of quality – appeared to prefer Japanese component manufacturers to the exclusion of all others, global credentials notwithstanding. Whenever HMI felt that existing Indian component manufacturers required technology or process upgrades, Lee enabled joint ventures with HMC's component suppliers from Korea. Ultimately, HMI started operations with sixty existing Indian and multinational component manufacturers and fourteen Korean entrants. As it turned out, this approach also ensured that product development timelines were fully met by the selected vendors.

The active involvement of HMI in the vendors' development phase often started at the project report stage itself. I recall accompanying Min Ho Lee at his request, on more than a couple of occasions, to meet with the project finance teams of banks evaluating the investment proposals of vendors, to apprise them of our marketing and sales strategy – which was the basis of their evaluation of project risk. But the real display of commitment came in the handholding of the vendor partners in attaining the desired quality levels of the products by focusing on improving processes. One recollection I have is the case of Ennore Foundries (now merged with Ashok Leyland), which had been selected as the supplier for engine crankcase castings. Their initial supplies at the prototype proving stage had a rejection rate of over 25 per cent because of porosity. Beyond the expenses on account of loss of machine time, power expenses, labour cost and the breakage of tool bits, this was effectively slamming the brakes on production itself. Lee immediately had a group of three metallurgists come in from Korea to work alongside the engineers at Ennore Foundries and make suggestions for improving their processes, which ultimately helped bring crankcase casting rejection rates comparable to global industry standards. Obviously, the learning from this interaction would have benefited Ennore Foundries on supplies to its non-Hyundai customers too, but what it did in the process was to create the foundation for a lasting relationship based on trust and mutual respect. It was this that enabled HMI to later roll out various quality initiatives along with its vendor partners, including the 100 parts per million (ppm) and 50 ppm quality improvement programmes aimed at cutting down rejection of products from Tier 1 and Tier 2 vendors, and thereby lowering direct material cost by as much as 7 per cent on an average in a bid to become even more competitive on a direct cost basis than the parent company and later enabled HMI to succeed in its export strategy. Even before the structured quality enhancement initiatives at vendors, standards matching the parent had already been attained when HMI successfully exported its first set of in-house manufactured components back to the parent company in 1999. It might be interesting for the reader to look for even one other case in the Indian auto industry where this has been achieved – and as rapidly.

Beyond the speed of project implementation and the achievements in the area of vendor development, it was the 'people factor' that provided Hyundai India with its other source of sustainable competitive strength. Setting up in Tamil Nadu automatically ensured a regular supply of well-trained industrial workforce, but actually putting it together and building it into a cohesive, highly productive, quality-oriented group was part of a significant effort overseen by G.S. Ramesh, among the earliest Indians to join the company, who came from the Collieries Division of Tata Steel to initially handle the industrial relations function and later the human resources initiatives of the company. Despite his non-precision-manufacturing engineering industry background, Ramesh adapted quickly to the needs of the fledgling company. Recognizing that the production technologies that HMI would bring in would require a completely different skill level from those generally available in the area, Ramesh rightly convinced Y.S. Kim and Moon Hee Lee about the tougher option of picking freshers being trained under the government's apprenticeship scheme and then training them in the systems and processes of Hyundai. The base of the workforce was thus made up of graduates of technical institutes located all over the state. This approach of spreading the selection net state-wide ensured that location-based or caste-based groupism among the workforce was avoided from the very start of operations. Since the government defrayed a part of the salaries paid under the apprenticeship scheme, the financial implications of this approach were also extremely beneficial. Above the technician level, supervisors and the graduate engineers, generally with prior work experience in automotive, auto components and engineering units, also typically came from the state. The Indian employees in the production and engineering management function came mostly from Tamil Nadu or one or the other southern states, and primarily from MUL. Moon Hee Lee very clearly recognized that the absorption of Japanese production management techniques (though, of course, in the Korean company it would have been sacrilegious to call it anything other than 'mass-production techniques') and the ability to adapt them to Indian conditions was at the time the best practised by and among the engineering and production managers of MUL. He decided that as far as possible the leadership of this top layer, which would directly work in parallel with the Korean engineering teams and oversee the day-to-day operations, would come from MUL. A group of highly committed, Indian engineering management talent, all well trained in Japanese production methods and quality systems including T. Sarangrajan, N. Kumar, K. Asokan, V. Subramaniam, Vishu Behl, R.K. Pal, S. Vaithyalingam, R. Sriram, B. Ganesan, A. Duraisamy and C.S. Gopalakrishnan, among others thus came in from MUL to build the production management capabilities of HMI.

At the level just below the senior Indian production management personnel, Moon Hee Lee had very perceptively got Ramesh to bring in as supervisors trained staff from the production lines of the Indian automotive component manufacturing companies already in Chennai. Many of these companies, primarily due to their involvement with MUL as suppliers, had also absorbed Japanese quality and production systems, and some had won accolades for their quality-oriented manufacturing processes even in Japan, along with managing to create a significant global export thrust. Moreover, with what might have been considered near exploitative wage levels in those companies (at least by the standards of other regions of the country) the cost of skill acquisition for HMI was very affordable. Given their identical or at least similar linguistic background as the technicians, the entire Indian production management and supervisory group was able to adapt Hyundai systems and give practical direction to the technician training programmes and make them particularly suitable and effective for the local workforce without the communication nightmares that Hyundai had faced at Bromont. As a result of this approach the learning curve ascension of the Indian technicians was at least as good, if not better than, those in Korea. This became evident in the manufacturing of fully made-in-India prototype powertrain components, and engine and transmission assemblies, right on schedule and in accordance with all the stated quality norms.

HMI started 1997 with a total employee count of just over 440. This rose rapidly to over 1600 when production of the Santro started, in 1998, and grew thereafter to more than 1800 by the time the Accent was launched in October 1999. By contracting out all supporting activities, from material handling and intra-plant logistics to housekeeping, the direct workforce count was always kept within what were considered safe and manageable levels – both cost and discipline-wise. The age profile of the young and enthusiastic workforce brought with it a certain homogeneity and when layered on with a caring, if somewhat paternalistic, attitude to their welfare, ensured a rare discipline and commitment with absenteeism in the early years never crossing the 3 per cent mark – most of it being chalked up in the agricultural harvest season when the largely first-generation industrial workforce went back to their villages to meet familial and societal demands. Issues that arose among employees were handled by factory committees, with intervention requests being presented to the human resources team in a formal forum and then opened up for debate to enable a speedy resolution. In this manner, in many ways, a truly ideal industrial work environment was created.

In the midst of such a high-quality team of Korean and Indian production and engineering professionals, I invariably found most members of the early finance team, with exceptions like Sun Joo Hwang and S. Varadarajan, quite a far cry from the exceptionally high-quality finance professionals I had always worked along with in TML. One particular memory that still stands out was a bizarre and convoluted tax-saving solution that the team had apparently conjured up for the expats' taxable income in India. A couple of years later when the government of India launched a crackdown on multinational skulduggery for hiding the true extent of expat salaries and remuneration, HMI was unfortunately one of the companies hauled up – the only instance of any real and deliberate deviation from regulatory confines during its first decade. The only other major concern of the finance team leadership always seemed to be how to convince the parent company about the hardships involved in living in India, in order for the Korean expats to qualify for a larger 'hardship allowance'!

The first instance of an acute sense of frustration with the finance team arose when we sat down to discuss why a deferral rather than a waiver of sales tax would be advantageous to the company. As mentioned earlier, as part of the fiscal incentives made available to HMI the Tamil Nadu government had offered either a sales tax deferral or sales tax waiver. The deferred sales tax amount equal to concessional Central Sales Tax (CST) of 2 per cent ad valorem, and the Tamil Nadu state sales tax collected on sales in the state would be repayable interest-free in twenty equal quarterly instalments from the fifteenth year to the nineteenth year after collection. The waiver, on the other hand, would have applied only to vehicles sold in the state of Tamil Nadu, whereby HMI could have collected the local sales tax amount from the customer and kept it with itself or not charged any local sales tax and given the benefit to the customer in terms of a lower ex-showroom price.

Most members of the finance team argued that if HMI chose not to charge the sales tax on sales in the state, the Santro could obtain a higher price realization for the company while still being competitive against the Maruti Zen, and since customers from all the neighbouring states would make a beeline for Tamil Nadu, the resulting sales spurt would lead to a huge gain. It took several rounds of often frustrating discussions on the strategic need to have a balanced growth of dealers and markets across the country, and the real possibility of other states levying an entry tax on vehicles being brought into a state by its residents, to be able to convince the finance team that the waiver would not be in the interest of the company. (Incidentally, it was the use of the sales tax waiver option that led Daewoo to focus so heavily on Uttar Pradesh, its home state, which in turn proved to be its Achilles heel. In the effort to dislodge Daewoo, the competition had to only pick one geographical market to attack the brand, and sales crashed.)

HMI finally opted for the deferral. Thus, on the taxes collected on the sale of cars in FY 1998–1999, its first year of commercial operations, Hyundai started paying the Tamil Nadu government the CST and TNGST collections of about ₹6 crore, at a rate of ₹30 lakh per quarter, starting FY 2013 and due to end in FY 2018. Over the period October 1998 to March 2006 alone, HMI probably collected and held with it over ₹500 crore in deferred sales tax and exempted input tax benefits – essentially providing interest-free working capital in near perpetuity.

Probably the biggest failing of the finance team, however, lay in their inability to work independently to raise debt funds for the company from the Indian banking sector. In line with government regulations then governing corporate forex debt, HMI was required to have a significant portion of its debt denominated in Indian currency, requiring the company to borrow from banks in India – not that it could borrow much in the global markets in those days. Even as the finance team appeared to think it needed only to work with the likes of Citibank, Bank of America, ABN Amro and Standard Chartered, and their Indian operations, none of these banks appeared willing to do anything except lap up the cream on inbound forex remittance transactions. They had a raft of convenient excuses: the Korean financial crisis was full-blown, the Korean won had slumped from 800 to 1300 to the US currency, and that they had already reached their exposure limits to the Hyundai Motor Group. With their favoured banks unable to deliver, the finance team was completely at sea. HDFC Bank did come in with a small commitment, but that at best amounted to moral support in those days. It thus fell to Y.S. Kim and me to knock on every possible door to convince the banks to lend to HMI. The list was long and included State Bank of India (SBI), ICICI Bank, IDBI, IFCI, Punjab National Bank and Union Bank. Ultimately, K.V. Kamath at ICICI Bank, M.S. Verma at SBI and Rashid Jilani at the Punjab National Bank came to the rescue of HMI.

It was ICICI Bank that set the ball rolling. After a detailed presentation on the product, the marketing strategy and production strategy, Kamath seemed convinced and immediately gave his in-principle approval, but said he would like to come in and see what we were doing before finalizing the loan or its covenants. A week later, accompanied by Lalita Gupte, then the deputy managing director and S. Mukerji, then executive director, Kamath visited the plant, already a beehive of activity, feverishly racing to meet deadlines. Engineers and development bankers at heart, the upper crust of ICICI walked through the entire plant discussing in detail practically every single machine that had been installed, then went out to the test track to drive the prototype Santro. Finally, Kamath turned around and said to me, 'I think you've got a winner.' The sari-clad Lalita Gupte was very impressed, too, particularly with the ease of ingress and egress, exactly as I had told her. (Though Kamath waited till the launch of the Terracan to actually get a Hyundai product, I recall Lalita Gupte bought a Santro Automatic, probably for one of those very rare occasions when she drove herself. Talk of the bankers' ultimate vote of confidence!)

The loan of ₹100 crore from ICICI Bank proved to be the proverbial lifesaver, and though it came at near-usurious rates of interest, reflecting very appropriately the then current global risk perception of HMC, this was one good turn HMI owed a lot to. ICICI charged HMI at least 700 basis points over the then applicable PLR even as it apparently lent money to some established Indian companies in the auto industry at 25 basis points over the PLR. But, most important, it gave the other banks confidence in the Hyundai project. (HMI ultimately repaid the loan in a little over one year, and ICICI's present top brass came over to request HMI to keep utilizing at least ₹25 crore of the originally sanctioned amount!)

M.S. Verma at SBI was equally supportive after a one-hour session during which he only discussed HMI's marketing and network strategy to take on TML and MUL before he gave an 'in-principle' nod, though he wanted the detailed project appraisal to be done by SBI Caps. I recall the SBI Caps interaction being a very formal though polite and somewhat theoretical exercise. When I said something about how the market would move 'in my opinion' and how the 'Zen segment', for want of a better word, would grow exponentially, the analyst from SBI Caps, obviously brought up on a diet of more structured global market research studies, told me, clearly articulating the difference between my 'opinion' and his 'analysis', that his studies suggested a much smaller volume growth in the segment. I believed that my qualitative opinion was worth more than his quantitative analysis, but kept my counsel – you can't really argue with bankers when you are a borrower. SBI Caps did give the project their green signal but noted that HMI would in all likelihood sell no more than 18,000 units in its first full year of operation with an optimistic ceiling of 24,000 units and a pessimistic floor of 12,000 units. HMI's first full-year sales were, of course, more than double the optimistic projection made by SBI Caps. Then, as later, SBI continued to be a strong supporter of HMI. With the initial loans in place, HMI finally managed to take a breath.

Not more than a handful of people realized just how serious the financial situation at HMI continued to be even after the loans came through. The ₹450 crore or thereabout collected via the 'bookings' route in October 1998 did provide a huge and unexpected cushion, though this came about with no thanks at all to the finance team. In fact, their management (if you could call it that) of the customer booking adjustments and refund process only earned HMI a fair deal of customer disaffection and, worse, a lot of suspicion from financiers, both of the company's ability and intent even as it struggled to distance itself from, and rise above, the widely prevalent and generally unflattering image of Korean companies.

The inability of the HMI finance team was quite distressing. By refusing to allow correlating of the customer booking form numbers with the receipt numbers generated by the company's ERP system, the team turned what ought to have been a rather routine payment reconciliation and refund exercise into a nightmare for customers, dealers, financing bankers and the front end – the sales team – of the company, who had to resort to manually sorting things out. After that windfall, however, in all my years at HMI, its finance team practically never had to borrow significant sums of working capital and earned their strutting rights with bankers purely as net lenders to the banking system, without having a say in treasury management strategy or policy, which in any case was generally dictated by HMC.

The first year of commercial operations, FY 1999, ended with a loss of ₹50.44 crore. Though the loss was much lower than budgeted, and the sales operations were run on a proverbial shoestring budget with not a single day of channel credit to support even the introductory phase – undoubtedly a first in Hyundai's global experience – the simple fact was that there was little support that could be expected or received from the parent company even as HMI entered the seventh month of commercial operations.

Entering 1999, still desperately strapped for cash in the wake of the Korean meltdown, but needing significant investments to cover the planned introduction of the Accent in HMI, HMC had actually started looking at the possibility of a significant dilution of its equity holding in the Indian entity, even going to the extent of making specific applications to the Foreign Investment Promotion Board (FIPB) for offloading of 14.2 per cent of the ₹812-crore equity. The investment bankers handling the proposed private placement transaction had managed to obtain a confirmed interest from the Unit Trust of India (UTI) and indicative interest from the global insurance giant American Insurance Group Inc. (AIG). While UTI had reportedly indicated an enterprise equity valuation of about ₹1,625 crore, making for an effective premium of ₹10 per share, AIG was rumoured to be willing to consider a marginally higher valuation of ₹2,000 crore, yielding a premium of ₹14 per share, subject to achieving certain profitability parameters. The investors also sought veto rights on further equity infusions and a commitment that an IPO would happen within five years. AIG on its part had a further condition: that of ensuring that the management team would be awarded employee stock options. AIG's concern probably emanated from the fact that HMC's position in Korea was seen as significantly worse than difficult, and they arranged matters so that in the event that the parent company had to exit HMI there would be a group of professional stakeholders in place to ensure a relatively less hard landing, or at least to handle a fire sale process. HMC was extremely vocal about not accepting the AIG condition on employee stock options since it believed rewarding employees was its prerogative and no potential investor had a role to play in that. There was a lot of toing and froing even on the other conditions, but as things started getting tougher in Korea, HMC appeared to climb down on the veto issue and the potential investors showed a willingness to agree to a structure with a share buyback at a price that would yield an internal rate of return (IRR) of anything ranging from 15 per cent to 20 per cent, with an indication of flexibility on those rates too, in the event the company did not go through with an IPO. But just as things appeared to be heading towards a resolution on the equity dilution issue, HMC's Korean creditor banks, perceiving an undervaluation of the equity, refused permission for the deal.

Though it is very difficult to confirm, the problem appeared to be (from distant India, and with no knowledge of the Korean language) that the banks believed that the equity or the underlying assets had been provided to them as security, albeit in different economic conditions, at twice the implicit enterprise equity value of the proposed transaction. The Korean banks on their part, thinking that HMC was at the edge of the precipice, were probably keen to hold on to the security for a disposal if conditions so warranted – and, as it was whispered those days, they showed a clear willingness to look for buyers too.

By the middle of 1999, the story went, a global investment bank, rumoured to be Bank of America, apparently approached both GM and, hold your breath – MUL – ostensibly on behalf of Korean banks, to acquire the banks' majority stakes in HMI that they, held as collateral. While the proposal to GM apparently stayed stuck in its decision-making maze, an advisor to SMC, a person I have always considered one of the foremost strategists in the Indian automotive industry, sensing an unbelievable opportunity, was rumoured to have moved with alacrity for the kill. SMC probably did not then have the liquidity for the acquisition and in any case would have had to contend with the government of India, the co-promoter in MUL, giving consent and approval (in accordance with the terms of Press Note 1, the ruling that governed such matters) if they wanted another plant in India. But Suzuki's advisor apparently figured the company could, instead, route the proposed share acquisition through MUL. However, access to MUL's not inconsiderable cash hoard would require the approval of the government nominees on the board of MUL. That clearly could not have been taken for granted. But, according to investment bankers in the know, Suzuki's advisor had apparently thought through that as well and had crafted a detailed note explaining how, in the event of a possible meltdown in Korea and the collapse of HMC, the acquisition of HMI equity was essential to protect 1,600 jobs in the then DMK-ruled Tamil Nadu, an argument they were absolutely certain the then union minister for commerce and industry, himself from Tamil Nadu, could never have ignored. In the informal negotiations that followed, confident that there was simply no other potential buyer in India, SMC's advisor apparently did not budge beyond ₹30 per share, offering, however, to put the MUL cheque on the table within a week of concluding the transaction. He had been following HMI closely, thanks to feedback from the SMC and MUL export teams, which consistently reported on Hyundai's products and export pricing approach. The reports apparently noted that in European markets, the Korean company was rumoured to spend on marketing and promotion on every single car, an amount equal to the sale price of the car itself, all in an effort to gain market share. SMC's advisor had apparently opined that despite the Korean market being both protected and oligopolistic, it would be difficult for HMC to sustain such pricing aggression in the export market without taking a debilitating hit on the bottom line. He probably reckoned that the then highly leveraged Korean chaebol's global dream run could well come to an end during what the Koreans invariably referred to as the 'IMF crisis', even as it was just gathering momentum, and resultantly thought that ambitious investment in India might well be available for the asking. The Korean bankers, it was then rumoured, might have settled for a number 50 per cent higher than what Suzuki's advisor had informally offered, but when they realized their asking price was unachievable they decided not to monetize their security and opted to sit out the much-feared carnage. On the other hand, given Korean sensitivities about everything Japanese, they may well have baulked at the altar. But then the tide turned – and quite unexpectedly.

Meanwhile, the sales of the Santro, which had averaged a modest 2,800 units per month in the last quarter of 1998, stumbled by almost 15 per cent in January and February 1999 reeling under the onslaught of the just-launched Tata Indica (for which bookings had opened), but then picked up smartly in March as the astronomical number of bookings for the Tata Indica and the possible two-year-long waiting list scared away buyers. Then at the end of April 1999, came the Supreme Court ruling on emission norms, and the announcement that HMI would launch Euro 2 compliant vehicles by the end of May. The 'Engineered for Euro 2' gambit worked beyond our wildest dreams. Sales of the Santro in the second quarter of 1999 rose 38 per cent over that in the first quarter, and then rose a further 50 per cent in the third! By September 1999 the Santro's sales were within touching distance of the Zen's, after having been less than half of it in January. The monthly average of the third quarter was thus a phenomenal 108 per cent above the run rate of the first. Best of all, every single car sold added positively to the bottom line. In August 1999, if I recall correctly, HMI made its first cash profit – never to look back. Suddenly, the extreme financial pressures eased up without much dependence on the parent company, and, HMI had enough funds from customer advances to meet even its working capital requirements. With the extremely profitable Hyundai Accent joining the party in October 1999, in FY 2000 – only the first full year of commercial operations – ended with a profit after tax of ₹59.34 crore – a feat no company entering the Indian market, before or since, has been able to match.

3

The Guns of War

At the risk of sounding blasphemous to some of my politically inclined friends, and perhaps completely bizarre to 'marketing' purists, I have for long believed that the thoughts of the Great Helmsman on military and organizational strategy could provide very insightful approaches to corporate strategy, though I'm quite certain he would never have intended his thoughts to serve such a purely capitalist pursuit.

Consider the following quote, for instance. It could well be a good starting point for a discussion on product development.

To link oneself with the masses, one must act in accordance with the needs and wishes of the masses. All work done for the masses must start from their needs and not from the desire of any individual, however well-intentioned. It often happens that objectively the masses need a certain change, but subjectively they are not yet conscious of the need, not willing or determined to make the change. In such cases, we should wait patiently. We should not make the change until, through our work, most of the masses have become conscious of the need and are willing and determined to carry it out. Otherwise we shall isolate ourselves from the masses. Unless conscious and willing, any kind of work that requires the participation will turn out to be a mere formality and will fail... There are two principles here: one is the actual needs of the masses rather than what we fancied they need, and the other is the wishes of the masses, who must make up their own minds instead of our making up their minds for them.

THE UNITED FRONT IN CULTURAL WORK
Mao Tse-Tung, 30 October 1944

Replace the word 'masses' which the word 'consumers', and there you have it – the essence of getting the first step right.

Much of the initial curiosity surrounding the Hyundai Santro stemmed from the fact that it looked rather unusual. There was a British television show, I can't recall which, that had panned the looks of the Amica (as the Santro was called in the UK) and, with tongue firmly in cheek, said something to the effect of 'the car's looks did not really bother the reviewers because they were returning the car at the end of the television shoot – but people who owned the car, and had to live with it, would not be so fortunate'. The Indian media was decidedly less impolite but did not hesitate to call the car 'gawky' and 'ungainly'.

Writing in *Auto India* after his first long-distance drive in the newly launched Santro, Hormazd Sorabjee observed, 'The car's appearance is no doubt futuristic and distinctive, but I find its looks too drastic to digest. Hyundai has been trying to convince me that the Santro is a work of art. I beg to differ. The styling is forced and exaggerated, with an overdose of creases and curbs. The huge headlamps give Marty Feldman a complex and the scowling front grille makes it far from happy. From the side, the extraordinary height of the body is accentuated by the short overhang and the small wheels on which it sits. The rear end is the saving grace and looks quite trendy.' He went on to admit, 'But looks are highly subjective...like it or not, the Santro design is the way forward into Y2K, where maximising space in a minimal footprint will be the name of the game... In truth Indians don't want small cars. They want affordable cars that are as big as possible.' As I joked then with Hormazd, and I think went on to write sometime later, he had earlier got it wrong with the 'breadbox' looks of the Tata Sumo and he would again. But both of us agreed that the great thing about the Santro was that once you sat inside the car it just did not matter what it looked like on the outside! And then Hormazd promptly went and said just that in print.

Consumers who had got used to feeling cramped in both the Maruti 800 and to a lesser extent in the Maruti Zen suddenly had an overwhelming sense of space with Santro's 'Tall Boy' design. The interiors of the Santro were absolutely world-class. Nowhere did they seem plasticky. Whether it was the grain on the dashboard, or the feel of the gear knob, everything was significantly superior to what the Indian consumer was used to experiencing with similarly priced cars. But that wasn't going to be quite enough. On the one hand, the Santro had to contend with the very popular, much loved and well accepted jellybean design of the Maruti Zen, and, on the other, it had to fend off two very good-looking new products with an Italian styling pedigree launched within days of the Santro hitting the streets. The first was the exceptional Guigiaro creation, designed by Italdesign, the Matiz from Daewoo, which was already making waves after bagging the Best Small Car Award at the British International Motor Show and the title of the World's Most Beautiful Car at the L'Automobile Pin Bella Del Mondo in Italy. The second was the striking (if closely resembling its design stablemate, the Fiat Palio) Indica from TML, designed by I.DE.A.

The Santro itself had no such pretensions to styling lineage. Its design had started life in the Namyang design studios of Hyundai as an attempt by the designer's there to take on the very successful

Daewoo Tico. The Tico was essentially based on the third-generation Suzuki Alto and looked like a cross between the Maruti 800, then being sold in India, and the Suzuki WagonR, sold primarily in Japan. The result of that attempt by Hyundai designers was the Hyundai Atoz. Even its greatest supporters would not suggest that the Atoz was a good-looking car. A well-rounded front suddenly transformed into a boxy rear to give the Atoz a peculiar, unbalanced look that made it the object of much derision. Purists in the global auto press had a field day ravaging the styling, and overlooked some of the best features of the vehicle – a fairly refined engine, and a relatively smooth ride and handling to name just two.

I first saw the Atoz in the clay when I was invited to Namyang in August 1996, after a long meeting with B.J. Park, then president of HMC, at the company's global headquarters in Seoul, for preliminary meetings regarding the job they had in mind for me. (The clay model is the culmination of the 'traditional' method of layering large amounts of clay over a foam core, then spending days and weeks shaping every line and curve, by hand, to get a physical mock-up of what the car would ultimately look like in flesh and blood. As Virtual Reality (VR) and Augmented Reality (AR) technologies have become more ubiquitous, styling experts have tended to forsake this 'art form'.) B.J. Park, Y.S. Kim and I had just gone through a long discussion on how India's car market would evolve, the tastes and aspirations of the growing middle class and the ideal entry product for the Indian market, when Park phoned the head of the research and development wing to tell him that an Indian guest was coming over. He asked his team to show me around the styling studio, particularly the one where the MX (the design code name of the Atoz) was being worked on. I was rather surprised – I was still working for a potential competitor, so to speak – and it probably showed on my face, because B.J. Park smiled and said, 'I'm sure that as a professional you will forget what you have seen inside in case you don't join us.' The sheer confidence of this company that was evident in its senior-most management and its employees then reminded me in many ways of the TML I had joined in 1978.

The sheer scale and modernity of the Namyang studio was impressive. Clearly, Hyundai was a company in a hurry. The styling studios were world-class; the average age of the design and styling teams – all in their mid-twenties – created a very favourable impression. Quite in contrast, the Atoz in clay was a major let-down. I recall telling J.D. Bae, who accompanied me, that I didn't believe this styling would work in India, and that they would probably need a more conventional treatment of the rear, tapered out perhaps. Bae agreed with me and revealed that another styling approach was very much in consideration and, after some hurried consultations on the phone, showed me the alternative styling iterations of the MX. In the MX version, the rear end was dropped abruptly in a straight line – much like in the Suzuki WagonR, which it was clearly inspired by. In the alternative styling approach (which ultimately went on to be adopted first for the Indian market, and then for much of the rest of the world), the rear hatch angled obtusely from a roof that sloped gently, almost imperceptibly, thereby not sacrificing much of the headroom clearance for passengers on the rear seat. One look at the first artist impressions, and I realized there was a lot that could be done with it. I did not hesitate to tell Bae as much. Soon thereafter, when, in a clear change in strategy, HMC decided on a 'small car' entry route into India, this alternative styling was badged the MXi – the MX for India! Hyundai's product planning process seemed reasonably robust and well-defined. It was the marketing management that led the initiation of the product development effort, exposed as it was to both global market trends and the Korean consumer.

Though TML had started to institutionalize a structured product development process under the leadership of Arun Maira, during the creation of the Tata 407, I realized that there was still a lot to be learnt from this young Korean company that I was considering to move to. I believe TML was equally, if not more, competent and creative on strategy formulation, but the product development process and implementation discipline that I witnessed at Hyundai was a revelation. TML too listened closely to the voice of the consumer while planning a product, went on to engineer products to fulfil the needs and desires of consumers, rapidly created availability through competent production systems and then went further to communicate the values of the product back to consumers, thereby creating brand preference. It backed all this up with an exceptional ability to support the customer through the life of the product. The clear belief in TML those days was that markets had to be dominated, and this was best achieved through the provision of superior product or business solutions via the core product, and then enveloping it in best-in-class pre-sales and post-sales support. However much of a motherhood-and-apple-pie statement this may appear to be, the fact is that this remained the secret to the sustained market leadership of TML. The simple, straightforward, seat-of-the-pants approach, bereft of consultant-style jargon also helped bring exceptional speed to implementation and often proved to be the decisive factor in ensuring victory. Perhaps the most obvious examples of this competence were the Tata 407, the Tata 2213 and the Tata Sumo – all three unmatched winners. While the 407 and the Sumo slotted in perfectly into existing market segments, the 2213 stood out, because it effectively redefined India's road freight market.

The Tata 2213 was created entirely based on consumer feedback gathered by a marketing team that had the humility to listen (just as Mao recommended!) and to try to understand what the customer was saying. The fact that the product obtained a green signal from top management and went from first prototype to serial production within six months despite significant opposition from technical purists within the company, is a reflection of the quality and intrinsic strength of the strategic process in TML and Ratan Tata's foresight. Arguably, the Tata 2213 was to some extent a reconfigured product presentation, but the overall packaging and what it ultimately did in and to the marketplace is the stuff of legend. Hugely successful? A definite, yes. Born of a structured development process? Not so much.

Creating the Santro from the ground up was a completely different experience for me. By late February 1997, just weeks after the ground-breaking ceremony for the manufacturing plant in Chennai, and days after I joined HMI, J.D. Bae and I were back to meeting analysts, auto experts, auto dealers and potential customers in India to get a better idea of consumer perceptions on the initially proposed MXi styling. The result? Not quite the resounding vote in favour of the MXi styling and design language that everyone in Hyundai had fervently hoped for. The bold stunning twenty-first-century look held the viewers' attention, albeit with reactions varying from 'ugh' to 'wow', with the former being preponderant. With space being high on the consumer wish list, however, the tall and wide packaging clearly evident from the artists' impressions, helped create and reinforce an image of a multi-functional small car. The potential consumers who liked the design recognized the utility and the versatility of the styling. Its light dynamic silhouette probably helped to favourably project a possible multi-functional character. However, overall consumer reactions to the styling were not entirely favourable during consumer interaction. No one had seen anything quite like the styling of the MXi. In order to gain a little respectability and acceptability for the design, we started drawing comparisons with the then recently launched Mercedes-Benz A class. This often occasioned polite sniggers and sometimes not-so-polite laughter. But the suggestion of such an association ultimately worked, and slowly but steadily the level of acceptance of the styling seemed to improve, though just marginally, in the clinics. It was clear to the small group that made up HMI's marketing team then, that getting consumers to accept the styling would be a significant challenge.

From those days to the first clay models of the MXi, things moved very rapidly and in mid-April 1997, just over two months after I had moved to HMI, and even as the concrete was being poured into the foundations at the plant site, Y.S. Kim, J.D. Bae, Yong Sung Kim and I went back to Namyang to see the first iterations of the MXi. It was, indeed, a very distinct improvement on the MX, and all four of us, united in our relief, believed for the first time that we had more than an even chance of conquering the Indian market. Starting with the deliberately simple front view, the MXi's massive C pillar tapered upwards in a definite curve that managed to impart an all-important element of tension and volume to this 1.5-box concept. The door lines imparted a further element of visual tension in the side view. The trailing edge of the front door was a straight vertical line, while the rear door line was curved. A cinched effect on the lower rear fender flowed into the rear door creating a muscular, sporty look. The front grill came with two options – a horizontal one, which was carried by the models displayed at the 'global launch' at the Auto Expo in 1998, and the toothy vertical line grill, which the product was ultimately launched with later that year. This then was the car we had to conquer the Indian market with. I must admit we were not wildly exuberant – but we were excited enough! The unspoken hope was that Indian consumers would feel the same way about the looks, as we did. Following this, the product development work started in earnest.

A lot of attention was focused by the product development group on consumer requirements of space. Making good use of its 1.5 metre width, 2.38 metre wheelbase and 1.59 metre height, the MXi was able to provide unrivalled front and rear headroom, legroom and hip room. A host of learnings and consumer insight on building a car to suit average Indian physiques rather than East Asian body types were internalized by the product development team. The ease of ingress and egress that Indian consumers so adored about the HM Ambassador were clearly issues that would help the MXi stand apart. The seat engineering group pushed relentlessly to deliver wide and comfortable seats and then worked on at least four iterations of the rear seat rake angle to get the perfect rear bench seat. Going beyond mere steel frames and multi-density seat backs, the group brought in anti-submarining designs for the first time in small cars in India. In hindsight, a little more could probably have been done by hollowing out the backs of the driver and co-driver seats in order to create a wee bit more legroom for occupants of the rear seat, but the cost and time implications may have constrained the group.

Another clear message that had emanated from potential consumers, with whom the product development team constantly interacted, was a silently muttered but faintly audible expression of dissatisfaction with even the Maruti Zen when it came to engine power and performance. During market research interactions, consumers opined that the engine of the otherwise reasonably competent Maruti 800 sometimes tended to struggle with the typical large Indian family load, particularly with air conditioning being switched on during India's unsparing summers. In essence, expressed in many ways, this was the consumers' stated and more often unstated desire for better drivability. All these learnings from consumer interactions helped create the definitional standard of engine performance for the product development team. I referred to it as the 'Peddar Road Syndrome'. The marketing team's ask of the technical team thus became the desire to have an engine with enough torque to enable five passengers to drive through peak-hour traffic on Mumbai's Peddar Road on a monsoon evening with the air conditioning on and without constantly shifting gears. Only those who have endured such a situation, particularly in the driver's seat, can appreciate the demands it puts on a car's engine and the driver's patience. To power the MXi, Hyundai therefore proposed the use of the 999 cc, four-cylinder, 12-valve Epsilon engine that was being designed in-house to fully comply with Euro 2 emission standards rather than the 770 cc engine offered on the MX in Korea. The light and compact engine design was to be created with a multipoint fuel injection system offered as a standard for India, rather than sticking to the conventional wisdom in India that unfortunately pushed for low-cost but relatively poor-on-emissions carburettor technology. The medium tuning and dual-intake valve technology proposed for the engine was an attempt to optimize fuel delivery, ensure better fuel economy and achieve a cleaner burn.

Consumers, however, seemed less than excited, in fact even a little concerned, about the proposed multipoint fuel injection which we were touting as a major technological advancement. Much of their concern emanated from the often overstated horror stories of the fuel-guzzling habit of the Daewoo Cielo, which was probably the first car to be launched in India with multipoint fuel injection system. It had managed to put the Maruti Esteem in the shade in the then 'luxury' car segment in India. Gummy Indian fuel tended to block the near microscopic holes of the injectors within months, if not weeks, of usage. This invariably led to the injectors dribbling and sent the fuel efficiency plummeting. Quick to seize the initiative against the Cielo, the staff at the competitors' dealerships ensured that this apparent failure gained wide publicity, highlighted the resulting abysmal fuel efficiency and used it to reinforce in the minds of the Indian consumer the 'virtues' of carburettor technology.

The Hyundai solution was simple and elegant. Without forsaking the talking point of multipoint fuel injection, Hyundai's engineers skirted the gummy fuel problem by opting for two relatively larger holes in the injector instead of multiple microscopic holes. The engine proposed for the MXi thus came to represent a significant step forward for small cars in the Indian automotive industry, and the transmission mated perfectly with the MXi's Epsilon engine.

A basic five-speed affair, its emphasis was on smooth and effortless gear shifts. The product development team had also internalized the one big unspoken desire of every Indian urban small-car driver – to take off from the traffic lights like a Formula One driver in a hurry. So they kept the throws short and the steps just tall enough to match the engine's power output curve characteristics.

Yet, it was the work on the heating ventilation and air conditioning (HVAC) that probably won the MXi the greatest initial applause. During interactions with consumers, a recurrent complaint pertained to the quality and efficacy of the air conditioning, even in so-called premium cars. The Opel Astra was often mentioned by consumers for its alleged failure on this front and a common refrain from customers was that the least they expected was a comfortable environment during the drive, particularly in a 'luxury' (read high-priced) car. Recognizing that the AC compressor used on the MX would be woefully insufficient for Indian climatic conditions, the HVAC design team standardized a 135 cc AC compressor for the India-specific product. The product development team recognized that this could mean a marginal penalty on the fuel consumption front, but considering that the MXi was destined primarily for urban Indian agglomerations, where traffic congestion would have a much greater potential negative impact on fuel efficiency, the decision was to opt for greater climate comfort. During the testing phase, the air conditioner was subjected to a gruelling fourteen-hour daily test drive cycle on the road from Jaipur to Jhunjhunu during the peak summer when day temperatures typically stayed above 48°C and the heat from the road surface could well have been over 55°C. Small wonder then that when the MXi finally got into consumers' hands, the climate control scored a perfect ten!

Concerns on occupant safety also often became the focal point of consumer interaction as soon as they learnt that the proposed product would be a 'small' car. Often the product development team found accident experiences of either consumers or their friends dominating the discussion on product features. It was clearly an imperative to ensure that the active and passive safety features in the MXi set new standards for this class of cars in India. The MX had already been built with a highly optimized body design that created a passenger safety cell of unmatched efficiency: a single-piece side panel made of high-tensile SPRC 35 steel, side-impact protection beams built into each of the four doors and the specially designed engine sub-frame made with ultra high-tensile steel to safely absorb crash forces had all combined to create a highly rigid enclosure that met the 30 miles per hour crash-test requirement in the US. Much as the India team preferred otherwise, a deviation in design, away from the MX, became essential. The single-piece side panel was replaced by a two-piece design with a weld in the middle. Though technically this was a globally accepted practice, the deviation robbed the MXi – on just one count – of being truly global and contemporary in terms of safety standards. For a start, the cost of creating a die for the single-piece side panel was an important deterrent. Further, the bed of the barely used Hitachi Zosen stamping presses that had been moved from Hyundai's shuttered plant in Canada may not have been appropriate for the job. There were a few other cost-related design deviations which did not, however compromise the safety features inherent in the original design of the MX. Yet, compared with the Maruti Zen and Maruti 800, the MXi was literally years ahead in terms of side-impact safety. Right through consumer interactions, explanations of the side-impact beams and their role in ensuring passenger protection were listened to with great interest and often led to debates on why MUL had not done the same with the Zen. Interestingly, the sound of the door closing appeared, in most conversations, to be the indicator for a heavy/safe versus a flimsy/unsafe door. Almost as if a dam had burst, consumers brought out their safety concerns and spoke animatedly about braking efficiency, braking distance and brake pad life. Each of these factors was studiously worked on by the product development team while putting together the MXi. And we discovered one more MUL's Achilles heel from the consumer's point of view.

Along with understanding the mind of the Indian consumer, the product development team was also constantly learning the reality of Indian road conditions. The most obvious implications were for the design of the suspension system. Working on the overall reinforcement and strengthening of existing front and rear suspension design, the product development team laid specific emphasis on an oft-encountered consumer pain point – the breakage of the ball joint – which appeared largely related to the Maruti 800 and Maruti Zen, and the expense of replacing the entire assembly. This was redesigned in such a way that the ball joint, the arm and the bush were made separately replaceable. Another concern was the body rattle that seemed, from consumer reactions, to be more pronounced in cities and areas with poor-quality road surface and on vehicles over a year old. A thorough analysis of existing vehicle models led to a reduction in weld pitch (the distance between two spot welds) on the body of the MXi, which in turn improved torsional rigidity and the ability to take torsional twists and stresses. What this meant was that the number of weld points per metre of length would increase by almost 50 per cent. Obviously, this would marginally increase both the time and the cost of manufacture, but there was complete unanimity within the team on the need to do it. It was the level of detail that the product development team went into that eventually led to the plaudits earned by the MXi even before its first birthday.

Through all this, one thing was getting clearer to us – we would soon have a potential winner on our hands. This, I believed, was the time to start thinking and behaving like leaders, rather than give in to a certain Korean tendency to remain somewhat in awe of Japanese companies. I sometimes caught fleeting glimpses of this. Obviously, the history between the nations had something to do with it. But now it was time to up the ante. In the first of its many dares to MUL, HMI moved its marketing headquarters to Delhi in November 1997. As marketing director, I firmly believed that in the imminent battle for market share the company could ill afford the polite conservatism of Chennai to permeate its spirit, and would have to fashion itself in word and deed in a manner more akin to the barely concealed aggression and the make-it-happen spirit of Delhi. (I recall telling a Chennai industrialist of our need to 'give up the Mylapore mindset in favour of the Punjabi Bagh paradigm', and I remember that neither his wife nor he were amused.) However, going head to head with MUL was something of an imperative and I repeatedly argued that in order to be accepted as a credible market leader we had to adopt the appropriate stance. I spoke in cricketing terms of the Rahul Dravid approach of lofting Alan Donald at his most aggressive over his head to the long-on boundary, an analogy that was completely lost on my Korean colleagues but fully understood by my compatriots. I think, in retrospect, that my aggressive posture may sometimes have bothered Y.S. Kim, who, I suppose, in keeping with his own externally calm personality, wanted to live down the well-known Korean penchant for aggression. A joke in the *Economist* in 1997 probably spoke most eloquently of that aggression:

> 'In Seoul, where queues are for wimps and elbows are for other people's noses, this joke is popular: A South Korean, a North Korean and a Japanese are sitting in a restaurant. The waiter comes up and says, "Excuse me, but I'm afraid we have no more meat." Perplexed, the North Korean asks, "What's meat?" Even more puzzled, the Japanese asks: "What's 'no more'?" Most puzzled of all, the South Korean asks, "What's 'excuse me'?"'.

I must honestly admit, though, that all the Koreans I interacted with in the early days, with probably a couple of exceptions, were the very epitome of courtesy and generally practised an old-world formal interaction. I recall a Korean colleague I was always friendly with being ticked off by Y.S. Kim for having addressed me by my first name rather than the more formal name and designation style generally favoured in corporate Korea in those days. But as their numbers grew, I did unfortunately get to see some truth in the *Economist* joke on more occasions than I care to recount. Yet, anyone who has stood at any enquiry counter in Delhi, only to be elbowed aside without so much as a by-your-leave, might just remain unfazed with that particular behavioural trait, simply because it would not seem very unusual.

When the MXi was finally unveiled as the Santro at the Auto Expo in Pragati Maidan in Delhi in January 1998, it was introduced as 'India's Small Little Big Car', and the unveiling itself was dubbed 'the global launch' – which it was. Though the Atoz (as the MX was branded) had been launched in Korea a few months earlier, the distinctively differently styled and engineered Santro was displayed for the very first time in Delhi in 1998.

But the event almost never happened for Hyundai.

Namyang had made just two exhibition prototypes and air-freighted them to Mumbai. Both units were received with just days to go for the exhibition, singularly damaged by the atrocious cargo-handling at the Mumbai airport. They were clearly unfit to be exhibited. With absolutely no facilities on the ground to repair the vehicles, it almost seemed that the global launch would be a damp squib. At this time, car designer Dilip Chhabria stepped in as the saviour. Despite being up to his eyebrows in work building concept cars for a bunch of Indian auto biggies, and putting together his own show creations, Dilip agreed to help out, purely as a personal favour to me, by rebuilding the vehicles to exhibition standards. Eventually, all the pyrotechnics of the Tata Indica launch notwithstanding, the Santro became one of the highlights of the 1998 Auto Expo. For one, it brought with it the element of surprise. *Business World* magazine had noted, in an article at the end of 1995, 'Ratan Tata, in fact, believes that there is no small foreign car that can be a perfect fit for the average Indian customer.' The article went on to quote him as saying, 'A Japanese car does not have the durability for Indian roads. Possibly not even a European car...because they design for a different set of circumstances – they are smaller in size because they are usually owner-driven and not chauffeur-driven. These cars do not handle the kind of family size that exists for most Indian travellers and yet be economical, fuel-efficient and have the economies that a small car like the Maruti (800) has (sic).' Tata's beliefs probably had a role to play in TML taking its eyes off what was happening in distant Chennai. But, without doubt, the derision and scorn that apparently greeted any mention of Hyundai during project meetings at TML's Pune plant probably evaporated instantly, even in the bracing winter of Delhi.

The Auto Expo of 1998 gave HMI the perfect opportunity to launch an attack against MUL – at the psychological level. Taking a cue from Genghis Khan's well-chronicled strategy of creating 'shock and awe' before his conquests of Bukhara and Samarkand, the pricing strategy of the Santro was clearly announced in an advertising supplement issued with the *Times of India* during the Auto Expo as early as in January 1998. The approach was very simple. Y.S. Kim agreed with and wholly supported my contention that HMI ought to get intending car buyers to postpone their commitments to MUL products as long as possible till they could actually touch and feel the Santro. I was convinced that each postponing buyer would actually end up converting perhaps five more and this cognitive ripple could end up forcing MUL to reveal its true hand on product and pricing strategy before the scheduled October launch of the Santro. MUL's apparent strong belief that the pricing, the product offering and the positioning of the Maruti Zen needed no tinkering with and any sort of correction in the price product matrix was not required only further served to help.

The opening photograph of the cover story in *Auto India*'s February 1998 edition said it all. A surging sea of humanity surrounded the raised circular podium on which the Santro stood in the middle of the Hyundai stall, completely oblivious to the arresting concept car and sports coupe Tiburon placed strategically close by in order to give viewers an idea of Hyundai's capability. It was the first time that a global auto company had chosen India as the venue for a global preview. Even with the tsunami of nationalist fervour created by the launch of the Tata Indica sweeping away almost everything in its path in terms of media coverage, the Santro still managed to get a lot more than merely passing mentions in all sections of the media.

Much of the credit for the supportive media coverage went to the young Oxford-educated then chairman of Hyundai, Mong Gyu Chung, who unveiled the Santro at its 'global launch' and tirelessly interacted with the media, fully reiterating everything that Y.S. Kim and I had been telling them over the past months. He spoke at length about becoming a volume player by creating cost advantages through localization in order to become a major alternative to MUL. He reiterated that India would be the global production base of the Santro, even exporting back to Korea if required, and then went on to categorically assert that the new Accent would be launched in India almost simultaneously with the launch in Korea. Given the doubts that constantly swirled around the sustainability of Brand Korea itself, his media interactions helped infuse enormous credibility in the brand. The support from the print and electronic media, members of which I had personally known well for many years, was to become an enduring part of Hyundai's India story and success.

A market survey that we conducted among customers at the Expo – away from the Hyundai stall – also helped to significantly bolster our confidence. About 30 per cent of the respondents showed a preference for the Santro, followed very closely by the Indica, with the Matiz and the Zen trailing some way behind. Together, the Santro and the Indica accounted for a whisker short of 60 per cent of model preferences. What lent this finding some credibility was the associated finding that the Santro and the Indica were neck-and-neck in straight preference comparisons with the Zen. Obviously, the survey could hardly be considered representative of either the nation or real customers because of the village mela atmosphere that had come to be associated with the Expo. After the Expo concluded, one display vehicle was left behind in Delhi to gather feedback from independent users on its performance in regular city driving conditions, with a view to ironing out any glitches in the product before the final launch scheduled a few months later.

The launch of the Santro was a glittering function in Delhi's Taj Palace Hotel on 23 September 1998, on the third day of the Navratri festival – another Indianization that I had brought in from TML. Some weeks earlier, I had proposed that the launch function would consist primarily of a public auction of the first five cars to roll off the production line, with the entire proceedings, along with a matching contribution by all the Hyundai dealers, being donated primarily to the Army Wives Welfare Association (AWWA), with smaller contributions going to the corresponding Air Force and Navy organizations to create technical training scholarships for the wards of martyred defence personnel. Thanks to my days at TML, concepts of corporate social responsibility were an integral part of my mental make-up. I discussed the concept of the auction and the support to the AWWA with Y.S. Kim as being an important part of building a truly Indian image for Hyundai. Though none of my other Korean colleagues were even remotely supportive of the idea, Y.S. Kim listened carefully and said that, among other things, it ought to be seen as a thanksgiving contribution from Korea for the role of the Indian Army at the time of the creation of South Korea and the building of the Demilitarized Zone, and agreed that we should go ahead.

Soon enough, Sanjiv Shukla, who had joined the marketing group a few months earlier, got in touch with the Colonel coordinating AWWA activities who in turn arranged for us to meet with the leadership of AWWA in early September 1998. Even today, the recollection of that meeting brings a smile.

Dr Veena Malik, wife of the Chief of Army Staff, General V.P. Malik, was the president of the organization. It would be the understatement of the year to say that she and her colleagues were suspicious of our intent when I first told them we wanted to make a contribution to create a scholarship under the control of AWWA. Even as Dr Malik asked me how much we were intending to contribute, her face said she was probably expecting me to quote a modest figure – maybe a couple of lakhs at the most. When I replied that we were hoping the contribution would be at least ₹20 lakh or so, I could clearly sense the suspicion mounting rapidly. A flurry of questions followed, including whether HMI had any business links with the Army. Everyone visibly relaxed when I told them we had absolutely no involvement with supplies of anything whatsoever to the Army, the Air Force or the Navy. In fact, we were not even considering registering for supplies to the Canteen Stores Department (CSD) because I saw no point in wasting our time dealing with its infuriating bureaucratic systems. But Dr Malik and her colleagues continued to probe till I clearly explained my intent to them.

I told them that as an Indian I felt that civilians did not quite appreciate the sacrifices of our men in uniform. We had become so dehumanized as a nation that news of the martyrdom of a young soldier in some place like Kupwara unfortunately merited much less attention from the average Indian newspaper reader than stock-market news or Sachin Tendulkar's innings against Bangladesh or even a comic strip. Dr Malik looked at me even more quizzically and asked if I had an SSC (Short Service Commission) background, or if I came from an Army family. With my answers to both her questions being in the negative, she seemed even more unwilling to believe that we did not have an agenda. She proceeded to ask if we wanted to use some Army facilities for the launch or perhaps even the Army band, and finally relaxed only when I said there was absolutely no quid pro quo. I added for reassurance that we would have no say in the management of the fund since we believed they were best placed to do this. On the spur of the moment, I offered that every child qualifying for a technical training scholarship under the scheme would automatically be eligible for a suitable job in HMI. Probably used to people offering collections from a charity premiere show of a movie, often little more than a 'society' fun event at best, the AWWA leadership continued to consider us with just a hint of a question in their gaze even as they thanked us and we left the meeting. On the day of the launch, the entire top brass of the Indian Army in Delhi, and much of the top brass of the Air Force and the Navy was present, having graciously accepted our formal invitation. Their presence at the event gave us a huge boost of moral courage.

I was reasonably confident that the auction would be a success. While Mumbai has had a culture of corporations donating for causes, in Delhi there seemed more of a tradition for big spending rather than big giving. Yet, my belief was that given Delhi's big spending habits and its desire to forever get ahead of the Joneses and, more importantly, to be seen doing so, we would not have too much of a problem racking up bids from our invitees, which included, among others, our dealer partners, vendor partners, bankers, a host of people from the industry and, of course, the media. I expected that, for the pride of being able to claim ownership of one of the first five Santro cars produced in the country, we'd be able to garner bids of at least 20 per cent over the retail price – all for a worthy cause.

The proceedings started with a terrible gaffe by the late theatre and film actor Tom Alter, our MC for the evening, when he twisted the acronym AWWA, but he was graciously pardoned and promptly corrected by Dr Malik and things went swimmingly from there.

Neither the donee organizations nor any of us in HMI were quite prepared for what came next. Following exhortations by Tom Alter and me for the guests to loosen their purse strings beyond what they would at their upcoming Diwali-night card bashes, the invitees got into the spirit of things and the first Santro went for an unbelievable 100 per cent premium over the list price. It was when the fifth car was auctioned for a whisker over ₹8 lakh that I really felt the evening's proceedings had been a huge success. The highest bid of the evening came from Raj Chopra, the owner of Competent Motors, one of MUL's largest dealers in the country and someone I had known professionally for over a decade. (I later learnt that he had a lot of explaining to do to the top management at MUL!) Eventually, after adding the matching contributions by the Hyundai dealers, collections totalled up to well over ₹75 lakh, with AWWA getting, as per our commitment, the major portion. Despite a lot of pressure from some of our Korean colleagues, Y.S. Kim and I made sure that the contribution did not become a trumpet-blowing public relations exercise for HMI. To this day I believe that a large part of Hyundai's success in India probably started with the goodwill that we got from this little gesture.

The media, sections of which had already participated in test-drives, appeared generally impressed with what they saw of the pricing strategy for the Santro and the overall implications for the Indian consumer. On 24 September 1998, in his column headlined 'Modelled to make Maruti curl up its tail', Veeresh Malik wrote on Rediff on the Net, 'The Hyundai Santro…is going to scare the pants off the bossmen at Maruti, for sure. They – the Maruti men – were expecting a bit of a flutter in their dovecote whenever they took time out from their internecine battles, but this?… It is not just going to compete with Maruti Zen but going to wade into Maruti 800 territory… Everybody expected a car war in the small car segment… Santro does not mark a flanking attack on or a salvo across the bows of the battleship Maruti Udyog Limited. It is more like the raid at

Pearl Harbour by the Japanese in World War II. People knew it was coming but the ferocity was unexpected...' Hailing the launch as 'good news for the customer' he observed, 'The Indian buyer of small cars will now, finally, have something to choose from. And if the Santro is representative of the shape of things to come, then look out for a replica of the computer industry hitting the motor industry soon. Next month will always be better and cheaper...' Fortunately for HMI, the market leader was less concerned with the imminent threat the challenger would soon pose, and MUL held on to both its distribution and pricing strategies for the Maruti Zen.

But there was no running away from the truth that we in the company were so painfully aware of, and Malik so pithily observed: 'On the downside is the rather downmarket image that Hyundai has the world over, their currently low service network...and, ahem, the fact that this multi-point fuel injection system still has to prove itself on Indian petrol. And there lies the catch. Will it pass the acid test of the Indian roads? Now that is going to be something to watch [out for].'

The Hyundai Santro finally opened for bookings against full payments from 8 October to 12 October 1998. The start date was selected because it was Karva Chauth, a ceremony which I personally believe is regressive, but one that has been decked up and pushed into social acceptance in a big way by Bollywood and Indian television serials. Deliveries were effected across the country from 18 October 1998 and that year Hyundai celebrated Diwali with India!

This was only a start. In an article titled 'War of the Wheels' published the week of the Santro's launch, *India Today* magazine spoke of the unfolding competitive scenario in the automobile market without really calling a winner. In the article, R.C. Bhargava, former managing director of MUL and then an industry consultant, was quoted as saying 'the difference between Maruti's financial advantages and those of the other producers is really quite enormous given its high volumes. It will take very long for the others to catch up.' But the article observed presciently, 'Maruti will have to factor [in] the cost of improving its technology to match what almost all new cars will offer.'

A few days later Ratan Tata told the *Time* magazine that pricing would be key to the success of the Indica, and appeared to acknowledge the arrival of tough competition when he said, 'I am more concerned about the Koreans, whose pricing is more aggressive. They will try to be below us, to beat us but I doubt they will go below us because they will then upset a lot of buyers who have already booked their cars and paid up in full.'

But the pricing reaction ultimately came from MUL without any warning. Two months after the Santro's price was announced, and literally hours before the launch of the Tata Indica, in an unprecedented move, MUL cut Zen prices by almost 15 per cent. But consumers had by then already signalled their acceptance of the pricing strategy of HMI, and sales staff at HMI dealerships were coached to tell prospective customers that the price cut meant that MUL was effectively acknowledging the impact of the Santro. 'Woh darr gaye (They're scared)' was the message that was beamed out by the foot soldiers. I silently thanked MUL for giving HMI a breather and for taking the easy way out by just fiddling with the price. Any product level intervention at that stage – including the technically feasible option of launching a Maruti Zen variant with a 1.3 litre Maruti Esteem engine under its hood, could have queered the pitch for the 'superior engine performance' promise of the Santro. But that was not to be, and the Santro's performance remained a talking point among prospective consumers.

In January 2000, at the start of the new millennium, just fifteen months after its launch, sales of the Santro at 7,442 units conclusively overtook that of the Maruti Zen at 6,337 units, keeping up the momentum to end higher in that year, and every year thereafter. For good measure, sales of the Hyundai Accent, then just four months on the road, overtook that of the Maruti Esteem.

4

Digging Trenches, Building Bunkers

HMI's dealership network was definitely one of its greatest strengths. Everything about it – its people, its spread and its structuring were all very different from those of the rest of the entrants in the industry in the 1990s. But, to my mind, it was the people who made all the difference.

Young, fiercely competitive and committed to making a mark, every member of the group worked towards just one objective – market dominance. Those who eventually came on board as dealers were highly qualified bond traders from Wall Street, US-educated management consultants, technocrats who ran their own precision-engineering manufacturing enterprises and first-generation entrepreneurs in the automotive service business. Yet, the list also included wives, daughters and sons from established automotive dealership families keen to make a mark on their own. The majority of the dealers were first-timers in the business, and I wondered even then how many of them would ever have stood the chance of having their application forms analysed and properly assessed – let alone being interviewed by the established companies – through the conventional, structured process of analysing dealer application forms. A record of sorts was set when we went ahead, notwithstanding several raised eyebrows, and selected as dealer principals Ragini Sanghi in Indore, Bharti Desai in Rajkot, Geeta Talwar in Chandigarh, Kavita Himatsinghka in Calcutta (now Kolkata), Nandini Rangaswamy in Coimbatore and Rupa Parikh in Jamshedpur. Though all of them came from families traditionally in the automobile business, they were striking out on their own and all of them went on to set new benchmarks of success as businesswomen in what has generally been a male preserve in India.

Compared with HMI's approach, MUL's was, for instance, altogether different, thanks perhaps to the market conditions that existed at its inception, or the widely rumoured external involvements in its early days – or both. There are few documented details of the process followed by MUL for network selection at the start-up stage in the public domain, but since I had personally known many of the first batch of MUL dealers (some of them well-established TML dealers) I had heard many versions of the process from the selected ones and even more conjectures of unverifiable nature from others. On the whole it seemed that by the 1990s MUL had come to rely on a simple tender-type price-finding mechanism in its quest for dealers rather than looking for young achievers or people who would be categorized today as potential unicorns.

Applicants for MUL dealerships would be shortlisted, as per the company's criteria, and considered for site visits by company officials. Based on the site visits, some applicants would be invited for an interview with the company's top brass, and a final shortlist of suitable applicants would be invited to make sealed bids, indicating the amounts they were willing to deposit with the company for the opportunity or privilege of representing the market leader in a near-monopoly market with long lists of waiting consumers – the ultimate rent-seekers' paradise! One can only conjecture about the implications of this approach for 'customer satisfaction', but common sense suggested that an auction-based process could potentially lead to a quick-returns psyche dominating the business philosophy of the successful applicants. The growing demand–supply gap as the purchasing power of India's middle class outpaced MUL's production capacity additions only served to push the auction prices up, and potential 'investor interest' in MUL dealerships soared as even MUL 'car bookings' actually appeared to become an asset-class for investors in some markets. The concomitant rapid growth of 'brokers' who quickly metamorphosed into retail finance intermediaries (many went on to become extremely successful MUL dealers later) is probably another interesting piece of evidence of the play of new market forces that resulted from the MUL dealer-selection process. In the ensuing, highly controlled 'sellers' market' there appeared to be little real space for true customer satisfaction – let alone delight.

My personal experience as a potential customer at one of the largest MUL dealers in Mumbai gave me important insights into a consumers' true buying experience. A few days after quitting TML in October 1996, and being required to hand over the company cars a few weeks thereafter, my wife and I walked into an MUL dealership quite literally across the street from where we lived in south Mumbai to go through the car-buying drill. Two years earlier, wanting to buy a base variant of the Maruti 800 for use in her office, my wife had had her colleagues do the rounds of MUL dealerships and was told of a seemingly unending wait. On the advice of the dealership personnel, and in order to meet her time schedules, she had finally just gone to a well-known NBFC and got a Maruti 800 through them within twenty-four hours. Their only condition was that it could not be paid for up-front but had to be 'financed' by them at what was even then an absolutely usurious effective IRR of over 30 per cent per annum. Besides being a completely legitimate way of selling the car at a 'mark-to-market price' (read my lips, I did not say 'black-market rates') what that managed to do was to raise the earnings profile of the NBFC and enable it to command a wholly undeserved stratospheric share price when it sold a large stake to a global auto-financing major soon thereafter.

This time round, my wife was naturally sceptical of going to an MUL dealer, but reluctantly agreed. I recall asking at the reception for the Maruti 1000 or the Maruti Esteem sales desk. Without looking up, the young lady waved us toward a colleague of hers seated behind her, who asked us rather brusquely, 'What colour?', even as she plucked out a cyclostyled pricelist, indicating all kinds of 'charges' added on to the company price. When I replied, 'Black,' she just said, 'Four months waiting,' and went back to chatting with another colleague. Even as she remained completely oblivious to our continued presence, I asked if any financing schemes were available. Again, without wanting to be interrupted in her discussions with her colleague, she just pointed to a door to her far right and said, 'Next room.' Here I was, willing to splurge more than the entire pre-tax annual salary I got as TML's marketing head on a set of four wheels, and my wife and I were not even offered a chair to sit down. I personally knew two generations of the family that owned the dealership, but I had not told them I was going over to check out and buy a car from their establishment. So there we were, being treated like 'normal' customers.

We left without further ado, and as we walked away we noticed a car delivery in progress from the public parking lot that the dealership had clearly appropriated. Keys and papers of barely washed or unwashed cars, dusty after being transported from Daman, were being handed over to desperately eager and anxious customers – by the security staff! The same evening, rather than head down the NBFC route again, I spoke with another MUL dealer principal I knew in another part of Maharashtra, who ultimately managed to get me a car in three weeks, simply because of a demand–supply mismatch for the particular model variant at his dealership. I did not get the exact model variant I wanted, but had no option. That perfect reality check, and my memory of the experience of buying a car from that MUL dealership, though I realized that it may not have been the norm, taught me one thing – how I would not like to be treated at any car dealership. Some months later, when I joined HMI, I decided we would put the consumers' experience in our showrooms at the core of our dealerships.

It was during the initial weeks of my joining HMI in 1997 that the network strategy for the company was conceptualized and formalized. Over long deliberations with Y.S. Kim, our initial team of J.D. Bae, Yong Sung Kim, S.J. Kwon, V.K. Jain and I chiselled out the basic concepts around which we would build our strategy. The critical first step, we believed, would be to define the 'desired dealer personality' for a company that would have to be both aggressive and fleet-footed. By consensus, we agreed that we would try and select people whose basic qualification would be the passion to succeed, along with the fearlessness of youth – irrespective of gender. A family background in the automotive distribution business was a definite plus, as was a reasonably sound financial base but, we agreed, these *would not* be the sole defining traits. We concurred that we ought to ideally select committed people we could work shoulder to shoulder with, people who could well be on the same side of the table as us, and people who would complement us in our consumer interface rather than remain mere conduits of product.

'Weapons are an important factor in war, but not the decisive factor; it is people, not things that are decisive. The contest of strength is not only a contest of military and economic power, but also a contest of human power and morale. People necessarily wield military and economic power.' I recalled to myself from Mao's *On Protracted War*. But finding such a bunch of 'people' and welding them into an unmatched fighting force was a tall ask for any company, and even more so for an unknown company in India. I believe to this day that no one else in the group really thought it was possible.

It was abundantly clear to us by then that the first product from HMI's stable would be the small car. We would therefore be in direct competition with MUL and TML, and in order to be relevant to the consumer we would necessarily have to have a physical on-the-ground representation to match the local giants – but this would have to be done to a plan. For a start, we agreed that we had to go national from day one rather than adopt a cautious region-by-region approach. We also recognized we would have to be present in markets that accounted for at least 90 per cent of total sales volumes, if we were to make a go of it. We then went on to put in place a plan to establish a 75-location fully operational network within 18 months.

Y.S. Kim thought the plan was overly ambitious, maybe even audacious, and asked me if I really believed – first, that we needed so many, and second whether it was at all possible to create a nationwide network. GM and Ford had managed to establish networks of less than 15 dealerships each over two years and more. Both companies had come into the country in joint ventures with large, well-established automobile manufacturers, but still appeared to be struggling to build a significant network strength or market presence. I recall arguing that if indeed we had to make something of the project we would have to necessarily get into an eyeball-to-eyeball confrontation with MUL in order to acquire their existing and potential consumers rather than scrap for the leftovers with the likes of the Indian wings of GM and Ford.

I argued for a strategy of encirclement, mobile warfare and guerrilla tactics as the necessary cornerstones of our market-conquest strategy. Recalling again to myself Mao's *The Present Situation and Our Tasks,* I put together a forceful argument for a rapid build-up of a pan-India presence, which would enable HMI to 'attack dispersed, isolated enemy forces first; ...strive to draw the enemy into mobile warfare, but...lay great stress on learning the tactics of positional attack... Resolutely attack and seize all fortified points and cities which are weakly defended. Attack and seize at opportune moments all fortified points and cities defended with moderate strength...'

We spoke at length about how the growth of the services sector, particularly the knowledge economy, would create a whole new consumer class, with a much higher average education level, disposable income and discretionary spending habits that would mirror those of consumers in developed economies. These consumers, we reckoned, would be in places like Bangalore, Hyderabad, Chennai, Pune, and so on. MUL could not have been unaware of these trends, but it appeared constrained in making any concerted strategic moves beyond its Delhi NCR–Chandigarh–Punjab market focus. As a result, the informal market channels in the latter markets probably ended up meeting the true demand of the newly emerging growth nodes of consumerism.

The decision in HMI was that while we would project a strong presence in Delhi NCR and the Mumbai Metropolitan Region (MMR), we would make Hyundai the first choice of 'new' India. I also firmly believed that both the American giants and Honda (probably owing to their consulting company-inspired product strategy and a variety of other reasons) would, for a long time, have limited relevance in India, and that there was no reason for HMI to be overawed by them (or anyone else with a daunting global pedigree) or their strategies, because they had demonstrated little or no in-house understanding of the Indian reality.

Being in line functions across departments and handling network development at the operating level at TML had given me a detailed grasp of the practical issues involved in network-building and maintenance in an Indian context – albeit for an established and dominant market player. But the concepts that were to provide the basic framework of the Hyundai network design as it eventually evolved were probably first conceived in 1995 when I was attending a strategy workshop run by the consulting firm Arthur D. Little (ADL) in conjunction with ICICI Securities. While discussing the entry barriers faced by potential entrants to the Indian automotive marketplace, the problems associated with the high cost of creating a distribution network received a significant amount of attention and became the focus of an important team exercise in diagnosis and prescription at the workshop. Breaking away from the general thought pattern of solutions being proffered, the team I led put forward a facetious sounding thought, Jerry Lewis-style: 'If you can't raise the bridge, lower the river,' or, best, do both simultaneously. The team spoke of appropriate sizing for Indian conditions and essentially rubbished the large dealership infrastructure format, much in favour with automobile multinationals (including HMI's parent) who appear to find themselves most comfortable with a tried-and-tested cookie-cutter approach to network design and establishment – and generally end up treating innovation in such matters as network structuring as merely a theme for an off-site training programme.

The simple reality, the team observed, was that in a capital-scarce economy, a successful network design would be one that would ensure early break-even for dealerships by keeping initial capital investments low, while obviously pushing for a rapid growth in sales volume, which would in turn create sustainable, viability-inducing earning streams, even with the low dealership sales margins that are an imperative to keep sticker prices competitive. More importantly, the group disrupted the entire tenor of the theoretical constructs being bandied about by raising the question – ought not networks to be built with reference to and around the consumer? I recall speaking to the group about military design folklore, the apocryphal story of how during World War 2, the Americans put a soldier in the centre and built a tank around him, while the Germans built the tank and then put the soldier into it. The amazing agility of the former was often said to have won the day, despite the fearsome firepower and armouring of the latter.

Fortunately, conventional wisdom (or is it simply herd mentality?) ensured that the concepts propounded by the group were too radical to be 'borrowed' or used as a source of inspiration. Typically, new multinational entrants in those days required their dealers to provide large showrooms and expensively equipped workshops at vantage locations, and, in order to ensure viability through 'reasonable' sales volumes, offered large sales territories with a near-monopoly status for the dealer. This in turn ensured that intra-brand dealer competition did not negatively impact on either sales or service margins and earnings of the dealers. Ford, GM, Honda and Toyota clearly voted for this approach, probably also driven by their understanding of which way the market demand would move and what that would call for in terms of product support. Unfortunately, this managed to perpetuate a monopolistic mindset in both manufacturers (who constantly railed against the control regime in industry fora, and yet appeared strong votaries within their own businesses and benefitted the most from it) and dealers. Worst of all, it appeared to actively enable, if not encourage, anti-consumer practices in the industry – both by manufacturers and dealers – aided and abetted by the clutch of foreign banks and NBFCs active in the business of financing car purchases.

At HMI, we hoped to change all this. Our early in-house market research interactions showed that consumers appeared relatively neutral to, even unconcerned with, the distance of showroom location and were generally willing to make a maximum of two visits to the showroom during the purchase process. However, it was clear that since the 'small' car would typically be the first (and probably single car) for most buyers, and be owner-driven, the accessibility of service could become a major contributor to the ownership experience and a determinant of consumer satisfaction. Converting this thought while charting dealership locations, we decided that consumers should not be required to drive more than 7 kilometres on an average or a driving time of a maximum of 45 minutes to reach an HMI service point.

Considering that a trip to the car service centre probably ranks just after a visit to the dentist in its attractiveness, we reasoned we ought to try and limit it in the first instance. Fortunately, the product itself afforded us the opportunity to increase the mean time between services from what consumers were then generally experiencing. The engine design team had confidently recommended an engine oil change interval of 20,000 kilometres, but given Indian road conditions that would mean the engine operating at least four times longer to cover the same distance than it would in developed markets. Recognizing that oil change intervals in India ought to be determined by operating hours at low revs rather than by kilometres of operation, we decided to factor in things like dust levels and peg it marginally lower than the norm suggested by the engine design team. Of course, that would still keep us way ahead of the market leader and, in our communication to consumers, help us equate increased service intervals with better engine technology. Our studies showed that the average annual car utilization ranged between 7,000 kilometres in smaller cities and a shade below 12,000 kilometres in the larger cities. At these levels, we could effectively have offered a single annual service as a major product feature. Yet, when we spoke with consumers about the potential need to visit a workshop or service centre only once a year, the invariable reaction at the time was incredulity accompanied by a question about whether it was the lack of our service infrastructure preparedness that made us claim this. It was obvious that the visibility of the service network was going to be a critical contributor to consumer confidence in the brand. But the demands of visibility had to be tempered by the reality of economic sustainability – and so it was that HMI created the concept of the compact car dealership.

Recognizing a relatively common peeve of consumers on the need to visit dealer workshops to iron out small irritants in the days immediately following the purchase, we proposed to eliminate infancy problems (typically a result of inconsistent manufacturing-line practices) by putting in place a centralized pre-despatch inspection by the service team at the plant. The service team would, in effect, be the representative of the consumers at the plant and ensure a standardized quality when the consumer received the vehicle at the dealership. The proposed process would have meant that dealerships would literally only have to wash and polish the cars prior to delivery. With a clear emphasis on 'new entrants' into the business, this approach, we believed, would adequately de-risk the consumer and the brand. Obviously, that would in turn have implications for the size and spread of the service network that we needed to create.

I recall Gautam Sen asking me, if indeed such compact facilities could do the job, why would another new entrant of that era ask its dealers to provide for 4,000 square-foot showrooms and 10,000 square-foot workshops? Without batting an eyelid, I answered that it was probably because the people who designed the network facilities were so confident of their product's quality that they expected their cars to always be found parked either in the showrooms or in the workshops. I then went on to add that if I was to be charitable I'd simply blame it on their blind adherence to network standards created for completely different markets. Gautam, whom I'd known from his days at MUL, had a more positive take, and ascribed it to their aggressive product introduction and plans for ramping up their volume, which were all over the media at the time. As it turns out. I was not wide off the mark. Months later I learnt that the corporate identity (CI) handbook created by the other entrant's team was simply a rehashed version of another manufacturer's CI, with only the colours changed. For at least a couple of years, it turned out that my jibe on their planning for large showrooms and workshop spaces proved uncomfortably prescient!

In order to curtail huge upfront investments on real estate, which could ravage its dealers' viability in the initial years, the basic HMI workshops were conceptually designed with a small footprint. Relevant and appropriate automation was planned to ensure greater workshop-bay efficiency and manpower planning was done in a way that could easily accommodate working extended hours, or even the introduction of a second shift to meet consumer convenience and ensure a sweating of capital assets. To keep investments low when it came to spare parts stock and still ensure high availability, we proposed the creation of company-owned and -operated regional warehouses for spare parts. Mao's dictum in *On Protracted War*, 'Without preparedness, superiority is not real superiority and there can be no initiative either. … a force that is inferior but prepared can often defeat a superior enemy…' was clearly at the back of our minds.

This, then, was the concept that I eventually presented in Korea in April 1997 to Chairman S.Y. Chung, Vice Chairman S.W. Chon, President B.J. Park and Executive Vice President (International) N.M. Kim. Deciding against invoking Mao before my South Korean colleagues, I spoke instead of the Viet Cong's tactics against the military might of the United States, about travelling light being of essence in ensuring agility in guerrilla warfare and the logistics support that the Cu Chi tunnels provided to negate the problems of long supply chains that snaked down from north to south Vietnam. I then made out the case for well-trained, small, compact, strategically located, logistically well-supported dealerships, with a high degree of agility and commitment to take on the might of MUL and TML. The audacious innovativeness of the approach was clearly unexpected, and even as the debate appeared at one stage to be veering around why we ought not to follow the likes of GM, Ford and Honda, there came the clincher from the vice chairman, 'It's a new market we know nothing of, but he clearly does. New markets need new solutions,' (or words to that effect).

With our strategic approach to product, pricing and distribution getting the green signal from the very top, now came the tougher part – actually making it happen.

HMI's network partner choice was driven by our definition of the ideal dealer personality, the requirements inherent in the product strategy and the resultant network design. Yet, the truth is that when push came to shove, we just did not have as many choices as we might have liked while selecting dealers. At the time the first advertisement seeking applications for dealerships was published, the Hyundai brand was still practically unknown in the country and hardly anyone other than those who had visited the Auto Expo in 1996 or those who lived in Tamil Nadu (where Hyundai's entry was big news) considered it as a serious business proposition. HMI received barely 200 dealership applications of any reasonable quality for a proposed 75-strong network structure.

In stark contrast to the response to Hyundai's advertisement, which reflected its brand image then, Ford India, in a selection process that was at least partially run by one of the Big 4 audit firms, was rumoured to have received over 5,000 applications for 15 dealerships! I still recall the raised eyebrows and questioning looks I encountered from most TML dealers when I first told them the name of the company I'd decided to join. Yet, practically every single one of the biggest, most well-established TML dealer families in the north, west and east regions had unhesitatingly told me they would look forward to working with me wherever I went. These relationships, I believed, would provide the foundation for HMI's network. Arguably, in the process, they might have risked displeasing the operating management in TML's automotive division. The dealers' generally positive response when I broached the subject came as a pleasant surprise to me, but I sometimes wondered if depending on TML dealers in such a large swathe of the country could be tricky and fraught with risk. The Tata Indica was scheduled to be launched almost simultaneously with the Santro. Despite the excellent personal relations I enjoyed with the families of the TML dealers who had committed their investments to HMI, it often crossed my mind that their large, well-established truck dealership business interests might well have been put into jeopardy due to their involvement with HMI. Given the choice, I fretted, they may simply jettison the Korean challenger and, if that happened, perhaps just six months before the proposed launch, HMI could be in very dire straits. But in those days the reassurance brought by the vote of confidence from some of India's most successful automobile dealerships meant a great deal, and even the risk of withdrawal was well worth taking.

But the TML dealer families who committed their support stood firm in their resolve. The biggest and strongest among them – the Bafnas in Maharashtra, the Guptas in Uttar Pradesh and Madhya Pradesh, the Himatsinghkas in Assam and West Bengal, the Kales in Maharashtra and Chattisgarh, the MGF group in Kerala, the Nandas in Gujarat and Punjab, the Parikhs in Jharkhand and Orissa, the Sanghis in Madhya Pradesh – all put their faith in the prospects of the yet-unknown Korean company, with a name they could barely pronounce and the promise of a product they had not even seen! In most cases, it was the next generation, many already tiring from the 'culture' that was taking hold in TML, who came over to work on the HMI business. I had known many of them since their childhood, and recall telling one TML dealer, a good friend, much to his wife's joy and relief, that his child's business was now my responsibility and he should not interfere in any way beyond providing the capital. With his child and wife visibly elated at my stand, the irascible petrel quietly acquiesced. Much to my relief, TML did not put them through the wringer for doing that. This could be due to any one of three reasons. For one, I clearly recall Ratan Tata mentioning on more than one occasion during in-company meetings that dealers should be given the freedom to invest, even in competing brands, because the company should strive to ensure that its brand 'commanded' the investment attention of the dealer and did not 'demand' it by virtue of its hold over the dealer's existing business. For another, it was quite possible that TML's management could not have afforded to simultaneously alienate such powerful and competent dealers with the softening of the truck market already becoming apparent in 1997. And, lastly, it was equally possible that the operating management of TML did not take HMI seriously at that stage.

With the TML biggies getting involved, soon enough some of the best-known Bosch dealers – the Jagwanis in Rajasthan and the Puris in Jammu and Kashmir – people I had long known for their focus on fair practices and adherence to quality processes also came on board. Almost everyone else, to my recollection, were first-time car dealers, though a couple did operate highly competent and well regarded MUL service centres.

But even they did not make the switch easily. It took many meetings and considerable convincing to convert those in the north. In the south, the TML dealers quite characteristically and, expectedly, stayed within their comfort zone and away from HMI. After years of playing a battered second fiddle to, and constantly being harassed by, Ashok Leyland nipping at their heels, they had just started enjoying a protracted period of unimagined dealership prosperity and growth thanks to two extremely successful product introductions that my team and I, while at TML, had helmed. Clearly, they did not believe that throwing in their lot with me was a wise move; nor did they want to do anything that they feared might rock their boat. There were, of course, just two that I spoke with in the south, and their reluctance wasn't entirely unexpected.

The one big automotive distribution behemoth which did consider Hyundai but chose eventually to stay away was the TVS group. Known widely in the south for its adherence to quality processes, particularly in its workshops, and for its ethical if somewhat condescending conduct in its showrooms, the group may have made an impressive addition to the big names that HMI had managed to interest. But there was a fundamental difference in our approaches. TVS apparently believed that in keeping with their 'stature' in the industry, they ought to be given sole distribution rights for the (then) four southern states. Both Y.S. Kim and I, on the other hand, believed that would militate against both the consumers' and HMI's interests from the very start, and indicated our preference for an application for a dealership in Chennai and maybe one city (out of three) in Kerala. Probably miffed at the 'Johnny-come-lately' with a none-too-certain future having the temerity to lay down conditions, TVS preferred not to apply or involve itself with the dealership end of HMI's business. Manufacturing companies in the group, all very highly regarded for their production quality standards, built an involvement with HMI as vendor partners, probably with no great expectations from it and negligible investment risk, only to hit pay-dirt (and gain greatly in terms of social recognition too), when HMI's sales were soon larger than the combined sales of the 'big guys' that they appeared so enamoured by.

TVS's decision helped pave the way for the entry and subsequent rapid growth of a group of young US-based professionals returning to India, and a first-generation entrant into the automotive business, the K.U.N. Motor Company Private Ltd. K.U.N. is today probably significantly larger than the TVS group in terms of car sales volumes in the same geographical markets across all brands it handled.

From May 1997, the first expansion of the marketing, sales, service and parts teams was kicked off. The Koreans Jong Hyok Kim (J.H. Kim), Young Key Koo (Y.K. Koo), Young Jin Ahn, (Y.J. Ahn), Stewart H. Suh and J.H. Youn came on board over the next few weeks, soon to be joined by Vijay Kumar, Puneet Choudhry, Vasu Dev Bhasin, Mukund Srinivasan, Manohar Bhat and A.N. Prakash Rao. J.D. Bae, one of the finest people I have ever had the privilege to work with, moved back to Korea soon after. Along with Y.S. Kim, we split ourselves into one core group and four teams, with each of the latter handling the process of initial shortlisting of dealership applicants in one specific region, and the core group ensuring rapid approval. In what was probably the fastest automobile dealership finalization process in India, even to this day, letters of intent were issued to 70 applicants, and the teams busied themselves with handholding the applicants through the process, starting with the selection of location.

The core group members moved across teams and established clear policies with flexibility, ensured zero red tape with extensive delegation and gave near real-time decisions to resolve operational issues. Moving away, where required, from traditional 3S (sales, service, spares) facilities, multi-location facilities were approved – as long as a definite consumer benefit could be established. In the days before Google Maps and WhatsApp photographs, I had to often depend on my memories of places and streets in cities across the country, and give an instant 'go, no go' signal to the teams on prospective locations – sometimes as they stood on-site and gave me details of their location from their mobile phones. A cardinal principle in determining location was to ensure unhindered traffic flow in front of the dealership's proposed showroom or workshop. Any source of potential clogging was a non-starter.

One memory stands out. Yong Sung Kim was calling from a proposed location in Bangalore and, as he described it, I stopped him short, and asked him how far it was from the movie hall. He first said, 'What movie hall?' and after a pause and a quick consultation with the dealer principal, replied, 'It's about 200 metres, but how did you know?' I reminded him I'd grown up in that neighbourhood, and approved the location. Working with TML had taken me all over the country and I could claim a reasonable familiarity with cities as diverse as Ahmedabad and Agartala or Chandigarh and Cochin and the ground-level knowledge helped immensely in speeding up location approvals. HMI got some absolute gems for showroom locations, including the company's own showroom at the Mahalaxmi Temple crossing in south Mumbai. At what was then probably the busiest traffic intersection in the country, with the highest concentration of dollar-millionaire customers in a three-kilometre radius, we got an offer from a realtor and gave him an in-principle nod within ten minutes, because, as I reasoned, we were getting a full showroom at a monthly rental that was less than what it cost to rent the hoarding opposite it for a week.

As a logical extension to our expectations of the early adapters coming from the new growth centres and from among non-conventional consumers, a Kolkata dealership was located with accessibility from Salt Lake–Rajarhat; one in Bangalore came up near the information technology hub of Electronics City, Koramangla; one in Pune was set up in the vicinity of the cantonment at Khirki; in Chennai the cosmopolitan Anna Nagar saw its first car showroom being built, and in Ludhiana the spiffy new residential areas that had started coming up off Ferozpur Road became a first-time location for a car dealership. Travelling through the assigned region, the network development teams ensured not just an adherence to timelines, but also the dissemination of learning at one dealership that could have relevance to the project implementation process at other dealerships. Invariably, the last week of every month involved state-wise or regional meetings of the dealerships with the core group to iron out any issue that could potentially delay matters.

Guided, encouraged, coaxed and pushed hard by Prakash Rao, Y.K. Koo, Yong Sung Kim and Y.J. Ahn, their teams thought nothing of doing ninety-six-hour work weeks, not in front of computer screens and in conference rooms, but out on the road, for months on end, unmindful of the weather. Eventually, in early 1998, dealership facility construction got into full swing all over the country. Locations proudly displaying a banner announcing 'The Future Home of the Santro' started popping up all over the country. The four teams then started working with individual dealerships on fleshing out organizational charts and completed the process of personnel selection in order to meet the target of having fully trained personnel on board by the beginning of September 1998.

The haphazard method of managing construction projects so common to India used to often result in nightmares for our methodical and process-oriented Korean colleagues. I vividly recall standing with Y.S. Kim and Asheem Suri, who had been selected as one of two dealers in Ludhiana, at a construction site – an empty plot of land with a solitary bit of shade, an almost leafless little tree – on a blazingly hot summer afternoon. Asheem Suri had just about managed to get possession of the land and was on the verge of getting approvals for his building plans – and we were less than 120 days from the launch function. Even the generally unflappable Y.S. Kim looked very concerned and asked me, 'Do you really think he can do it?'

I can't honestly say I was not worried, but knowing the tremendous resources that the Suri family could bring to bear on the project, I tried to assuage Y.S. Kim's fears by simply saying, 'Don't worry he'll do it. Like the Japanese have Just-in-Time (JIT), in India we have what we call Somehow-in-Time.' After the stress-relieving levity, we spent the next hour under that tree, listening closely while Asheem convincingly detailed out every action he had taken and reassured us that everything would fall into place. Ultimately, he did manage a high-quality, true showpiece of a facility – obviously somehow-in-time!

HMI's own Motor Plaza in Delhi went one step further in giving all of us sleepless nights. The landowner, the MGF Group had everything including the architect, drawings, civil contractor, equipment and labour in place but finally got possession of the land through a Debt Recovery Tribunal (DRT) bench barely 100 days before the vehicle deliveries were scheduled to commence. T.M. Kumar, who had by then been drafted in to help with getting the Hyundai Motor Plaza projects in Delhi, Chennai and Mumbai on-stream and had worked with me on every aspect from identifying the plaza locations to completing the acquisition or tenancy, brought a new urgency and much-required project management skills to the Delhi project.

As important as getting the facilities completed on time was to ensure that, in line with our endeavour to achieve early dealership viability through improved capital efficiency, we minimize the funds that dealers would be required to invest on workshop equipment, showroom facilities and corporate identity kits, even while maintaining the highest industry standards. In what was definitely a first in the Indian auto industry, in an extension of something I had tried out in TML years earlier, HMI ensured that substantial capital savings accrued to dealerships through a programme of 'assisted procurement' of workshop equipment and special tools. A TVS group trading company that specialized in importing workshop equipment approved by global OEMs was our clear partner of choice. Their pricing, however, was totally out of sync with our approach. Just prior to our negotiations, V.D. Bhasin, Vijay Kumar and Puneet Choudhry did a detailed teardown analysis of two specific high-value items on our equipment shopping list – a two-post car lift system and a paint booth – in an effort to arrive at an estimate of actual manufacturing cost. We then presented the TVS team with our best price offer – between 40 per cent and 50 per cent below their list prices. What we offered them, however, was a single order for a quantity that was a multiple of their cumulative sales over the past five years and asked them to check with their Italian principals on the pricing – offering them the use of our office conference room and phones for the purpose. It was late on a Friday afternoon, but given the time difference the Italians had not yet signed off for the weekend. Bewildered at first, they quickly regained their poise and immediately started talking numbers. Ultimately, the following Tuesday, we got our price, they got their order and HMI dealerships got standardized, global-quality workshop equipment at prices significantly below what the near-monopoly Indian manufacturer of one item had then very reluctantly offered. The Indian workshop equipment market has never been the same since.

On special tools for the workshops, V.D. Bhasin and his team went a step further. After procuring five sets from HMC, they reverse engineered the products and invited quality manufacturers of garage tools in India to bid to manufacture them locally, again with the commitment of single-source procurement. The result: HMI dealerships ended up spending probably one-tenth of what dealerships of other global OEMs spent on special tools. When we had to get dealerships to invest in Emergency Repair Service (ERS) vehicles, we put together all the pre-production prototype Santros that the plant had assembled and billed them at a significantly discounted price that best reflected their prototype status.

To cut costs of showroom construction, HMI did not stop at recommending a colour or make for showroom floor tiles or false ceiling panels, but went ahead and negotiated a 'rate contract' price with manufacturers that would be applicable to orders received from HMI dealers for supply in any part of the country. In the negotiation with India's then largest manufacturer of false ceiling panels, we were able to obtain a price very close to what was offered in the winning bid in the tender for the Terminal 2 of Indira Gandhi International Airport in Delhi, then under construction, since the total area of the panels that we were procuring across all dealerships across the country was roughly similar. Dealerships ultimately ended up saving almost 30 per cent beyond the best wholesale prices they would have got in the most competitive markets in the country, and this lowered their initial capital investments even further.

A similar effort led by Yong Sung Kim, J.H. Youn and Manohar Bhat helped create a Dealer Management System (DMS), incorporating the best features of, and processes used in, Hyundai

Canada, MUL and TML. Working closely with a crack team headed by Pradeep Banerjee, a valued former TML colleague with highly regarded internal audit experience, at Bangalore-based software fledgling Datacons (later acquired by a subsidiary of ICICI Bank), the system was built and tested in record time and was probably the first integrated DMS ever to be developed entirely in India. The actual development cost paid out to Datacons was then divided equally amongst all the dealerships, and they ended up paying probably not more than 5 per cent of what other global OEMs were then charging their dealerships for similar software. Obviously, HMI did not build in the cost of the intellectual input that was provided at every step of process definition.

The IPR was in principle to be shared because HMI had developed the framework and Datacons had coded it, but we took near free annual system maintenance of the system at dealerships in lieu of royalties on potential sales – thus saving them revenue expenditure. Later, at least three multinational OEMs bought the software for their Indian dealerships, and I recall being told by Datacons that at least two of them sold it on to their dealers for a profit. All this was at a time when broadband availability in India meant only Sify and keeping operating costs under check entailed giving dealerships specific night-time slots for all uploads and downloads!

While the network development and service teams were focused on the front end, J.H. Youn and Mukund Srinivasan worked around the clock to create a parts support system that would at least match the well-established, extremely efficient and highly regarded MUL spares system in terms of order-fill rates and speed of supply. The high level of localization at HMI meant that except for some bearings, steering components and the ECU, everything else could be procured real-time either from the plant or from vendors in the vicinity of the plant and the mother warehouse of spare parts. But there was still the challenge of the road-freight-based supply line snaking its way from Chennai, with all manner of inbuilt cost-inefficiencies, transit uncertainties, damage risks and delivery delays. The obvious answer would have been to stuff the network with parts from the very start, but that would have only served to increase investments by dealerships in current assets and in turn impact their viability.

The spare parts team went on to create a network of parts depots across the country, starting with Delhi, Mumbai, Calcutta, Bangalore and Kochi, and then set in place milk-run systems that could supply dealerships with parts and meet any emergent requirements with leads of less than twenty-four hours. The commitment made to dealers was that any Vehicle Off Road (VOR) order received prior to 2 p.m. would be shipped the same day. Of course, this meant larger inventories being held by HMI, which would also be taking on a significant part of the freight costs, particularly for dealers in the north, west and east regions, but it also ensured a rationalization of inventory and enabled dealers to convey to consumers a sense of comfort on parts availability. This was, incidentally, the method TML had used very effectively against the Japanese manufacturers of light commercial vehicles in the late 1980s. A network of seven regional parts warehouses supported the Tata 407 and Tata 608 ensuring world-class spare parts availability that played a big role in the success of both products.

The real test of all the hard work and HMI's system capabilities probably came much later in 1999 when floods in Calcutta laid low about 60 cars, while potentially impacting at least another 320. Over a period of three days after the waters subsided, the electronic control units or ECUs were replaced as a precautionary measure on the worst-affected cars, along with a locating modification literally designed and implemented on the fly by V.D. Bhasin and his service team. On the rest of the cars in Calcutta, the replacements were completed over the next two weeks. The location modification went on to become a full-fledged engineering release and got incorporated on the production line – not just for Santro cars made in India, but also for the Atoz variant made in HMC.

Through a 'service campaign' ('recall' was a barely known and rather misunderstood word in India those days), ECU location modification work was carried out on Santros across the country as a product enhancement exercise. Similar support efforts during a spate of floods in Ahmedabad, Bangalore, Mumbai and Chennai over the few months thereafter established the operational capabilities and competence of the spare parts and service teams of HMI beyond any doubt.

All this was, indeed, a path-breaking effort. To start with, the 73 locations network – two short of what originally intended had been because of delays in establishing the network in Assam – was spread all over the rest of the country even at the launch stage, making it the fastest network establishment exercise by any car manufacturer – before or since. In comparison, MUL had cobbled together a 38 locations network over two years, 1983 and 1984. Even TML, which started with the unbeatable advantage of having one of India's strongest dealer networks, was slower off the blocks in setting up a dedicated initial network for the Indica. At a speed that was quite unparalleled, fully functional sales, service, spare parts and emergency response facilities were established by HMI to exacting globally acceptable standards and at costs well below those then prevalent in India. Yet, even more significant was the manner in which the exceptional team that made all this possible applied itself to the task of welding together a group of people, most of whom did not know each other earlier, into a highly motivated fighting machine, with a single focus – leadership in the marketplace.

Over the many months of preparation I'd had occasion to discuss with Y.S. Kim various issues on building dealer relations and the cultural sensitivities involved in Indian business. We had chatted at length on the manner in which TML, for instance, had fostered a very familial atmosphere within its dealer community, which was probably among its greatest strengths.

Y.S. Kim personally had exceptional cultural sensitivity and his politeness had become something of a legend not just among HMI's employees and vendor partners, but in the corridors of Fort St George, the Tamil Nadu government's secretariat, as well. His innate ability to relate at a very human level with people, even as he remained a man of few words, helped build an amazing bonding even with the dealer principals.

Together, we evolved a practice, very much like that of the TML I once knew, of receiving and treating dealer principals as honoured guests. At every dealer convention, right from the very first one at the Taj Fisherman's Cove near Chennai, we invariably stood at the door to greet them with a traditional 'namaskar'. I would constantly reinforce this with all our team members, reminding them that HMI's dealers were our first customers and that they helped pay our salaries. Time and again I reiterated to my colleagues that dealer principals were the true brand custodians, because they had put down their hard-earned money to help build the brand, they very often outlasted managements – and while employees always had the option of walking away, dealers rarely did.

I often pointed out that the value of the combined investment by dealer principals in land and facilities for the dealerships , if converted to equity in the company, made them shareholders with almost as large a stake as the parent company itself. But with the colleagues I had working shoulder-to-shoulder with me, I need hardly have worried. Each of them had a strong knowledge and experience base, which automatically ensured that arrogance had no part to play in their dealings with dealer principals, or for that matter with their staff. I believe this approach to its dealer partners, based on sincerity, complete transparency and mutual respect helped HMI build an extremely strong network foundation, on which it built the superstructure for future growth.

I don't believe HMI was entirely unique among the multinationals in that respect. But they were few. Ford India, though it had just a handful of dealers, was also known for the quality of its dealer principal interaction based on mutual respect and an exceptional openness, both under John Parker and Phil Spender. But one European multinational that just did not seem to understand, or care about cultural sensitivities while operating in India, probably took the cake. A few months after the HMI dealer convention at the Taj Fisherman's Cove, this multinational apparently organized a similar event along with a dinner on the beach. That's where the similarity ended, because while the dealer principals and the Indian staff were expected to line up for a buffet of regular Indian food, a special table was laid out for a sit-down dinner for the expatriate management team replete with the choicest wines and an elaborate seafood-based continental menu. Disgusted at what he considered obviously unacceptable behaviour, and what he saw as 'racist treatment', one of the dealer principals, also an HMI dealer, young, professionally qualified, outspoken, no financial pushover and extremely well-connected politically in his state, protested in no uncertain terms, publicly contrasting the situation with the way dealer principals were treated by HMI, and led an embarrassing walkout, joined by at least four more dealer principals. The expatriate company's management remained unfazed and continued with their dinner. Needless to say, the principal resigned from that dealership soon enough.

The untiring efforts of the HMI team at constantly guiding and supporting each individual dealer principal culminated in the perfect climax. Over a three-week period before the initial vehicle orders were sought in October 1998, dealerships were inaugurated all over the country – from Jammu to Thiruvananthapuram, and from Ahmedabad to Kolkata. Some months earlier, I had introduced another ex-TML colleague of mine, A.P. Gandhi, to Y.S. Kim and HMC, and he came on board as president just weeks before the commercial production of the Santro commenced. The complete HMI senior management team went around making sure we stood with the dealer principals in their first moment of triumph. The near-parenting approach that HMI brought to bear on its dealer development activity served the company very well as it helped build a strong two-way relationship based on trust and fair play.

Inauguration of the first Hyundai authorized service centre in Chennai established in October 1997 to service imported Hyundai cars.

First Row (L to R): The author; J.D. Bae, then marketing director, HMI; and Y.S. Kim, then managing director, HMI.

Second Row (L to R): Min Ho Lee, then director of procurement; and V.D. Bhasin, then general manager, service.

Third Row (L to R): Kamlesh Patel, ace rally driver and owner of the centre; Puneet Choudhury, manager, service; and H.S. Kwon, general manager, service.

At the rollout of the 500,000th car in December 2003. (*L to R*) J.I. Kim and the author.

Celebrating the rollout of the 200,000th export car in October 2005. (*L to R*) S.S. Yang, managing director, HMI; Dr V. Krishnamurthy, chairman, National Manufacturing Competitiveness Council; the author; and K. Suresh, chairman, Chennai Port Trust.

Change of guard at HMI: Bidding goodbye to Y.S. Kim and welcoming J.I. Kim in April 2002. (L to R) The author; Y.S. Kim; B.J. Park, then president, HMC; and J.I. Kim.

The author with HMC's chairman, M.K. Chung, in February 2006.

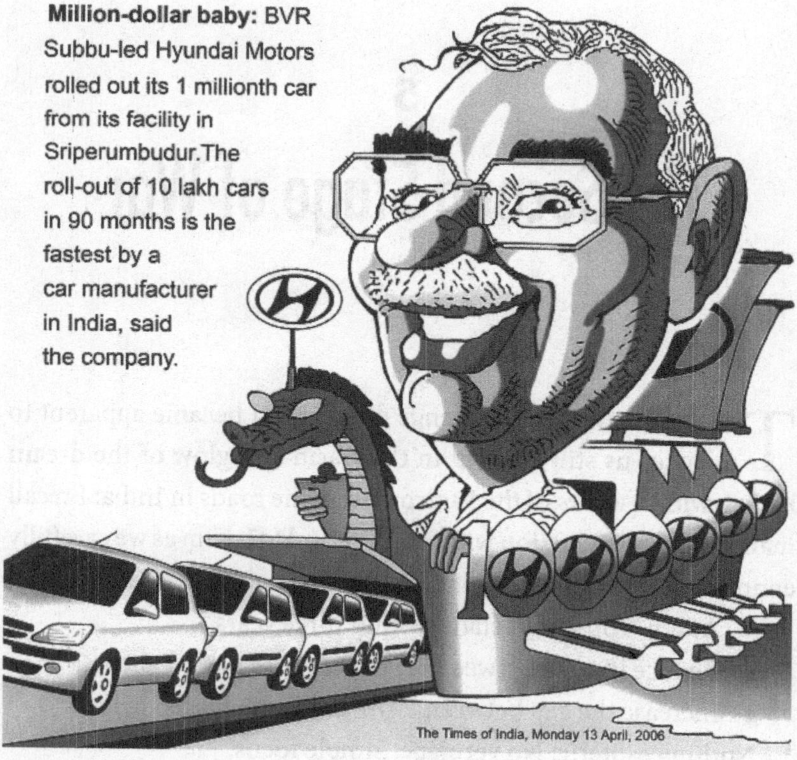

A *Times of India* creation commemorating the 1,000,000th car manufactured at HMI's plant near Chennai in 2006.

Source: The Times of India Group.

5

The Second Stage of War

The enormity of the challenge facing HMI became apparent to many of us still basking in the warm afterglow of the dream launch within weeks of the Santro hitting the roads in India. I recall many hours of discussion with Y.S. Kim and J.H. Kim as we carefully enunciated three simply defined marketing goals for HMI:

- Attain 'Top Three' status within three years.
- Reduce the gap between HMI and those placed above.
- Increase the gap between HMI and those placed below.

Nothing esoteric. No verbiage. Simple focus.

While most of my Korean colleagues seemed distinctly less prone to think in terms of achieving market leadership, coming as they did with an underdog or challenger mindset, I possessed the TML mindset, which believed leadership was a birthright because our capability of securing and retaining market dominance was an inherent one. Y.S. Kim tended to agree with me and my desire to inculcate this burning ambition for growth to ultimately overtake MUL, but tempered my exuberance with his rationality. Naturally, therefore, the goals we defined ended up somewhere in between desire and reality. But we were unanimous when it came to the three parameters that we would work on to attain market leadership – quality of the product, enhancement and application of technology and quality of consumer interface.

Going back to my readings of Mao, I was convinced that '*attack, is primary, while defence – a supplementary means of destroying the enemy and the means of self-preservation – is secondary. In actual warfare the chief role is played by defence much of the time and by attack for the rest of the time, but if war is taken as a whole, attack remains primary...*' (*On Protracted War*). Put into the context of the automotive industry, I read this to mean that we would have to use the product (and technology upgradations in the product) as the battering ram to ensure initial gains in market share, while at the same time using methods to garner greater consumer affection and confidence at every single point of contact for self-preservation. Moving both these in tandem, I believed, would create a virtuous cycle of self-sustaining growth.

Though I always implicitly believed it, I never imagined that outdoing MUL on marketing strategy was going to be a piece of cake. From the outside, MUL looked to me to be completely distanced from the consumer as it sat on the proverbial high horse of a typical near-monopolistic seller. With consumers seeking an upgrade from the Maruti 800, demand for the Maruti Zen had risen sharply, but allotments to dealers appeared to be based to a great extent on the number of 'bookings' at a dealership. Unofficial intermediaries, backed by NBFCs, in regions like Delhi NCR and the northwestern parts of the country used the 'bookings' condition to create an impression of insatiable local demand, cornered supplies and effectively appeared to redistribute the supplies at huge premiums to consumers in the rest of the country. A peculiarly regional phenomenon, the 'it commands a premium in the open market, ergo it is a good car' approach, appeared to me as an observer, rightly or wrongly I can't say, to have completely permeated the psyche of MUL's network and led to a lowering of its guard.

It appeared to outsiders like us that some part of MUL's network, probably confused the huge premiums that the Zen attracted as reflecting consumer affection rather than consumer desperation born out of a perennial shortage of supply and imbalanced product distribution – whatever the reason for these were. The truth was that the new Indian consumer – educated, professional, aspirational, particularly, the salaried middle class – simply hated the idea of having to pay a premium. That, I believed, was just the opening HMI needed. All we had to do was to engender a mass movement against the near-monopolistic power of MUL.

The task at hand was effectively to become the first choice of this new professional and aspirational India that MUL, in what appeared to me its lack of concern bordering on nonchalance and worse, had seemingly chosen to ignore. Tracking the Maruti Zen's 'unofficial' premiums across markets gave us a clear idea about where to make our product available, thereby giving consumers a choice that they did not have earlier. But there was still the job of finding those customers and reaching out to them. It wasn't quite in the realms of 'ambush marketing', but ended up having a similar impact.

Years earlier, in 1995, at TML, my team had used the occasion of a Mahindra-sponsored cross-country SUV rally being flagged off from the National Sports Club of India (NSCI) in Mumbai to string up, literally overnight, hundreds of banners extolling the just-launched Tata Sumo, spread all the way from Haji Ali to Lotus Cinema. It made the Mahindras see red, and a host of other shades associated with apoplexy, but that hardly mattered to us. The message was later reinforced by probably the first in-cinema car advertising, with the Sumo ad film showing to virtually the same target group in south Mumbai's Sterling cinema. The Sumo soon became the choice of south Mumbai's swish set and made it to bungalows in Lonavala or beach houses in Alibaug. And then in 1996, came Pepsi's famous tongue-in-cheek ad campaign at the time of the ICC World Cup screaming 'Nothing Official About It' at that had its arch-rival Coke, the official sponsor of the mammoth sporting event – and ambush marketing had come to stay.

At HMI I employed similar tactics. Surrogate advertising for car finance by Hyundai dealers, offering 'special, low rates' on financing purchases of the Maruti Zen would, I figured, introduce us overnight to hundreds of potential buyers of the Zen, including many who had booked the car at dealerships across the country and were waiting – not so patiently – for their chance to buy it. The dealers also used recently set up but as yet relatively underutilized workshops to offer customers of the Maruti 800 free car servicing on the weekends and conducted car-valuation clinics at petrol stations to gain access to a large number of customers who were considering their next upgrade.

When commercial production of the Santro commenced in September 1998, it was an absolute imperative to ensure that every single car that rolled off the Indian assembly line met the same standards of fit and finish that global consumers expected. After all, if Indian consumers were expected to pay prices for the car that were in line with global standards, why should they have to settle for anything less than the global standard in terms of technology, performance and quality? Hundreds of man-hours spent in training a highly charged and young workforce ensured that every car that went into the driveways of Indian consumers' had the perfect gap and flush and a paint job without even a hint of orange peel. Almost overnight, but not without adequate warning of its intent, Hyundai raised the standard for interiors, overall build quality, and fit and finish, in the small-car market. In order to drive home the advantage, the sales staff at HMI's dealerships was assiduously trained to point out to potential customers what they ought to look for when evaluating a car's aesthetics.

Automobile reporting was in many ways in its infancy in India then, and very few members of the media would look for, or write about, details like gap and flush in a car's build, or other such matters of finesse, unless it was deliberately pointed out to them. When it came to the Santro, looks were not the car's strongest feature, so we had to focus the consumers' attention on things that would really matter to them in the long term. But we recognized that this was only the start, and Hyundai would have to constantly strive to keep ahead in terms of safety, build quality, product technology and the quality of customer interface.

All our efforts at defining the product and ensuring exceptional fit and finish were noticed and given the thumbs up by auto journalists who test drove the final batch of production prototypes on a 450 kilometre run from Chennai to Bangalore and on to Ooty. As the cars breezed through Bangalore's traffic, the true power delivery capabilities of the perfectly torqued engine became apparent to all those driving, and as they hit the highway the ride and handling competence of the suspension system came in for unstinted appreciation. There were some comments on the softness of the ride, but recognizing that the car was primarily aimed at urban users, it passed muster all round. *Auto India* went on to note that 'for highway use, the Santro is more than good, thanks to a combination of straight-line stability, good acceleration, cruising ability, ride comfort and no noise levels.' Concerns, however, were voiced about the gear steps, seat ergonomics, pedal placement and gear shift accessibility in some driving conditions. But the overall verdict of the magazine was: 'The Santro is a better conceived car…as an overall package. It is great as a city runabout and just as good on the highway. Spacious, economical and driver friendly, it uses the latest technology – something Indians simply love. A lot will depend on the price.'

Yet, when customer bookings for the Santro opened in October, despite the humongous efforts by Hyundai's dealers – who contacted every single customer who had enquired about the car in the immediate aftermath of the advertising campaigns that had already been aired by then, the total orders seemed to limp ahead disappointingly. Even on the evening of the penultimate day, the number had just crossed 10,000 with almost zero real support in terms of publicity coming from the finance intermediaries, all firmly aligned with MUL, the source of their bread, butter and, unquestionably, jam.

Neither HDFC nor KMFL, both of which had formally become the first two finance partners of HMI, nor ABN Amro, which had muscled into the collection process probably owing to a familiarity with the finance teams at the parent company in Korea, had moved a little finger to help. Like good bankers they seemed only attempting to manage the potential risk of losing business if HMI took off by committing to a partnership in word but being reluctant to back it with much money.

Though some dealers were keen to make bookings in their own names, they lacked the funds to do so and many did not meet the credit parameters outlined by the banks. 'Dealer bookings' have been a strange peculiarity of the Indian automobile retailing scene. For years auto dealers had watched some of the most storied names in the NBFC sector develop into a fine art the process of booking cars with full payments, getting allotments in a supply-constrained situation, and then selling them at a 'premium' couched in higher interest rates to make it all legitimate. Some large dealers had taken the same path, and set up highly leveraged finance companies of their own to do just this. But they also used the 'bookings' that they thus held to further their core auto and other businesses – including, for instance, 'obliging' a long-standing customer, or officials that they invariably dealt with – without seeking anything more than the actual cost of funds employed for the booking. The 'goodwill' they thus generated was invariably of far greater consequence to the majority of them. But HMI's band of dealers, were for the most part, small newcomers – and the company's own future was not obviously considered worthy of too much funding by the official NBFC partners, who ran the normal customer booking schemes more as a low-risk , high-profit retail finance product than out of any real sense of commitment to HMI. This is when ICICI Bank stepped in.

Driven by a management that strongly believed in building and nurturing relationships, one that understood the manufacturing industry, ICICI once again dared to look beyond the transactional element of the business. In a replay of the earlier corporate finance support that it had provided, it again pulled out all the stops. With just a written commitment on the company letterhead and a written 'personal' guarantee from me that any cancellations would be refunded to the bank alone and that the bank's lien on the booked vehicles would be protected at all costs, ICICI funded dealer-backed bookings – by dealers they scarcely knew then – of well over 3,000 units on the last day.

Both ICICI and I knew that the company letter that I had signed at 5 a.m. that morning would have technically required ratification by the company bean-counters and definitely the board itself to have any real validity – and that there was absolutely no way I could have convinced people in India and Korea to agree to give that guarantee in six hours. But both the bank and treated it as a formality to be completed, because of our underlying trust in each other and a willingness to find unconventional methods of physically enforcing the lien by simply controlling access to the cars' keys! Just as we knew that the personal guarantee I had signed for funds covering over 3,000 bookings represented a sum about five hundred times my personal net worth. But that was the time to act, and we did. Thanks primarily to the enormous timely support from ICICI, HMI closed with 15,000 bookings at the end of the booking period. On that day I realized that HMI probably had only one true supporter in the financial service sector. About the others, I kept my counsel – as I still do.

When the bookings process was finally done, there was no time for euphoria because, internally, particularly the Indians in the sales and marketing teams – and Y.S. Kim – figured that the brand still did not have the strength to sustain itself in a long-drawn-out battle with MUL.

Though MUL had, by all accounts, initially rubbished the potential challenge from Hyundai in all its internal meetings, it hit back hard immediately after the launch. We had never underestimated MUL's control over their 'informal' sales channels, the Direct Sales Associates (DSAs) of finance companies and banks, because of the ability of the company and its dealers to provide the DSA's significant earning opportunities because of the product range and the brand pull. But the extent of it and its strength was still a revelation as the Santro's booking process got underway and the DSAs at best stayed away from the Santro and, at worst, bad-mouthed it to potential customers in no uncertain terms.

We knew, therefore, that the effective demand at the initial launch stage was probably only half of the bookings we had garnered, and people, by force of habit, were just gaming the system using two tries to make sure that they scored at least one hit. Making the pitch even more sticky, MUL, feeling the heat of real competition for the first time ever, cut prices of the Maruti 800 and the Zen in December, right on the day of the much-awaited launch of the Tata Indica. After knocking off a few bells and whistles, MUL cut the prices of the Zen by almost 15 per cent. Soon enough, by January 1999, bookings for the Santro had more or less evaporated after we had managed to supply just under two-thirds of the numbers booked. We were well and truly struggling.

Then came TML's Indica with a record 115,000 bookings or thereabouts in a week. A few months earlier, V.M. Raval, executive director of TML, had confidently told *India Today* magazine, 'We are trying to make the impossible possible. We expect to sell 1.5 lakh cars by the end of the first year of production.' The Tata Indica's positioning of 'More car per car' combined with styling, the advantage of diesel, the near unbelievable pricing and, of course, the lasting allure of India's most trusted brand, had, not unexpectedly, further queered the pitch for the Santro. As the enormity of the task at hand of building the Santro and the Hyundai corporate brands became even more pronounced, it became clear that HMI would have to move rapidly beyond merely imparting greater finesse to the quality of consumer interaction at the dealerships which had been an integral part of the effort by the sales and customer care groups in the company from its very inception – the defence, as Mao would have seen it.

In order to always maintain close interaction with consumers, Hyundai had already established three company-owned sales and service outlets in Delhi, Mumbai and Chennai, modelled after the Mercedes 'lighthouses' in Germany and TML's own variant of that model in Delhi and Orissa. Going further, Hyundai established its marketing headquarters right above its company-owned sales and customer care outlet, the Hyundai Motor Plaza in Delhi, thereby ensuring that the company and its management were never distanced, literally or figuratively, from the real reason for their existence, the person who in the ultimate analysis paid their salaries – the consumer. Yet, car sales remained sluggish.

It was at this time that it was also noticed that the company was getting saddled with a relatively large unsold stock of red cars. What had happened was simply that consumers, so taken up with the red Santro that Shah Rukh Khan drove in the television commercials, chose it while booking the car, but when they went for delivery many simply changed their minds and chose silver or white instead! HMI had clearly advised dealers not to push the consumer, and to accept any change in ordered specifications, without exception – or penalty. After selling 8,447 units in the October to December quarter of 1998, and just 9,201 in the January to March quarter of 1999, April 1999 opened without too much excitement.

It was a rather insidious disinformation campaign by an auto major in November 1998 that gave us the first indication that our product was spot on target and the entry of the Santro had got the competition a wee bit worried. As part of our programme to get as many influencers of public opinion as possible to test drive the Santro, I had requested Surajit Dasgupta, then, as again now, of the *Business Standard* newspaper, who covered the auto industry to drive the car over the weekend and give me his personal feedback on what we had done right and what we needed to improve. On the Monday morning following the weekend, Surajit had a visitor who claimed to be from a competitor and asked him about his new car. When he replied that it belonged to a friend and that he had only borrowed it for a test drive, the visitor told him he should rethink his choice of brand because the security of the car left a lot to be desired. When queried, he proceeded to open the locked vehicle with what seemed like almost no effort. Surajit thanked him for his advice, and minutes later called me to tell me about the 'finding'. I was stunned, because this was a fault that we had noticed on the prototypes just weeks before the launch and had proceeded to fix in all the cars that were being sold. Obviously, this 'demo' car had escaped the close scrutiny. When I kept prodding Surajit on how he had managed to find this flaw, he told me of his visitor of that morning without mentioning any names.

Having heard of one competitor's widely rumoured capabilities in the dirty-tricks department, I guessed the identity of Surajit's visitor's employer and, purely on a hunch, called its CEO, someone I had known and respected. I told him what seemed to have happened, and how. Since the visitor had handed over his business card to the journalist, I told him that a story in the next morning's newspapers was a near certainty. He lost no time in decrying the attempt, and categorically assured me on both a personal and professional level that even if, in fact, it had been done by his marketing team or its dealers it would never happen again. I had obviously called correct on the identity of the company, because they did go back to Surajit, and at their request and explanation of 'misguided employees', or so I assume, the story did not ultimately make it to the papers. Weeks later, when another major competitor had arranged a test drive for journalists at its own test track, it provided along with four of its own vehicles one Santro and vehicles belonging to other competitors. Hormazd Sorabjee, who was there, told me later that just as he took the keys of the Santro to get a near instant like-to-like comparison of the driving characteristics of the vehicles, the head of manufacturing of the company, a good friend of mine, told him to be careful when going around the corners because he had heard of a case of the Santro toppling over because of its height and its high centre of gravity. Hormazd, who had by then extensively driven the Santro, laughed it off, but nevertheless called me later that night and asked me if such a case had really been reported.

I assured him that no such thing had happened and asked him if, at any time during the test drive of the Santro he had made to Ooty, he had ever felt that the vehicle was unstable because of its height. He agreed completely and called off, but the next morning I called my friend at the competitor company and told him that if he did not call up Hormazd within the next couple of hours and tell him that the rumour of the toppling of the Santro, was just that – a baseless rumour – I would not hesitate to immediately make public photographs of his company's pre-production prototypes along with details of at least three engine failures. After remonstrating that he had only said stuff about the Santro in jest, he called up Hormazd and suitably clarified the matter. Needless to say, incidents of this kind did not happen almost ever again, till a burst of adventurism by an ill-advised MUL dealer in Hyderabad many years later, narrated in a later chapter, led to HMI filing a civil complaint, which the courts decided in its favour.

Then, in April 1999, all of a sudden, even as Hyundai was still struggling to get sales going, came the first real opening for a concerted assault on MUL – much before we had anticipated or even dreamt it possible. Anil Agarwal, the founder of the Centre for Science and Environment (CSE), a truly respected, committed and knowledgeable environmentalist, and his colleague Sunita Narain had been relentlessly waging a war against automotive pollution, particularly in the Delhi NCR area. Taking cognizance of their concerns, the Supreme Court of India had appointed a committee under the chairmanship of a bureaucrat, Bhure Lal, to study the problem and suggest solutions. As insignificant a player as it was then, I recall HMI was not even invited to meet the committee, let alone offer suggestions. MUL, on the other hand, was represented on the committee – ironically enough, it would later seem.

The committee, in its report of April 1999, estimated that more than 90 per cent of the nitrogen oxide (NOx) and respirable particulate matter (RSPM) from vehicular exhaust over Delhi was due to diesel emissions. It attributed impairment of visibility and haze-like conditions to suspended particulate matter and spoke of its potential to cause cancer, drawing heavily on findings from a study of California of the year before. Perhaps wrongly seeing this merely as part of a MUL-led conspiracy against the newly launched diesel Indica, TML tried to turn the tables and appeared, to industry insiders at least, to influence the stand of the SIAM, which till then appeared defensive and strangely ambivalent in its approach to addressing the issues of air pollution directly attributable to automobiles exhausts. Guided by its then president, TML's executive director, who was then president of the SIAM, the society indicated to the Supreme Court a willingness of the automobile industry, and its technological readiness, to bring forward the applicability of the Euro 1 norms in the Delhi NCR area, to June 1999, two years ahead of what the government of India had originally proposed. What everyone in the industry knew was that the lack of real capability of the 'volume leader' in petrol vehicles would thus finally stand to be exposed to the people of India. Even as I watched from the sidelines, I realized this battle of the Titans could throw up interesting opportunities for HMI.

On 29 April 1999, the Supreme Court ruled that all private non-commercial vehicles would have to conform to Euro 1 norms by 1 June 1999 and Euro 2 norms by 1 April 2000. More critically, the Supreme Court decreed that with effect from 1 May 1999 only 250 diesel-driven vehicles per month and 1,250 petrol-driven vehicles per month could be registered on a first-come-first-served basis in the Delhi NCR area. Given that car sales in Delhi NCR were probably close to 10,000 vehicles per month at that stage, the judgement was seen by almost everyone in the auto industry as truly apocalyptic. Without doubt, the judgement created unprecedented tremors in the industry. Sales of petrol cars by HM and PAL stopped virtually overnight. The petrol version of TML's Indica also took a battering – though, in any case, it was hardly selling. Both the diesel Indica and the diesel Ambassador just about managed to survive, primarily because of the relative ease in meeting Euro 1 norms as applied to diesel engines. MUL, still smarting from what was widely seen as a public rebuke by the Supreme Court, which asked why the company was exporting cars that met higher emission standards and denied them to Indian consumers, would have little option other than to start working feverishly to somehow meet the Euro 1 norms, which would probably mean falling back on using a carburettor that it had been using earlier on export models. That, when the world had clearly moved to multi-point fuel injection.

This was the moment for HMI to strike.

Industry insiders and observers alike, who reacted with alarm at the monthly cap on sales volume in Delhi NCR, seemingly did not bother to look at an equally critical earlier statement in the judgement which said that all private non-commercial vehicles that conformed to Euro 2 could be registered in Delhi NCR without any restriction.

With a view to facilitate registration in the manner indicated, the judgement provided that the registering authority could register the vehicle on a certificate of the manufacturer, duly authenticated by an authorized officer certifying that the vehicle conformed to the stated norm.

For Hyundai, this was the most important part of the judgement, and even as the rest of the industry appeared shell-shocked, I spoke with Byas Anand of the *Times of India*, when he called me just hours after the judgement, and told him that Hyundai was not really concerned about the impact of the 1,250 vehicle monthly cap on sales in Delhi NCR, and we in fact welcomed the judgement. I went on to tell him that in line with the court's directive, and its effort to move India out of the dark ages in technology, HMI would start selling only cars conforming to Euro 2 standards. I spoke of the Santro as already being 'engineered for Euro 2' (which ultimately became our advertising slogan as well), which I touted as the true mark of technological competence, and did not refrain from publicly contrasting it with MUL's position. The rest of the media soon latched on to the story and within a week 'Hyundai's technology leadership' became a matter of public discussion. Appearing on more than twenty television shows in four or five languages over the next thirty days, I reinforced this link between higher levels of emission compliance and better technology. Not content to stop there, I invariably spoke publicly of the possibility of resale values of non-Euro 2 vehicles ultimately falling through the floor as larger and larger swathes of the country would get covered by the higher emission standards. I also reckoned that fear of rapid erosion of capital values would not only move consumers towards higher technology standards, but would willy-nilly move the relatively technology-neutral – or technology-illiterate – financial services sector, even then in great awe of MUL, towards recognizing that the nature of the game was changing permanently.

Hamstrung by the immediate non-availability of a suitable technology response, MUL was soon on the backfoot, trying to rationalize its well-past-sell-date carburettor technology – not just to its own dealers, but on television discussions as well. Each time it did that, Hyundai won one more round in the perception war. Sensing that the tide was clearly in our favour, I derisively referred to MUL's desperate batting for carburettor technology on one television programme by using a common Hindi saying that is susceptible to being construed as rather pejorative: 'Majboori ka naam hai…' ('Desperation thy name is…') and stopped at that, without completing the sentence. But it was enough. The viewers had got it!

That was the easy part. Fulfilling the commitment I had made in the media, wasn't quite as simple. Minutes after my declaration that Hyundai would only sell cars that were Euro 2 compliant, I went back to the advertising presentation I was sitting in on along with Y.S. Kim and told him what I'd told the *Times of India* – I felt this was a heaven-sent opportunity for us to position the brand ahead of MUL by changing the canister in the exhaust system and essentially reprogramming the engine controller unit (ECU). I said I realized that there would be a cost implication because of the higher thickness of the palladium coating on the canister element, but I believed the impact on brand acceptability and sales would make it worthwhile. At a time when we were losing a small amount of money on cash basis on every car produced and sold, it was not an easy call to take, but Y.S. Kim's response was typical of him. He asked me three questions. First, would Indian customers indeed equate higher emission standards with better technology. Second, would we able to do it? And third, could we cut budgets elsewhere to make it possible? After listening to my responses to each of his queries, he just said, 'Okay,' and minutes later he and I had a long telephone conversation with Dr H.S. Lee, then head of R&D at Namyang. We told him that we had committed to offer the 'upgraded' products before 1 June, and though it appeared from the Supreme Court judgement that we would not need to go through the certification by the Automotive Research Association of India (ARAI) – which is a centre for automotive research and development, vehicle type certification, automotive testing and calibration – we believed that in order to enhance the credibility of our product offering we ought to get our vehicles certified by the ARAI as being Euro 2 compliant. Lee listened very patiently and his only question at the end was about the length of the homologation process and the potential logistics delays. The next morning a group of six technicians were dispatched from Korea with the components required to be changed on the batch of test vehicles to be sent to ARAI for the homologation tests to confirm compliance to Euro 2 emission standards. All this, without committees, without reports, without any waste of time! Just a simple goal – technology leadership en route to market leadership.

By the time the first batch of vehicles, retrofitted with Euro 2 components, were sent out of the plant to ARAI in Pune after detailed in-house testing, retrofit components for every single Santro in stock at dealerships had been airfreighted from Korea, received in Chennai and distributed thereafter to Delhi, Mumbai and Bangalore (our three biggest markets), Pune (only because it was TML's hometown, and I wanted to make a statement) and Calcutta (because a customer had actually called and berated me after my first public announcement on the Delhi launch, asking why I was discriminating against his city) to convert every vehicle held in stock by our dealers. Teams from production, quality, testing and after-sales service fanned out across the country and worked shoulder-to-shoulder with dealer principals and their staff to convert every single unit held in stock by them to a Euro-2 complaint one, finishing off literally days before the ARAI homologation certificate was received. On 31 May 1999, Hyundai started selling Euro 2 compliant cars across the country, with a little sticker pasted on the rear hatch that simply said 'Euro 2'.

Almost overnight, in a never-before occurrence in the automobile industry, an emission norm that was not yet mandated had been turned into a sub-brand. It firmly established Hyundai's technology credentials in the minds of India's consumers. Even more important, it conclusively put HMI well ahead of MUL, and gave the sales force a new mantra: Technology leadership is superior to volume leadership. 'We're not bigger, but we're better' was the call to arms that galvanized the entire company and its consumer-facing stakeholders. It was only a matter of time before consumers heard this primeval roar of confidence and nodded their approval.

From here on, the Santro's sales continued their upward trend. To my mind, this move to turn technology, quite honestly not its greatest strength, into an epaulette and wear it with the confidence of someone unto the manor born – and convince the Indian consumer about its right to do so – was the single most important point in the history of HMI. I strongly believed that consumers would recall only the first man on the moon – or, more rightly in this case, the first one to plant a flag there and send pictures back! The fact of the matter is that on the day we announced the Euro 2 model, Daewoo, Ford, GM and Honda were selling vehicles which, with just as little tweaking as we did, could offer Euro 2 compliant vehicles in India. But it was simply that none of them understood the consumer as well as Hyundai did. After growing only 8.9 per cent in the first quarter (January to March) of 1999, sales in the second quarter (April to June) jumped by 37.85 per cent and spurted sharply by 51.1 per cent in the third (July to September). Quite unprecedented in the annals of not just Indian automotive history but even globally, a second shift was introduced in Hyundai – a greenfield venture by a rank outsider in a fiercely competitive market – within ten months of the start of commercial production, and it laid the foundation for the launch of the Hyundai Accent and a reign of profitability that has not ended since 1999.

In its inaugural issue, *Autocar India* magazine took the Santro along with the Maruti Zen, Tata Indica, Fiat Uno and Daewoo Matiz for a head-to-head 10,000 kilometre test to pick the best of the pack. Before pronouncing its verdict, it looked at everything a consumer would, but under the magnifying glass of a very high-level professionally qualified scrutiny. Starting with design and engineering, the shootout focused on powertrain and performance, the quality of the interiors, the ride and handling, air conditioning, fuel efficiency and, of course, pricing. When the verdict came, it was unambiguous to the core:

> 'Throughout our test, the one thing we could not digest about the Santro is its looks, which we felt is its weakest point. But let's face it, you aren't buying one of these cars to enter a beauty contest, and looks are after all subjective. On the whole, this is the most versatile car of the lot. It's great in the city, competent on the highway and its flexible and responsive 12-valve engine is a strong asset that copes well under all circumstances. It provides good comfort, carries a decent amount of luggage and feels [like it is] the best engineered car in this segment. The Hyundai is also the least stressful car to drive and also has a great service backup. All this adds [up] to provide a high level of customer satisfaction. Despite the wide choice, we think the Santro wins by a fair margin.'

Surprisingly, the comparison did not consider build quality or finesse in fit and finish, because if it had taken into account elements like gap and flush, for instance, the Santro's margin of victory would have been considerably wider. *Autocar India*'s vote of confidence was among the more emphatic ones Hyundai had received, and when layered on top of the great things the general-interest media was writing it only served to further strengthen the morale of the entire network organization. The dealer principals and their frontline sales and service staff, persevered to add more to the momentum.

It had been abundantly clear to me that MUL would remain stuck in the technology backwaters for a while, what with its insistence on continuing to work with improved carburettor technology to attain Euro 1 standards on the Maruti 800, and the widely reported friction between its partners. Differences of opinion between SMC and the government of India with regard to localization, planned factory expansion locations and the funding sources of MUL had surfaced in public a few years earlier. In September 1997, in an interview with a journalist from *Nihon Keizai Shinbun*, Osamu Suzuki reportedly said, 'We'll have an abacus in our left hand and come out punching with our right. We don't need to compromise.' As Kazayuki Motohashi observes in his book *Global Business Strategy*, 'Insisting that the Indian government was violating the contractual agreement to "select appropriate personnel as company president", Suzuki went so far as to take action against the government in both the Delhi High Court and London's International Court of Arbitration. The Indian government did not think that Suzuki, a mere private company, would react so strongly. Finally, in 1998, the two parties settled. The dispute caused interruption to new car models, causing delayed management decisions on new car sales by Maruti Udyog.' This was clearly the best time to further drive home the advantage that HMI had seized with the Euro 2 gambit. Falling back on Mao's thoughts again helped me chart out our next steps – and this time, again, with defence!

The proximity to the consumer gave HMI, what I consider another one of the defining moments in its quest for glory. As part of a consumer feedback loop system that we had created, my colleague V.D. Bhasin and I made sure that between us we personally spoke with at least one service customer at the workshop under our office every morning. We had also decided to specifically keep track of customers who came back for a vehicle's second service within a twelve-month period. That first happened in Kolhapur where an absolutely delighted consumer in the insurance service sector had managed to notch up 50,000 kilometre on his Santro in just eleven months, primarily clocked up on the highway between Kolhapur and Bangalore. We missed speaking with him, but, soon enough, there was one in Delhi as well. Just two days before HMI was due to celebrate the first anniversary of its commercial launch, a retired senior Army officer who had driven his Santro extensively, particularly between Delhi and Chandigarh, came back to the company-owned and -operated workshop for his vehicle's second service at the 15,000 kilometre interval. When I spoke with him he was very pleased with his experience, but appeared concerned about the future. When quizzed further, he explained that his concern arose from the fact that one year of his ownership was going to end over the next three weeks and with that the warranty would end too. Speaking of his past experiences, he said the first vehicle he had ever bought had come with a three-month warranty policy and had started giving trouble in the fourth; his second vehicle had come with a six-month warranty, and started giving trouble in the seventh. It had made him wonder what would happen in the case of the Santro.

I spoke with him at length about Hyundai's quality systems, the inherent robustness of the Santro's design and the concept of 'infant mortality' in the automotive industry, and tried to assuage his fears with regard to a possible product failure. When after fifteen minutes he remained unconvinced, I suddenly asked him how he would react if I extended his warranty by a year because I believed in what I was saying about the product's reliability and durability. He gave me a rather incredulous look and asked me, 'But how is that possible?' I told him I would send him an official letter within the next couple of days to confirm what I had just told him, but he still did not appear convinced. So I took out a business card, signed on the reverse and handed it to him, saying that if ever he had a problem with the car's functioning all he had to do was to give my card to the dealer principal at any dealership workshop he took it to, request him to speak with me and we would not charge for any work done on the car or any part replaced. The only condition I set was that he would have to ensure that regular maintenance schedules were adhered to without fail at any authorized Hyundai dealer workshop. That finally appeared to satisfy him and he left, promising to call me if he faced a problem. With the idea for the extension of warranty still forming in my head, V.D. Bhasin, H.S. Kwon and I discussed the concept and S. Punnaivanam from the technical and warranty section of the service team got down to work on a detailed report on all the warranty failures we had faced since launch. The two most expensive warranty cases handled till then – technically, 'goodwill' warranty, because neither was related to design or manufacturing defects – related to a couple of instances of hydrostatic lock and consequential engine seizures when customers had, it would seem under the mistaken notion that the vehicle came with amphibious capabilities, attempted, of their own admission, to drive it in water depths exceeding 1.25 metres or close to 4 feet.

But the rest of the complaints were minor: a bunch of door-checker and lock issues for one, wrongly spliced wiring at unauthorized accessory-fitment shops leading to malfunctioning tail lights, or high-pressure fuel lines meddled with by chauffeurs (yes, even in Santros!) in a bid to extract petrol. Clearly, the India-specific engineering that had been done during the design phase had ensured that the Santro was distinctly more robust and durable than even our commitments to consumers during the launch and thereafter. Also, except for the incidents involving hydrostatic locks, all the others had happened below 1,000 kilometre of operation and most were largely due to obvious mishandling. The total number of warranty cases was in the low three digits despite the first full year's sale of over 50,000 units. Coming on top of these low failure rates, the 'real' indigenization achieved by HMI meant locally produced, rather than imported replacement parts, and that helped ensure that the actual total warranty expenditure in the first year remained below 0.05 per cent of the sales turnover! (Auto companies sometimes make larger warranty provisions in their books as a matter of abundant caution, and then write-back the unutilized sums in years of low profitability.) For a first-timer on Indian roads, that was a dream debut. Though verifiable, comparable data points for competition are impossible to obtain, component industry sources spoke in strict confidence about the travails of another entrant of that time. When its warranty costs were rumoured to have soared past the ₹100 crore mark in its first year, the manufacturer apparently tried charging most of them to the suppliers, despite having, dictated the component design in some cases, or just hidden the warranty expenditure among overall marketing related expenses in all publicly available documents.

The next day I proposed to Y.S. Kim that HMI ought to announce a unilateral two-year warranty on a retrospective basis to all its customers from the first car sold as a token of its gratitude to them for their unstinted support in its first year. I told him of the customer I had met the previous day and reasoned that HMI would be seen as setting the agenda in terms of customer orientation in India. Going beyond the mere financials, which in any case were decidedly favourable, I pointed out that the long-term strategic benefits of the act could be quite unprecedented. By making periodic servicing at authorized dealer workshops a prerequisite to enjoying the second-year warranty, we would be ensuring that we would identify even the smallest product complaint before it acquired the potential of reaching epidemic proportions, thereby reinforcing the image of the Santro as a reliable car for India's quality-seeking, aspirational middle-class consumers.

Moreover, a consistent growth in earnings on genuine spares and lubricants required for periodic maintenance services would accrue both to the network and the company, which would offset any unlikely rise in warranty costs. Going beyond this, the move would ensure that dealers would remain in touch with consumers in the early days of their involvement with the brand and use this to obtain referrals from existing consumers, ultimately moving consumers to the higher-end brands within the family that we expected to introduce over a period of time. Given the human propensity for looking for security through 'belonging' to a group, I reasoned that existing consumers could be counted on to help attract others into the fold. HMI was probably the first company in India to launch referral reward programmes for existing consumers, often handing out free service coupons or accessories in exchange for referrals.

But the clincher, I believed, would be that by ensuring that consumers brought cars back to authorized dealer workshops the increased warranty programme, would end up making sure that cars would be as close to their original condition as possible even after two years and this would reflect positively on the resale value of the cars whenever that happened. Given that resale value (then) came right after price, fuel efficiency and ease of maintenance as the most important determinants of brand choice, such a move would only serve to further cement the brand position both of the Santro and of Hyundai itself. There was absolutely no way that MUL would be in a position to match HMI on this.

I spoke at length about what TML had managed to achieve with the '3 years 300,000 kilometre warranty' on the 407 a few years earlier, in support of my contention. Despite the fact that HMC had announced a 10-year body warranty in the US market a few months earlier, there was a great deal of reluctance from many of my Korean colleagues, including, surprisingly, an otherwise always forward-looking J.H. Kim, because of the great unknown unknowns that India's road conditions presented vehicles. But Y.S. Kim first looked at all the facts and figures that I had marshalled, discussed the proposal primarily from the long-term strategy point of view, and agreed that it was well worth the risk.

Once the decision was taken, advertisement space was booked with all the major newspapers, and the artwork for a full-page advertisement with a simple straightforward message saying just 'Thank You' aimed at India's consumers for the trust they had reposed in us and for being a part of the Hyundai family. The artwork in the biggest, boldest typeface that would fit for the two words was created, approved and released by 8 p.m. that evening. The next morning, on the first anniversary of both HMI's, and the Santro's, commercial launch in India, history was made as India's consumers woke to a new dawn and the realization that receiving the respect they deserved from an automobile company had finally become their irreversible and inalienable right. The suddenness and ferocity of the blitzkrieg left the competition stunned.

While Daewoo, as expected, immediately announced its own version of an improved warranty, MUL, far from going retrospective in coverage, was not able to make an enhanced warranty prospective and ultimately settled for options of extended warranties on its models for two and three years, but at a cost. HMI had, once again, in a matter of less than six months, established that it was way ahead of MUL, now not just in terms of technology, but also in terms of its attitude towards the consumer, its most important stakeholder. In short, David had just walked up to Goliath and casually taken away his candy.

No sooner had the ink dried on the advertisement than both our resolve and abilities were subjected to a very sudden and severe test. It rained in Calcutta as probably never before, and hundreds of Santros got fully or partially submerged. The entire organization moved to get customers' vehicles back on the road with an alacrity that earned us tremendous goodwill. This was the time to put our money where our mouth was, and HMI gave full warranty coverage on any damage, despite it being caused by an act of God. No advertising campaign, however widespread and expensive, could have done as much for Brand Santro as that single decision.

Even as Hyundai kept its eyes firmly fixed on the target it was chasing, the team never forgot to look into the rear-view mirror. Beset as the Tata Indica was by myriad problems of build quality and performance, many industry insiders seemed to believe the car had flattered only to deceive. Even as TML struggled to ramp up production with a thrust on quality and reliability, negative word on the car's performance and dependability did rounds of the streets and the huge backlog of bookings faced the first signs of tired liquidation. By the end of the third quarter of 1999, in terms of volume sales, the Maruti Zen was 22 per cent ahead of the Santro, which in turn was 40 per cent ahead of the Indica. Even by the fourth quarter of 1999, the Indica remained well behind the Santro and the Maruti Zen. Yet, a burst of effort on the quality and build-quality front, and a broad acceptance of the product by the commercial (taxi) segment, ensured that it was catching up fast. The Santro's lead of 11.5 per cent over the Indica at the end of the fourth quarter of 1999 was already down to 9.5 per cent at the end of the first quarter of 2000. Of course, over the same period, the Santro had managed to narrow the distance between itself and the Zen from 12 per cent to just 2.5 per cent – but for a team that was perennially in a '*dil mange more*' (which literally translates as 'the heart craves more', the signature line of an unforgettable Pepsi ad series that has entered the common man's lexicon in India) mindset, this was small consolation. Always aware of the tremendous strengths of TML in terms of finance and technology, I remained, unlike almost all my Korean colleagues, reluctant to disregard the potential challenge from the Indica. At the same time two other cars, the Daewoo Matiz and the Fiat Palio were proving to be tough competitors. The Palio, particularly, was an exceptionally well-built car, let down only by poor leadership, and abysmal marketing and product support. The Matiz was amazingly good-looking and handled rather well, but suffered from having a pretty rough engine. Yet, none of these three cars could be taken for granted. (I have always believed that had TML come out with an absolutely bug-free and reliable product in 1998, Hyundai would have found the going much tougher.)

In the meantime, Daewoo had pulled out all stops in its attempt to catch up with the three market leaders, though the sustainability of their effort was doubtful. After a detailed internal teardown of the Matiz and an analysis of its import content, we decided that HMI did not need to concern itself with Daewoo India in the long term. The company had invested heavily in the expensive Special Purpose Machines (SPM) manufacturing capacity that could manufacture 250,000 units of the 1.6 litre engine suitable for the Cielo or Nexia. What it actually needed to satisfy the demand in the Indian market was the 800 cc engine suitable for the Matiz and this it had to import at a substantial cost disadvantage – rendering the final product, uncompetitive if it had to be priced profitably, and vice versa.

With the aggressive price positioning it had adopted for the Matiz, even a partially imported powertrain would only end up ravaging the company's financials. I recall sharing the essence of this analysis with a large group at ICICI Bank during a talk on risk management in the automotive industry. I called out Daewoo India then, just as I had called out PAL Peugeot a couple years earlier in the same lecture series. (Apparently, the Delhi office of ICICI corporate banking believed I was not being objective in my assessment since I was a competitor, and the bank continued its lending.) Ultimately, as Daewoo India's parent organization got mired in a host of problems, the company came unstuck in India too. Rumour had it that the company's entire capital investment in the powertrain division was originally earmarked for a plant to be set up in China but was suddenly re-routed on the high seas to India probably at a valuation much above the actual, because of a sudden change in China's rules. Since all the imports were under the Export Promotion Capital Goods (EPCG) scheme, they were in any case not subjected to customs duty. But given the high gearing of the project imports, overvaluation could have left a large profit reserve with the trading arm of the parent company, which had apparently supplied the equipment. This reserve could have then been used to supply CKD kits of the Matiz at specially deflated prices – thereby effectively evading customs duties – in order to sustain the aggressive pricing for the Indian market. If indeed the rumours were true, the approach to 'financing' the operation was clearly, to be charitable, unwise.

Fiat, the other major potential competitor, with what was, in terms of technical specs and performance, probably the best product in the market at the time, fell prey to the incompetence of its local management team and possibly their arrogance – after all, they did have Ferrari; Michael Schumacher, the reigning god of the Formula One motor sports circuit; and Sachin Tendulkar, the cricketing icon, speaking on their behalf to Indian consumers.

By the end of 1999, it had become amply evident that this was going to be a three-horse race – except that MUL had other ideas and had flanked the Santro with their Zen, on the one hand, and with the much-delayed WagonR on the other. As soon as it was launched, the only thing the new Maruti WagonR model managed to very successfully do was to suddenly make the Santro look like the winner of a beauty-pageant, particularly after the minor facelift of the Santro that came by in the millennium model.

By April 2000, it was clear that going back to attack mode was the obvious strategic choice for HMI, and we are not just talking about 'looks' here. One clear learning from an almost everyday direct involvement with customers at showrooms across the country was that while customers were taking test drives on variant of the Santro with power-steering, they were ultimately choosing the lower-spec variant primarily because of what they considered a steep increase in the price of the variant with power-steering. Convinced that a potential trebling of purchase volumes could drag the purchase cost of the power steering substantially below the rates current at the time, the product management team comprising Stewart Suh and Gagan Kohli worked closely with the vendor development team to achieve this. Thanks to additional volumes being ordered, the cost of replacing the manual steering with the power option resulted in a minimal incremental cost of ₹13,000. (Incidentally, six years earlier, a similar math had enabled TML to standardize power steering on all the 2213 variants, even as its main competitor Ashok Leyland kept plugging variable-ratio manual steering as the ultimate panacea.) The product engineering and vendor development teams at HMI worked closely with marketing and product management to reconfigure the regular second-level air-conditioned variant by dropping a few inconsequential bells and whistles and adding the power steering, thus making it appear that a third-level variant with a power steering was being launched at a price substantially lower than the top-end variant, which till then was the only one boasting the feature.

Recognizing that Indian consumers would be happier getting a completely new variant than what might appear to be a mere tinkering with an existing variant, it was rechristened the Santro Zip Drive and launched in May 2000. The combination of technology and performance, with spot-on pricing proved just right. Over the next three quarters of 2000, the Santro nosed past the Maruti Zen and built a resounding 43 per cent lead over the Indica, which appeared to show little signs of resolve or success in ensuring that the non-taxi individual consumer segment saw merit in what it purportedly offered.

But technology and market leadership gained something of a self-sustaining momentum for HMI only when it was backed by some unbelievable support that came from the financial services sector. Once again, it was ICICI Bank that pulled out all the stops. V. Vaidyanathan and Sachin Khadelwal of ICICI, were joined by Dipak Gupta and Gaurang Shah of Kotak Mahindra, and Shyamla Khera and A. Asokan, then of Centurion Bank (now a part of HDFC Bank after a series of mergers). As a group, these bankers, practising rare initiative and creativity as a norm, probably did far more to give financial stability and heft to HMI's dealers – and thereby to the company – than anybody can fully comprehend.

But neither MUL nor their Zen was willing to concede the race, and though the Santro remained ahead in 2001 it continued to face stiff challenge from the erstwhile champion and its new running mate, the WagonR. Despite the crisp throttle response of the Epsilon engine, it was becoming apparent that engine power was probably holding the Santro back to some extent. This is when HMI responded with the introduction of the larger 1.1 litre engine. Christened the Zip Plus, as a continuation of the Zip Drive theme, the architecture of the new engine remained identical to that of its predecessor, but with increases in both bore and stroke and a step up in the compression ratio. More important, the new engine came with a distributorless ignition system and a knock sensor, so critical given the quality of fuel dispensed at the retail level in India. At this time, the Zip Plus was being developed simultaneously both in Korea and India – and the development in India was completed forty days earlier. Very soon thereafter, India, first on account of quality, then cost and now the speed of implementation of the new project, was confirmed as the global production base of the Santro! Though the Zip Plus probably fell well short of the Fiat Palio in terms of top speed, the overall city performance of the Zip Plus was on par with some mid-size cars. The higher engine compression ratio and marginally tweaked gearing combined perfectly to aid performance in the 55–70 kilometre/hour speed range, and coming on top of the immediate throttle response

THE FIGHT FOR MARKET LEADERSHIP

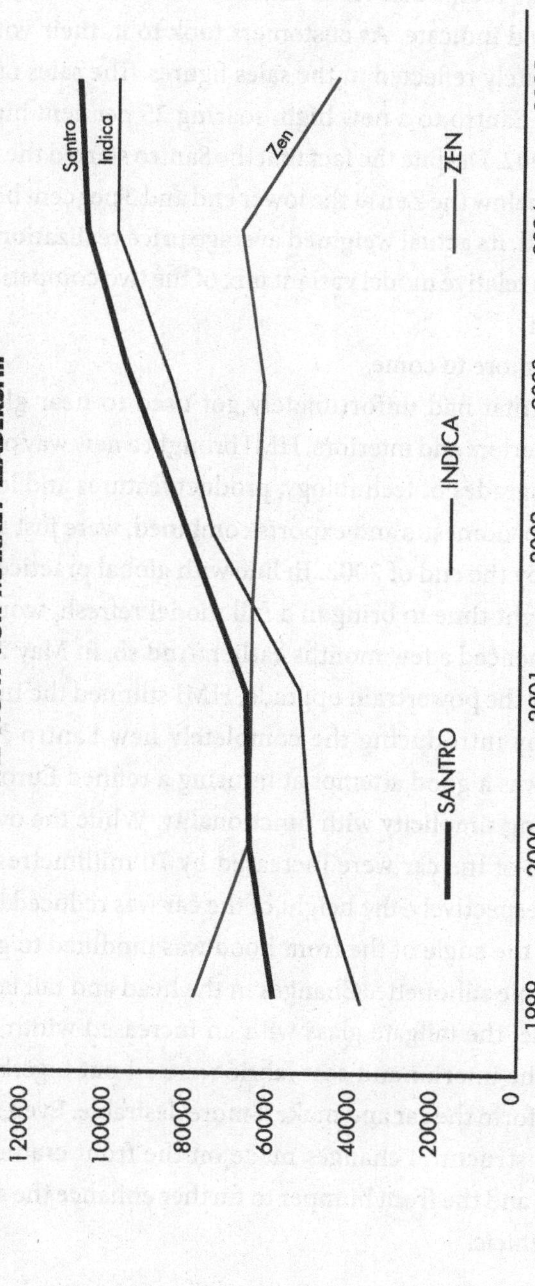

	1999	2000	2001	2002	2003	2004	2005
SANTRO	58650	65492	66359	80706	93854	104748	107205
ZEN	77786	64998	64578	64351	62296	67820	44960
INDICA	38627	50248	53253	74120	84120	98318	97926

and rapid acceleration at start, so characteristic of the Santro, ended up making the car feel much faster than actual numbers on the speedometer would indicate. As customers took to it, their vote of approval immediately reflected in the sales figures. The sales of the Zip Plus took the Santro to a new high, soaring 25 per cent higher than the Zen in 2002. Despite the fact that the Santro started the year priced 2 per cent below the Zen at the lower end and 3 per cent below it at the higher end, its actual weighted average price realization per unit, based on the relative model variant mix of the two competitors, also surged ahead.

But there was more to come.

To a country that had unfortunately got used to near glacial changes in car exteriors and interiors, HMI brought a new way of life. With constant upgrades of technology, product features and looks, sales of the Santro, domestic and exports combined, were just short of 300,000 units by the end of 2002. In line with global practice this was clearly the right time to bring in a full model refresh, work on which had commenced a few months earlier. And so, in May 2003, just one year after the powertrain upgrade, HMI stunned the Indian auto consumer by introducing the completely new Santro Xing. The new model was a good attempt at infusing a refined Euro chic to the car, blending simplicity with functionality. While the overall length and width of the car were increased by 70 millimetres and 30 millimetres, respectively, the height of the car was reduced by 10 millimetres, and the angle of the front hood was modified to give a much more likeable silhouette. Changes in the head and tail lamps, the radiator grille, the tailgate glass with an increased width, new key colours for the interior and seat fabric were all put together to completely transform the car and make it more desirable. Even more critical were the structural changes made on the front cradle, the dashboard panel and the front bumper to further enhance the safety features of the vehicle.

India loved the new look, as did the rest of the world. Domestic sales rose over 16 per cent in 2003, as supply constraints kicked in, with a spectacular 400 per cent growth in exports to over 30,000 units. Even as the Santro's sales performance in both the domestic and export markets continued to remain healthy, and production ran at 100 per cent capacity utilization, the practice of constant product upgrades had become a part of the ethos of HMI and served to further raise the expectations of India's consumers. Obviously, HMI did not disappoint, and before reaching the one-million production mark yet another upgrade of the Santro's engine was unveiled – this time branded the eRLX. The company had made it a habit of setting high benchmarks, achieving them and raising them all over again.

Finally, the Santro had made a permanent place for itself in Indian hearts and on its roads. It successfully put HMI on a cycle of self-sustaining growth, first by racing to a monthly run rate exceeding 6000 units in the tenth month of production, and then maintaining monthly production at a level at which costs generally became globally comparable even within the first year of production. The company followed up on this by crossing the quarter-million cumulative sales mark in just its fourth year. Within the first decade of its production the Santro had crossed the million-cars-sold mark, ensuring that the replacement demand that kicked in, along with loyal upgraders within the large family, were enough to propel HMI into self-perpetuating growth as the company moved up the value chain to make and sell an array of larger, more sophisticated cars.

6

War and the Art of Communication

It wouldn't be out of place to say that both brands, Santro and Hyundai, were built, to a large extent, by the way the company communicated with its consumers and stakeholders. In its communication, there were three elements that really stood out – its brand ambassador Shah Rukh Khan who agreed to become a part of our eventful journey in March 1998; the straight-shooting advertising professionals from Saatchi & Saatchi led by Shanta Kumar (Shanta), Bhargava Krishna (Bhags) and Shubabrata Ghosh (SG), who came on board in August 1997; and the enviable support the brands received from the media – print and electronic, English and regional language, general and special interest, since late 1997, but particularly after the Auto Expo in January 1998.

SRK, the thinking person's brand ambassador

It has, for some time now, become almost *de riguer* to use brand ambassadors in advertising products ranging from cosmetics and cars to soaps and scooters. Quite a change from the days when movie stars modelled only for Lux and it was considered revolutionary when Sunil Gavaskar modelled for Digjam Suitings, or Kapil Dev for Palmolive Shaving Cream. Unlike today, products of the time rarely, if ever, drew life from the people who endorsed them.

For an unknown brand, in particular, the role of the brand ambassador attains great significance. It starts with aiding brand recall and, thereafter, if the brand ambassador is well-chosen, her or his reputation and credibility tend to rub off on the brand. A great deal of the credit for ensuring rapid recognition of the Hyundai brand in a world devoid of social media and YouTube goes undoubtedly to the magic that Shah Rukh Khan (popularly SRK) brought to our communication. It was almost literally after he started pronouncing the brand name in his own inimitable way in the second in the series of introductory commercials that anyone outside the automotive industry and readers of business dailies started paying attention to Hyundai.

We knew from the word go that creating name recognition was going to be our biggest challenge. This came home to me in no uncertain terms when I visited the marketing headquarters of Indian Oil in Mumbai in mid-1997 to meet their Sales Director and Chief General Manager (Lubricants) and work out the broad contours of an exclusive lubricants filling service agreement, something I had done once before in my TML days. Despite the meeting being pre-arranged, I recall having to wait endlessly at the reception and repeat the name 'Hyundai' four times over while the lady at the desk kept saying 'Honda', till finally I just handed her my business card and asked to see the gentlemen in question. She took a long look at the card and said, 'Oh, you make scooters.'

Later that afternoon, I was recalling the events of the morning to Shanta and Bhags at Saatchi & Saatchi. We all agreed that the problem of the Hyundai brand not being recognized was serious enough, but what complicated matters further was the confusion with 'Honda' and the difficulty we could have in getting people to recognize the slanted 'H' logo as opposed to the straight one that Honda used.

To say that Hyundai was an unknown brand in India circa 1997 would have been the understatement of the decade. Worse still, we were up against two very formidable brands – the incumbent market-leader Maruti, which had come to define middle-class mobility in India since 1983, and Tata, then simply the best-known and most-admired brand in India. Not to mention the automobile brands also in the fray: Daewoo, Fiat, Ford, GM and Honda – in alphabetical order. To top it all, we came with a near-unpronounceable name and it reminded those few who had heard the name, of Jay Leno and the uncharitable and often hilariously overstated comments made by him on Hyundai products and their performance on his famous, eponymous American television show. That's when we decided we needed a very recognizable popular Indian, to get out there and introduce the brand to India. Given that the most recognizable Indian faces are generally either from cricket or the movies, at least we knew where we had to look.

Late the same evening, Shanta called me and told me of his idea of approaching a particular Bollywood star to be our brand ambassador. The name he suggested was a star well-known for his love for cars and his stable of exotic wheels. After listening to all the reasons why we should work with the particular gentleman, I remained unconvinced. In my opinion, the star in question did not fit the image of Hyundai that I thought we ought to project – that of a fearless challenger. Our brand ambassador would perform the crucial task of creating an impression on all our potential customers, so he or she had to be someone whom people would want to emulate and aspire to be like – intelligent, witty, urbane and sophisticated. Yet, at the core, the person would have to be 'family-oriented' and essentially be able to reflect the personality of the target market – the aspirational Indian middle-class moving beyond its first set of wheels. Someone who could effortlessly, and with style, relate to consumers across both age and gender – someone like the 'Raj' of *Dilwale Dulhaniya le Jayenge* (*DDLJ*), a film that decades later continues to be a favourite among millions of Indians (evident in the number of ad spots that run with its repeat telecasts even today). It was very clear in my mind that we ought to have someone like SRK, a star who had achieved unalloyed success on his own steam, with no family connections in Bollywood (read, like Hyundai with no Indian industrial group partners) and no legacy in the business (read, like Hyundai, an unknown brand in India, with no government backing) – just a possessor of style, class and power-packed performances that people could relate to and believe in.

Always keen to debate an issue, Shanta turned the discussion around and reminded me that a few years earlier SRK had featured in an ad for a moped, a product that had not really made much of a mark in the marketplace. This could impact the image that we were trying to build for Hyundai, he said. I countered that that was probably before the *DDLJ* effect had become apparent – with a couple of films after that SRK seemed to be set for a significant future. We decided to think it over and revisit the issue the next day. At dinner that night I asked my wife, Meenakshi, and my children Advait and Indira (at the time teen and pre-teen respectively) their opinion on the choices before us. Meenakshi reminded me that in the latest movie we'd watched of the other Bollywood star, not only did he look old and worn out, but he also did not ultimately get the girl – and as far as the public was concerned he was a 'deserving loser'. The clear favourite at home was SRK.

Over the next couple of days, we did a straw poll on our choices for a potential brand ambassador covering the entire marketing, sales and service team (then perhaps a grand total of just twenty-plus Indians) and dealers who had already been selected across the country. Again, the result was overwhelmingly in favour of selecting SRK. When this was discussed by Y.S. Kim with Indian colleagues at the plant in Chennai, someone came up with the suggestion to consider one of the reigning southern 'megastars', and got a not-entirely-unexpected near-unanimous vote from all those polled.

Y.S. Kim asked me to consider this suggestion, particularly given that the numbers of 'Indian' voices from Chennai were at least ten times the total from the marketing team! Fortunately, our marketing decisions at HMI were not based merely on structured, quantitative data and when I told him that the response he had got from Chennai did not really reflect India as a whole, Y.S. Kim was a trifle perplexed. Those were the days when a Hindi film that was a blockbuster in most parts of the country probably showed for just one week at cinemas in Chennai that specialized in screening Hindi movies – but no one could deny SRK's star quality that had swept through the major part of the country.

So SRK it was! But one problem remained. SRK 's office was not quite as well-organized and efficient as it no doubt is today, and the only option we had was to try and make a 'connection' work – Indian style. Enter Lalit Kapoor, who had just been appointed as a dealer in the Bandra suburb of Mumbai. Lalit made up for his complete lack of car-retailing experience by a keen understanding of consumers and knowing, it appeared, almost everyone in Mumbai's filmdom, thanks to the movie halls his family owned in Mumbai and Delhi. Lalit immediately got in touch with Saeed Mirza, who spoke with SRK, and three days later, Shanta, Bhags and I met the superstar.

To begin with, SRK was reluctant to get involved with a completely unknown brand at a time when he was carefully building his own. His association with Pepsi had made him a very likable face of the 'now' generation, and Hyundai certainly did not have the brand cachet of the cola giant. So I had to take SRK through the whole spiel about the 'Hyundai approach' that I had earlier given to Saatchi & Saatchi, when I requested them to pitch for the HMI account (more about that later in the chapter). Shanta and I told him that the way we saw it, HMI's brand ambassador had to be familiar with the company and the brand and believe in it in order to make the advertising convincing for the consumer, so it was necessary to give him all the details of the global conglomerate, the Indian entity, the manufacturing plant as it was envisaged, and the products. In fact, SRK was probably one of the first few people outside the company (and those at Saatchi & Saatchi) to be told that the Santro was going to be launched ahead of the Accent, even though, as mentioned earlier, as a matter of strategy, in all our interactions with the media, both Y.S. Kim and I continued for a long time to deliberately obfuscate issues and often give out contradictory and conflicting views on which would come first.

Yet, he continued to have his doubts. Voracious reader and well-travelled, it is unlikely that SRK was unaware of the rather lowly brand image of Hyundai in markets like the US. I recall he asked me pointed questions about the company's monumental Canadian failure. Obviously, something about what I said must have convinced him. In fact, our initial conversations with SRK ultimately became the story of the ads introducing Hyundai to India – except that there was no 'Mr Kim', as in the ads. It was just Shanta and I telling SRK the plain, unvarnished truth about Hyundai.

He took his time to respond and, almost ten days after we first met him, agreed to become the brand ambassador for HMI. Things went smoothly thereafter, and finally SRK and I sat down one Saturday afternoon in his study at home and he put down on his laptop what was to become the defining document of his relationship with Hyundai – on a single sheet of paper. The actual contract document was signed weeks later on one of his visits to Chennai. His fee, of course, raised a whole lot of queries and discussion, primarily from and among my colleagues in the finance team in Chennai, which almost created a bit of difficult situation with SRK.

On the day when we were to decide on the number of days for the shoot, the dates and so on, we met at Mehboob Studios, where SRK was shooting a commercial for Bagpiper, if I recall correctly. Our colleagues in the finance team were insistent that we at least try for some last-minute 'bargaining' with SRK. When I refused point blank, because we had already shaken hands with him on that, the unfortunate responsibility fell upon my colleague J.H. Kim who, albeit very reluctantly, broached the subject rather indelicately with SRK telling him what a great honour it would be for him to be associated with the Hyundai brand and why he should consider a reduction in the fee already agreed upon.

SRK was not amused. Stunned and speechless for just a fraction of a minute at the brazen attempt to renegotiate terms we had already shaken hands on, he told J.H. Kim that in India, at time, he was the bigger brand and it was an honour for Hyundai to be working with him. SRK then switched to Hindi and expressed his disgust to me in no uncertain terms, and for an instant it almost seemed like all our discussions and negotiations of the past three weeks would come to nothing. In order to save the situation, I hurriedly took J.H. Kim away, and even as he spoke with the finance team, went back to soothe SRK's ruffled feathers. In that instant, I learnt an important lesson in diplomacy, which I must admit has never been a vice of mine!

Despite this near-hiccup, SRK remained the very epitome of professionalism. He was, in every way, what I would consider the ideal brand ambassador. He worked closely with the director on every little detail from helping tweak the script to suggesting set design, figuring out the lighting, the camera angles – just about everything to get the final product absolutely right. This sense of ownership and involvement from the very first day laid the foundation for what has been an enduring relationship between SRK and HMI. No sooner was the product launched than SRK had a Santro parked in his driveway and, on occasion, I think, had his son dropped to school in it as well.

(Much like the Pepsi fountain, or was it a can-dispensing machine, that he always had in his study!) Invariably, when SRK decided to gift a car to a close relative, it was a Hyundai Accent that he chose. Later, when he decided to give one to his producers and directors, the choice was the Hyundai Sonata. This is the kind of commitment to the brand that one hopes for from a brand ambassador. Hyundai reciprocated by ensuring product placements in all his films, whenever approached.

Another little-known facet of SRK that made him a dream brand ambassador was his knowledge and appreciation of the finer points of marketing and brand communication exercises. Somewhere along the way, SRK had branched out into film production through his company, Red Chillies Entertainment, now a powerful creative and production banner in its own right. Given that SRK himself would be closely involved with all aspects of the making of the commercials, Hyundai became one of the earliest clients of Red Chillies. It was soon proved that the trust was not misplaced when the 'Sunshine Car' was launched in 2002. The creative treatment of the ad series was conceptualized by Saatchi & Saatchi and production was handled by Red Chillies. The film was shot in Malaysia, where SRK had managed with his exceptional popularity and personal connections at the highest levels of government, to actually get the authorities to close down a highway for a couple of hours in order to complete the filming on schedule!

Despite the best intentions of all concerned, and partly because of a delay in getting the cars over to Malaysia for the shoot, there was a fairly significant cost overrun on the production budget. SRK called me one morning from Malaysia, sounding embarrassed at Red Chillies having to seek a price reset. He was relieved when I asked him to just go ahead because, as I reasoned, the overrun was a very small proportion of the overall launch budget. I had all but forgotten about it when ten days later my colleague Sanjiv Shukla came up to me with a CD mailing envelope for me from SRK. Intrigued, I opened the package to find a note saying, 'Thanks for your support,' and a DVD which contained three fifteen-second short films starring him, Preity Zinta and, of course, the 'Sunshine Car', which he had personally conceptualized, written and produced completely free of cost – and outside of the production contract. No doubt, perhaps in deference to SRK's request, even Preity Zinta had done the films at absolutely no cost to us. Incidentally, while the launch films conceptualized by Saatchi & Saatchi were used over a month-long period primarily in the electronic media and cinema halls, the short films that SRK conceptualized and created played every day for well over six months both on dealer showroom screens and as paid advertising – and helped reinforce the much-needed 'Sunshine Car' boost to a brand that had started showing the first signs of fatigue. His understanding of Hyundai's customers made those films exceptionally valuable communication tools.

SRK's commitment as a brand ambassador was also marked by his willingness to invest in the relationship and build it for the future. I don't believe there is another example, in India at least, of a relationship between a company and a brand ambassador lasting over two decades. One particular incident probably best exemplifies this commitment. In April 2003, Hyundai was working on the launch of the Santro Xing – the first full facelift of the brand. At the time, SRK, who had been suffering from a prolonged back problem, had undergone surgery once and was on the verge of going back to London for the second. Recognizing just how important the facelift launch was to the company, he agreed, despite his physical condition, to do the shoot for the launch film. There was just one caveat – he would not jump or run in any of the frames.

The most remarkable thing about his sense of commitment was that his contract had expired before we shot the film, and he and I had only just started discussions on the new contract. I recall that for one reason of schedules or another, he and I were unable to meet to finalize terms. We finally scheduled a meeting at his house, located halfway between the airport and my home in Mumbai. When I called him on landing, he apologized saying he wasn't at home, and instead proposed to come over to my place, which was located halfway between the south Mumbai location he was in and his home in Bandra. Sure enough, he came by. After three hours, endless cups of tea and witty, sparkling, friendly and perceptive conversation on a range of issues from economics to politics to history, philosophy, food – and Delhi – we forgot all about the contract. He had promised to meet someone, so he left saying simply that we could discuss it another time. That sense of trust was the bedrock of the relationship. Some days later, he flew to Bangalore, did the film, completed the dubbing the next day, added a film of a personal message for the launch function and left for his surgery the same night. That was the film where 'Mr Kim' comes back with a menacing looking Cat Woman-like aide to take away the keys to SRK's Santro, leaving him stranded on the road – actually an air strip just outside Bangalore – and then returns to hand him the keys of the brand new Santro Xing! Ultimately, the terms of renewal were finalized between him and me on SMS probably four months later while he was still in London, and a new contract reflecting the financial terms, with retrospective validity, drawn up and sent to him in September of that year.

But commitment is a two-way street and Hyundai remained equally committed to SRK. When we were offered the chance for an in-film placement of the Santro in a renowned producer–director's new film, which went on to become a blockbuster, we declined the offer politely, without a second thought. When asked if we'd work with the 'new star' after the movie was declared a hit, I categorically told the media that we were clear about the personality of the car, and did not see any need to alter it and confuse our consumers. That simple public vote of confidence from Hyundai, particularly when SRK was then being incorrectly and unfairly tarred for a Pepsi ad which featured a lookalike of another actor, was the very least we could have done in the circumstances. I don't believe it would be an overstatement if I said that both the HMI approach to the brand ambassador and the relationship that we managed to build with him were unique. After Hyundai, other car companies in India have tried to involve brand ambassadors. The list is long – Maruti with Amitabh and Abhishek Bachchan for the Versa; Fiat with Sachin Tendulkar for the Palio; Toyota with Aamir Khan for the Innova; GM with Saif Ali Khan for the Optra; and Ranbir Kapoor for Nissan – but none have been even remotely as successful. The difference probably lay in the completeness of the Hyundai approach – in our communication the brand ambassador was 'the customer', not merely a prop to gain viewer attention. Or perhaps it lay in that undefinable something, that *je ne sais quoi*, that SRK transferred so selflessly and consistently from his persona to the Santro brand.

HMI did occasionally have others from the entertainment industry working along with SRK in the process of communicating with our consumers. A then little-known model, Mallika Sherawat was seen with SRK in the Zip Drive commercial, for instance, and Gayatri Joshi, who was SRK's leading lady in what was probably her only movie, was also paired with him in a Santro ad. But Preity Zinta was the only other Bollywood personality, after SRK, whom HMI worked with for a relatively protracted period. Saatchi & Saatchi believed she was the perfect choice for the Sunshine Car campaign, but they were concerned that there was, apparently, a widely rumoured lack of professional alignment between her and SRK, who had not worked with her after *Dil Se* her maiden movie with him. I thought the best way out was to broach the subject with SRK, which I did one afternoon in his van at a shoot. After he listened to the ad concept in its entirety, he told me in detail the reason for the 'misalignment' and his reluctance.

I didn't press the issue further and, between endless cups of standard SRK-issue chai, the chat meandered along about a couple of films he was working on. Suddenly, he stopped short and said, 'You know, I think the ad concept is timed perfectly for the brand, and Preity will fit the bill. Forget what I said. Let Saatchi & Saatchi bring her on board.' His professionalism, and his ability to constantly put the needs of the brand before any other consideration, was absolutely exceptional. Preity Zinta did both the Sunshine Car and the World Car ad series with SRK, bringing her own brand of aplomb and gaiety to the proceedings.

I must admit that apart from hitting the veritable jackpot by bringing in SRK, we were a relative disaster when it came to choosing a brand ambassador. Primarily as an attempt to give the Hyundai Getz a young, uber-cool image, Hyundai decided to bring in Sania Mirza to help promote the brand at a time when she appeared well set to get a sub-20 world ranking. Perhaps, as an organization, we did not invest enough thought and involvement in the relationship or the creative treatment of the brand, or Saatchi & Saatchi could not put together a creative treatment that matched the brand ambassador, or perhaps because Sania Mirza showed little interest in the proceedings and the product itself – or maybe because of a bit of all three – the end result of that series was unconvincing and wholly forgettable. HMI has never again looked beyond SRK for a brand ambassador for any of its products.

Saatchi & Saatchi: Creativity with Passion, Panache and Professionalism

Unbelievable as it may sound today, when many would probably give their right arm to get onto the HMI bandwagon, the fact is that in 1997 Hyundai did not manage to attract any of the larger advertising agencies in India to even pitch for its advertising account. In March 1997, a few weeks after I had joined HMI, J.D. Bae, Yong Sung Kim and I literally went around calling on ad agencies in Mumbai, telling them what the company was all about and requesting them to consider working with us on building an unknown brand. Invariably, the one issue that seemed to concern most of the agencies was the size of the advertising budget and when they heard of the pitifully small sum (from their point of view) that an unknown company with an unpronounceable name was considering, many were too shocked to even snigger. Obviously, most of the larger, better-known ones politely declined the opportunity, on one pretext or another. Ishan Raina at Euro RSCG, whom I knew reasonably well, was one of the very few who showed more than a modicum of interest. Sista's Saatchi & Saatchi was the other.

I'd known Shanta, Bhags and SG – part of the famous 'Give Me Red' gang at Rediffusion – since the time when they'd worked on the TML corporate campaign. They had just moved out to establish Saatchi & Saatchi in India. After a series of presentations, HMI chose, by a very narrow margin in a quantitative score-card of attributes, to work with the Euro RSCG folks, who did some of the very initial advertising, including one inviting applications for dealerships. While during our initial selection process Euro RSCG appeared to the majority of people on the committee to be ahead by a small margin in terms of comprehending our strategy and designing a communication framework for it, it was always clear that the Saatchi & Saatchi team was in an altogether different league in terms of creativity. Ultimately, by the latter part of 1997, after an interaction of the Saatchi & Saatchi team with the then HMC chairman, M.G. Chung, the HMI account moved to Saatchi & Saatchi, and I was back to working with a group of professionals I had known, respected and enjoyed working with earlier.

Saatchi & Saatchi got down to work almost immediately and among the first brainstorming exercises with them was the one in which the brand name 'Santro' was finalized. After a fairly lengthy iterative process Saatchi & Saatchi came to the meeting to discuss branding, armed with a few shortlisted suggestions headed by 'Diva'. All of us were on the same page in terms of the personality of the product that we wanted the brand name to communicate. We wanted it to signify modernity, youth, a sense of fun, sophistication, style – and, for want of a better word, Euro chic! We were also absolutely certain that we would not go with the parent company's branding of Atos/Atoz because of the phonetic similarity with the word 'autos', a very Indian term for a three-wheeler. (Almost all respondents who had seen the initial styling renderings during customer clinics had spoken disparagingly of the original Atoz design, saying that it reminded them of the non-aspirational and very downmarket 'auto'.)

Saatchi & Saatchi were clear that the brand ought to remind customers of the French Riviera, the very epitome of a stylish lifestyle. The group considered 'Nice' for a start, but gave it up because of its rather generic quality when pronounced as an English word rather than a French name, and its association with a well-known brand of sugar-coated biscuits. And then, voila! J.H. Kim took the first part of the French phonetics of both words in St. Tropez, and created 'Santro'! But to give it some semblance of likeness with the branding of the original Atoz by the parent company, the styling of the letters was retained. (Of course, the parent company sold the car, even when sourced from India, as Amica, or Atoz Prime, or even under the Kia or Dodge brand names. The only other country that used the Santro brand-name was Pakistan, and though they could never admit that it was a made-in-India car, dealers there too – apparently, and not so surprisingly – used SRK in their advertising though obviously without authorization).

The challenge before the HMI marketing team and Saatchi & Saatchi was to create brand awareness and build brand equity without the luxury of a blank cheque book – in fact, with so little in money terms that we perforce learnt to use our combined imagination. On one occasion, a few months after the Santro was launched, still desperately short on promotion budget, HMI produced a point-of-purchase poster using one of our colleagues, Saif Siddiqui, and Sanjiv Shukla's toddler daughter to depict a happy Santro family, just so that we could save on the fee that professional models would charge. I don't believe there will be a parallel to this kind of cost control in any other automotive company globally.

Even before the first public viewing of the Santro, the HMI and Saatchi & Saatchi teams rose brilliantly to the occasion. Using stock footage from the parent company's archives, for instance, Saatchi & Saatchi first created a collaged representation of the Hyundai global product portfolio with a simple sign off – 'The Winds Have Changed' – and put it onto channels that typically had younger viewers hooked, without their finger on the remote. This was followed up a few months later, in the run-up to the 1998 Auto Expo, with an even longer commercial focused on the parent company's capabilities and the new tagline – 'Our Future Is Yours'! Only then did the first serious Indian advertising production start; a very low-cost film, shot in two days flat at Famous Studios in Mumbai, to be shown at the HMI stall during the 1998 Auto Expo with very catchy lyrics set to tunes inspired by popular chartbusters by the Spice Girls and a music video-type routine centred around the star of the show – the Santro.

The very lean marketing team that handled both the advertising and promotion consisting then of just Stewart Suh, Sanjiv Shukla and Rohit Khurana was often stretched to near-breaking point with the inevitable bunching up of pre-launch activities. Stewart Suh, an extremely intelligent and perceptive, if often abrasive marketing professional (who still managed to look after his own team with a rare empathy and the spirit of a teacher), had handled both the advertising and promotion functions in developed markets and therefore came with a good understanding particularly of the analytics, management and production processes involved.

Yet, he often appeared to struggle to come to terms with cultural issues in communication or understanding the nuances of both English in an Indian context, particularly where the communication was based on a mixture of emotion and humour, and obviously Hindi. Sanjiv Shukla admirably filled this gap and together they provided the perfect day-to-day interface with the creative group at Saatchi & Saatchi. Sanjiv's role was particularly critical because of my insistence that, as far as possible, advertising in Indian languages was to be created separately from English advertising. Invariably, much of Hyundai's advertising was conceptualized and written in conversational Hindustani, and then translated into various regional languages by Saatchi & Saatchi offices in other parts of the country, working closely with HMI employees and dealers in various states to get the idioms absolutely spot on.

The advertising strategy that Saatchi & Saatchi and HMI jointly developed evolved from detailed and structured qualitative research (and, of course, our collective gut-feel) into the process of choosing brands, the buying practices of small car buyers and potential upgraders in Delhi, Mumbai and Bangalore – which we believed would be markets with the highest volume/growth rates, and display the greatest likelihood of accepting change and signal early shifts in brand preference. Given its importance, Shanta, SG and I stayed personally involved at every stage of the study, including the face-to-face interactions with our survey respondents.

The research appeared to suggest that, in an era when detailed information on automotive technology or performance aspects of cars was limited in its spread and availability among mass buyers, the choice of brand and the decision to purchase lay substantially in the male domain. Additionally, purchases seemed to be influenced significantly by informal information channels, primarily word-of-mouth at the workplace or the broker ecosystem that had developed as a by-product of the demand–supply mismatch of MUL products.

To give HMI, or any other new entrant for that matter, a fighting chance to enter and thrive in such a market environment, this had to be changed. Demystifying cars and getting the lady of the house and children involved in every aspect of its purchase was an urgent imperative – but obviously only after addressing the typical male buyer's doubts on the sustainability of the company itself. (That, at a time when PAL Peugeot and PAL were already beginning to somewhat shake the Indian consumers' long-held belief that car companies were too big to fail!)

The advertising strategy was structured as a four-stage process. During the first part of Stage 1, we decided that the overall advertising approach would be built on introducing the brand, creating brand recognition and acceptance. In the second part we focused on making the family the core around which the actual product would be created and presented, before showcasing the product itself. This serialized approach to building the brand was definitely a first for the Indian automotive industry, perhaps even for the advertising of consumer goods in India. The ad series started with 'Mr Kim', the Korean actor representing Hyundai, gate-crashing an SRK shoot with a request that he advertise the company's new car, and then went on, in the next episode, to have 'Mr Kim' recognized by SRK. In later episodes, the story got him to apprise SRK about the company's investment in plant and equipment, production capabilities, vendor development efforts, and the sales and service backbone. We reckoned that these were exactly the doubts and questions that could arise in the minds of India's consumers and with SRK seemingly assured by 'Mr Kim' on what were possibly also their concerns, they would move towards trying the product, exactly as he did in the last of the series of advertisements.

In a very unobtrusive way, the ads also introduced pester power into the process of buying a car by focusing on children flocking to SRK for his autograph. We hoped children belonging to a generation weaned on a staple diet of television, with whom SRK was already a big hit, would also identify with SRK's future car. The series ended with SRK – helped by his dog – defining the Santro as the 'complete family car' and effectively trying to push Indian consumers towards making the purchase decision process into one which involved the entire family.

With SRK's well-chronicled six-to-sixty female following, the implicit hope was that we would be able to bring in evolved and finessed feminine choices and children's electric involvement, to layer over the staid, herd-comfort-seeking and relatively boring male element in the brand choice exercise when it came to cars. As the Santro's sales volumes showed a continuous upward trend every month through the first year after its launch, the launch campaign was declared the best campaign by the *Business Standard* Brand Derby, and marketing professionals across the country sat up and took notice of the trail-blazing efforts. Even earlier, the New York Festival for Advertising Effectiveness had given the campaign global recognition by awarding it the Campaign of the Year in the Best TVC Automotive category!

Immediately after the launch of the product, as SRK's presence moved from television channels and the print media to audio-visual aids and point-of-purchase collaterals in dealerships, Stage 2 of the advertising strategy came into play with a focus on product technology and product benefits, direct from the consumers' standpoint and comparing it with competition. With brand recognition established, a series of short television commercials that focused on simple consumer benefits like the ease of ingress and egress, the safety afforded by impact beams in the doors and just the feeling of interior space served to bring the Santro into the consumers' list of potential choices. Simultaneously, a conscious effort was made to further build on the high-tech image already created for the product in order to contrast the level of technology that the Santro offered with what was on offer from MUL and TML.

Building on the multi-point fuel injection theme of the launch period, the advertising focused on the new tech-savvy India with the 'Genius is Inside' campaign that referred to the ECU which had almost as much effective computing capability as desktops had a few years earlier. A comic book extolling the technology edge of the Santro was widely distributed at showrooms across the country to kids who accompanied their parents to see the vehicle. We figured that technology-grasping millennials would propel our growth – and hasten their fathers' acceptance of our product. (Years earlier, in TML while preparing to launch the Honda Accord proposed to be manufactured in a joint venture with Honda, in a bid to acquaint a generation with Honda's much-talked-about engine technology, I had posters of Honda Formula One cars distributed in the elite schools in Mumbai and Delhi. Needless to say, the effect was instantly visible. Soon enough, the Honda Accord became the most imported car in India!)

Younger consumers who invariably perceived computers as the very epitome of technology could not help but notice the stark contrast with MUL's carburettor-based engines. With the intention of creating a surrogate web presence to serve as an automotive technology chat room, Saatchi & Saatchi and HMI then created the character of 'Dr Sheer-Genius', to be directly run by SG and I. But it's unnecessary (and unapproved) use in a regional tactical ad unfortunately meant that the character's identity cover was blown and had to be dispensed with soon enough.

Given that this was also the period that witnessed the launch of the Tata Indica, it proved to be one of the most trying times for the Santro's sales volumes. Though the launch of the Euro 2 product in

May 1999 had barely any advertising support except for a solitary 60 column centimetre ad on the last page of the Delhi edition of a newspaper, it reinforced the technology edge of HMI and took the Santro's sales from one new peak to the next.

The launch campaign for the Hyundai Accent further cemented HMI's image as a technology leader. Starting with a simple fact that HMC had spent about US $1.2 billion on research and development in 1998 and 1999, and that this was the period when the new-generation Hyundai Accent was developed, Saatchi & Saatchi created a memorable tagline hailing the Accent as 'The $1.2 Billion Car', and developed a series of ads that spoke primarily about the research and development focus and spending of the Hyundai group, weaving into it details of the product that was launched in October 1999 in India, barely a couple of weeks after it was introduced in Korea and before it was launched in Europe. The launch campaign advertising for the Accent probably fell somewhere between a corporate and a product campaign, because even as it created a superb launch platform for the new model it served to further impress upon non-Accent consumers that the new car's stablemate, the Santro, was equally pedigreed in technology terms because of the parent company's research focus. Achieving complementarity between two campaigns for two products, in two very different market segments, in such a manner as to create a virtuous cycle of brand strengthening was also unique in the Indian automotive industry at that stage. With the two brands now complementing each other perfectly, HMI entered the new millennium.

Just when the media was applauding HMI for attaining pole position in both its product segments in the first month of 2000, Saatchi & Saatchi and HMI felt we ought to build on the advantage with yet another advertisement-led corporate brand reinforcement effort that would further bolster sales volumes. Having worked in TML in the days when it believed in a rapid ramp-up of product sales volumes in the early stages of product introduction followed by a product life-cycle that was perpetually extended by technological interventions, which in turn made for consistent profit generation, I fully endorsed the old auto industry adage 'Jo Dikhti Hai, Woh Bikti Hai,' loosely translated as, 'The more it's seen, the more it sells.'

The network and sales teams had been pushed hard to achieve what even my Korean colleagues considered a very aggressive sales ramp-up, and by January 2000 cumulative sales of the car had crossed 77,000 units within sixteen months, well beyond what had been committed to the parent company. The big '100,000 units sold' milestone was within touching distance and provided the perfect opportunity for some trumpet-blowing. For this purpose, Saatchi & Saatchi created the very memorable 'Kab Hoga Ek Lakh' ('When Will We Get to One Lakh?') contest to focus the consumers' attention on the event. A humorous FM radio, television and print media campaign that was built around a contest open to Hyundai's consumers invited them to guess the date when the magic sales number would be achieved and helped unleash a wave of consumer involvement very early on in the life of both the corporate and the product brands.

Personally, I had always felt market-share growth was the more important metric for a marketing organization. But achieving a cumulative sales volume of 100,000 units out of a market-segment volume of 400,000 over the same period, by a company that had not been seen on Indian roads barely twenty months before that, was definitely something to crow about – and consumers ought to be made aware of. It was, to my mind, a far greater achievement than perhaps attaining the same milestone in a market with an annual volume of 2 million units, for instance.

Broadcasting volume milestone achievements can play an important role in building brand credibility and consumer confidence, simply because everyone loves a winner. And when the 200,000 units cumulative sales figure achievement came up very soon thereafter in

2001, Saatchi & Saatchi worked to recreate the magic with the 'Dekhte Dekhte Do Lakh' ('Two Lakhs in a Jiffy') contest and campaign to further build corporate brand strength along with the product brand. Given the serious fund constraints HMI constantly faced in the early days, this ability of Saatchi & Saatchi to work together with us to stitch together amazingly cost-effective campaigns was the ultimate test of their professional competence – and they invariably came through with flying colours.

In attaining cost efficiencies in our advertising, HMI worked closely with Saatchi & Saatchi to break new ground. I recall in the early 1990s, when my wife Meenakshi had reviewed the state of the Indian advertising industry for *Advertising Age* magazine of the UK and spoken with ad bigwigs about the possibility of media buying being separated from creatives even in India, the idea was pooh-poohed and dismissed out of hand. But advertisers had obviously already started questioning the rationale of what was widely perceived as a mere intermediation effort of an advertising agency that put in probably a month of cerebral and creative effort and lived off it for as long as the campaign held. Reflective of competitive realities, at least in the automotive space, advertising campaigns generally seemed to defy age in those days. The extremely tight financial situation of HMI, which then did not have the luxury of a parent company with deep pockets and the willingness to support media-buying extravagance meant that we had to be creative – in the positive sense of the word – while building the reach we wanted with the paltry pennies we had. The non-conformist Saatchi & Saatchi gang clearly saw the logic from HMI's point of view, and even in the absence of a well-developed media marketplace, actively supported HMI moving towards a structure that demarcated creative and media-buying responsibilities. The results of this amazingly open attitude and willingness to avoid any potential conflicts of interest, even when the HMI advertising budget was relatively insignificant in value terms, helped create media-buying initiatives that ended up giving the Hyundai brand far greater visibility than the actual expenditure might have suggested. Working closely with HMI, Saatchi & Saatchi helped stitch together path-breaking ad space deals with the likes of Bennett Coleman & Co. Ltd, *Dainik Jagran* and *India Today* that enabled mega brand visibility at local brand spends.

Through this period, the technology-focused communication for the Santro brand continued with the Santro Zip Drive ad series, through the unfortunate parting of ways with Saatchi & Saatchi (albeit temporary, as it would turn out), a relatively short involvement first with Bates and then SSC&B Lintas, the market contraction of 2001, till the Santro Zip Plus campaign broke in the middle of 2002 and the eventual return of Saatchi & Saatchi to take back stewardship of the brand. Once again, the Santro was applauded by *Business Standard* Brand Derby, this time for being one of the three most successful brand launches since the inception of the Derby.

One of the most important developments in terms of consumer psychographics of the Indian market became very obvious from about the beginning of 2002, and marked the beginning of Stage 3 in the evolution of Santro advertising. What we observed quite clearly was that the average age of our consumers was drifting below thirty, and very often the Santro was the first car for upwardly mobile young professionals. The confidence that the brand had been able to create with banks and finance companies, particularly in terms of asset-value retention, and the widespread support it received from ICICI Bank (and thereafter, inevitably due to competitive pressures, from others as well), had led to a situation where very minimal down payments, if any, were called in from potential consumers at the time of financing the purchase.

The low consumer equity requirement from banks on the purchase of a Santro served as a virtual force-multiplier for a new, consumerist generation of Indians that had clearly come to embrace the Freidmanian permanent income hypothesis while spending with never-before gusto. The Nobel Prize-winning economist Milton Freidman hypothesized that people will spend money at a level consistent with their expected long-term average income, which tends to then be thought of as the level of permanent income that can be safely spent. Communicating with this group, already reasonably well-informed because of the rapid spread of Internet-based information, we figured, would need to go beyond the allure of technology.

At this point Saatchi & Saatchi conceptualized and created the 'Sunshine Girl' in an attempt to bring in a higher emotional connect with consumers. The television and print campaign featuring SRK and Preity Zinta, supported with attractive point-of-purchase collaterals, created a new wave of enthusiasm among consumers and the results soon showed up on sales charts as well. Going further with the emotional pitch was the advertising oriented towards lady users for the Santo Automatic that was launched in September 2002, addressing fathers and husbands who cared. The advertisement featuring hands and feet decorated with mehendi in particular, along with the other ads in the series soon had lady drivers warming up to the car as their first choice of wheels. An earlier attempt with the Tulip Club, a special service for lady drivers, had withered away, simply because lady drivers probably still could not appreciate what their husbands or children saw in the car – except perhaps the ease of entry when they wore a sari. But this time it was different, and emotion took us closer to the real decision-makers in households. The Santro's sales volumes grew at twice the rate of the Maruti Zen and the Maruti WagonR combined. Albeit, sales of the Tata Indica did grow faster in that particular year, but since it appeared to primarily address the commercial use or taxi segment, HMI did not consider it a direct competitor for purposes of performance comparison or while formulating competitive marketing strategy responses. The emotional connect continued as a part of the overall advertising message till early 2003, when the full facelift model, the Santro Xing, was ushered in.

As the company and the brands had evolved broadly in line with the plans and expectations, HMI and Saatchi & Saatchi believed that the advertising in Stage 4 ought not to focus merely on the product but attempt to use the product to further build corporate identity, which would in turn provide an even greater boost to the product itself. Importantly, the launch of the Santro Xing in April 2003 was an event that had no precedent in the Indian automotive industry. In a country where intervals between car model changes were typically measured in decades, HMI had completely changed the look of the Santro in a space of just over fifty months after its launch, a move that was in line with the normal product life-cycle interventions of the global automotive industry. A television ad series showing SRK getting a Santro Xing in exchange for his older Santro told in the by-now familiar serialized format helped create the platform for the new model to be rapidly accepted. Once again, for a remarkable third time, the Santro Xing campaign was applauded by the *Business Standard* Brand Derby, this time as the best brand re-launch. This was important, for it clearly established that HMI was committed to ensuring that Indian car consumers were treated on par with global consumers. Even more important, the Santro Xing was slated to soon enter the markets of Western Europe – from India – with styling, ride and handling, and powertrain specifications identical to those that were offered to the Indian consumer. This combination, we believed, positioned HMI so far ahead of MUL that the latter would find it impossible to catch up, let alone overtake the Santro, and decided that it needed to be brought to the attention of consumers. The approach was thus to position HMI and the Santro as the choice of the 'global Indian', and by implied contrast to relegate competition to the group with the lower-ranked products. TML had, in the meantime, announced very ambitious plans to enter the

UK market, but the short-lived nature of that foray and its rapid disintegration only served to add further lustre to the achievement of HMI and the Santro Xing. While television campaigns featuring SRK and Preity Zinta in a variety of global locations served to build this global image of the Santro Xing, the reinforcement probably happened during the summer of 2005 when Indian tourists started seeing the car widely during their travels in Europe. The emotional treatment was once again brought back via the 'first car' campaign to further cement its volume gains, from mid-2005. By the end of Stage 4, as HMI rolled out its millionth car, again setting a record of being the fastest to do so in India, both Brand Hyundai and the Santro had firmly established themselves in the minds of Indian consumers. HMI was now simply referred to by India's consumers as the 'Santro company'!

Comparative (read Combative) Advertising

It probably wouldn't be out of place to say that Hyundai brought comparative advertising to the Indian car industry – an act for which we were vilified and mocked by the advertising fraternity in particular, and elements of the mass media in general.

I never did understand what the brouhaha was about and why there was so much reluctance to bring out advertising that compared a product with its competition. In the battle to grab the buyer, much worse has allegedly been done by companies in India, in the detergent space, in the soft drink business and in the automotive industry itself. The preachy, sanctimonious, pretentious statements that emanated from advertising professionals and the attempted intervention of the Advertising Standards Council left me unfazed. I firmly believed that the consumer had the right to know what was on offer and as long as there was no falsehood in any communication no one ought to complain.

Fortunately, the Saatchi & Saatchi gang and the Hyundai marketing team were on the same wavelength and, soon enough, in a range of tactical, if rather combative, advertising that we hoped would also give greater credence to the brand, Santro took on the Maruti Zen and everyone else. The way we figured it was that if our competitors' partners in the financial services industry and their direct sales associates could spread misinformation, often bordering on canard, by word of mouth, Hyundai had every right to place the relevant facts in the public domain. The information asymmetry that existed then, primarily because the Internet was still not as widespread and content on the net remained limited, had to be addressed through informative advertising even if it ran the risk of appearing to be confrontational. We just had to make sure that the comparative advertisements used printed information from company brochures already in the public domain and were then positioned only as an attempt to provide a common platform for evaluating the various features of the cars mentioned.

Soon enough, others started to see and understand our viewpoint and even a hallowed name like Ford got into the act. Faced with the slowing growth of the Ikon, Ford probably believed it had to get its volumes from the segment just below where the Ikon was placed, and came out with an advertisement addressing potential 'small car' buyers and suggesting that they would do well to compare their choice with the Ikon. We may have let it pass, except that we believed that the 'small car' they showed looked like the Santro. Our own advertisement in response was as fast in coming as it was brutally hard-hitting, after which we completely stopped attacking Ford in print, and they returned the compliment. But Ford had already committed the cardinal error of punching below its weight. This is all that Hyundai needed. From the next day, HMI's sales personnel at dealerships across the country were trained to tell undecided customers who were considering the purchase of an Accent, but still comparing it with the Ford Ikon, that they ought to actually compare the latter with the Santro because the Ikon was aimed at that market segment. Photocopies of the Ford ad and the Hyundai response were both handed over immediately to buttress the point. Needless to say, among customers who came to Hyundai showrooms and attempted to compare the Ford Ikon with the Accent, the impact was near instant and, in a matter of months, if not weeks, the Ikon's downward spiral started in the non-taxi segment in the important markets of Delhi, Mumbai, Bangalore and Chennai.

The comparative ad war with Daewoo India, however, turned ugly. It had started as a minor scrap in Calcutta in September 1999 when, in the aftermath of the floods there, even as we were working overtime to provide a few affected consumers with a solution and had cast the net wider as a preventive measure, Daewoo India released a series of ads questioning the claims made by Hyundai of the Santro's technological prowess. Focusing on the problem at hand, of fixing customers' cars, HMI did not react. Even after other minor provocations, including one that claimed the Matiz outsold the Santro 3:1 and added in small print that the data referred to the UK. Refusing to be drawn into a slanging match, and deciding that we should wait our turn, we decided Mao-style that we should '*concentrate an absolutely superior force, that is to say, a force six, five, four or at least three times that of the enemy, concentrate the whole or the bulk of our artillery, select one (not two) of the weak spots in the enemy's positions, attack it fiercely and be sure to win. This accomplished, swiftly exploit the victory and destroy the enemy forces...*'

Such an opportunity ultimately came when reports about large-scale financial wrongdoing at Daewoo India's parent company, and the source of all its Matiz CKD kits, first surfaced in the Korean and global press. As things unravelled in Korea, it was clear that Daewoo India would not remain unaffected. Using typically mobile warfare and guerrilla tactics, a series of salesman-talking-point slides which focused on the problems that customers could potentially face if they chose to buy the Matiz, were released to dealers in markets where the Matiz had started building something of a presence. This was particularly done in Uttar Pradesh, Daewoo India's home market and only real stronghold due to it exercising its ill-advised sales tax waiver option. Written in colloquial, conversational Hindustani jointly by Saatchi & Saatchi and HMI, the hard-hitting sales aid was very creatively structured for a relatively simple conversion into tactical advertisement by dealers or a hand-out to consumers. First used in Gujarat and then in Uttar Pradesh, the ad insertions (the cost of which HMI typically reimbursed to the extent of 50 per cent) with the headline 'Car Aapke Ghar, Company Sadak Par' – loosely translated as 'The car's in your driveway, but the company's headed for the streets' – was just the spark needed for the intended conflagration. The copy repeated the points in the sales aid, and 'informed' potential customers that the parent of a company manufacturing 800 cc cars had just been declared bankrupt. It effectively asked them to ponder who would provide them with spare parts and maintenance support in the future if they bought such a product today, exhorting them to buy intelligently and simply choose India's best small car, the Santro.

An incensed Daewoo India first threatened the concerned dealers with legal action and then threatened to sue Hyundai and me in my personal capacity. It was rumoured that the company even sought the intervention of the Korean embassy to ask HMI to stop the attack. Y.S. Kim ultimately spoke to his compatriot at Daewoo India, promising to stop dealers from publishing the particular advertisement. The extent of the panic reaction at Daewoo India meant that the ad was having its desired effect. Determined not to let up on the pressure, we turned the screws tighter. Tongue firmly in cheek, a new missive was sent out to HMI dealers purporting to explain the sensitivities involved in the proposed asset valuation exercise by HMC following the formal invitation extended by the creditors of Daewoo Motors.

The letter went on to say 'you are strongly advised to refrain from using any news on this front as part of any advertisement campaign under any circumstances whatsoever', leaving one thing unsaid – that the copy of the letter itself could be handed over to customers.

Daewoo India which felt that the headline of the ad was indirectly referring to it and was both disparaging of it and misinforming potential customers, sought and obtained an ex-parte injunction from the Monopolies and Restrictive Trade Practices Commission (MRTPC), restraining Hyundai and its dealers from issuing the controversy-creating advertisements. The MRTPC bench observed, 'In our opinion, this prima facie amounts to unfair trade practice within the meaning of the MRTPC Act. The applicant will suffer irreparable loss not only in its corporate prestige but also in the sale of its cars.' It awarded the injunction to Daewoo, restraining HMI from publishing the offending advertisements in print, visual, electronic media and hoardings, and posted the next hearing in the following month. HMI had complied even before the hearing was held, and the resultant media coverage of the restraining order was just what we needed to ensure that curiosity about the details of the 'offending' advertisement appearing to allege Daewoo India's imminent demise and the company's panic-stricken response, seemed adequately whetted. The intended message spread all over the country, courtesy news reports. A few days later, Daewoo India once again approached the MRTPC alleging that HMI's advertisements comparing the Santro with the other small cars in the market had misrepresented facts and was tantamount to unfair trade practice. But this time, after hearing the complaint, the MRTPC refused to grant an injunction restraining HMI from issuing comparative advertisements.

Daewoo India then, apparently, decided on direct action and sent about four hundred of its workers in company-contracted buses to demonstrate at the Hyundai marketing headquarters in Delhi. Rather well-known for their 'not-so-peaceful' ways, the Daewoo

India workers surrounded the premises and indulged in some very high-decibel sloganeering along with threats of stoning and burning down the building. Led by a few of their union office-bearers, they appeared to be aware of the legal implications of trespass and continued to stand just outside the main gate of the premises, which had by then been locked. But a few hot-heads in the rear were already getting restive by the time V.D. Bhasin accompanied me downstairs to speak with the congregation. My Korean colleagues, generally very queasy about taking on their compatriots, and therefore often not in agreement with what they perceived as my sledgehammer tactics had, in the meantime, seen this crowd, probably thought it was my war anyway and decided to high-tail it back to the guest house where they had earlier gone for lunch. My willingness to walk down and meet with the gathered workers, and the fact that Bhasin, who had earlier worked at Daewoo India, knew some of the union office-bearers personally, helped to marginally defuse the situation.

I (Satan personified, as projected to Daewoo India's employees) invited the group's leaders to come upstairs to the conference room to hear me out and understand my point of view, even as I asked our administration colleagues and the facility security detail to provide water and refreshments to the crowd outside. Completely disarmed by HMI's decision not to call for local police help, they reluctantly followed us upstairs. Then, after one of them in a very Bollywood-style dialogue said he considered it 'a sin even to drink a glass of water in the enemy's house', they sat down and listened while I gave them critical details of the financial situation not just of Daewoo India but of its parent company as well – all from Korean and global media reports, along with copies and translations of Korean news reports. In a statement that unfortunately proved to be prescient, I told them that they and their comrades ought to take care of their own long-term benefits then lying in the company-managed provident fund account. The ensuing silence made me confident that the management of Daewoo India would now have an even bigger worry to contend with than HMI's advertising. The seeds of suspicion had now been sown not just in customers' minds but, far more dangerously, inside the Daewoo India plant as well. The approach borrowed from Mao was simple: '*Complete annihilation demoralizes the enemy's troops and depresses his followers; it raises the morale of our troops and inspires our people. A quick decision makes it possible for our troops...to wipe out the enemy reinforcements one by one...*'

When the next MRTPC hearing came up a few weeks later, the lawyers representing Daewoo India sought an end to the proceedings since they had received neither any directions from the client nor payment for their services. Within weeks Daewoo India started sputtering to a halt. By April 2001, it was clear that all was not well with the company when it stopped reporting on its performance to the industry body, SIAM. As Daewoo India got sucked into the quicksand of its own and its parent's financial misadventures, the Serious Fraud Investigation Office (SFIO) started an inquiry into the operations of the company. On one fateful evening in May 2002, all the Korean expatriate management personnel allegedly left the plant, sent their chauffeurs home early and left India the same night with their families and their personal belongings before any legal action could be initiated against them in their professional capacities.

Was HMI at fault for informing customers about spending their hard-earned money wisely? Even today, after all these years, I think it was absolutely the right thing to do. A few weeks after the ad war with Daewoo India initially broke out, Saatchi & Saatchi parted ways with HMI. It was then perceived as a fallout of the ad fisticuffs. Nothing could be farther from the truth. In reality, Saatchi & Saatchi opted out of the contract renewal process because, as it later transpired, they were unwilling to accept some blatantly unethical 'requests' allegedly made by a couple of our colleagues, both of whom played an important part in the overall marketing decision-making process. Unwilling to lose such valued members of the team as the Saatchi & Saatchi trio that had helped build the Hyundai brand in India, both Y.S. Kim and I personally met with Shanta to request him to reconsider the decision. But a clearly upset Saatchi & Saatchi held its ground, something that few professionals would probably do. A few months later, Saatchi & Saatchi moved to MUL in search of business and created a campaign that helped breathe new life into the WagonR brand. Some months later both our colleagues involved in this unsavoury episode left the group, and Saatchi & Saatchi eventually returned to handle HMI's advertising in 2002.

Early in 2005, another comparative ad issued by HMI appeared to get another competing brand hot under the collar. While focusing on the safety features of the Santro Xing, sales personnel at the dealerships had been advised to draw the attention of potential consumers to the fact that, unlike the WagonR, the Santro came with a seatbelt for the middle passenger in the rear seat. The model in particular remained unnamed in all the communication, but it was obvious to any intending car buyer to which company it belonged. Technically speaking, putting a third passenger in the rear seat of the WagonR could be construed both as a safety hazard and as a violation of the Motor Vehicle Act. If policemen all over the country could haul up 'traffic offenders' when they caught three people riding a two-wheeler, they ought to have been doing exactly the same thing if they found three people in the rear seat of the Maruti WagonR. The ad that upset people pointed out just this, referring to the fact that the Automotive Research Association of India (ARAI) had certified the Santro Xing as a five-seater and refrained from naming the competitor that was technically only a four-seater. Quick to take umbrage at being named, ARAI demanded an explanation from HMI and asked for the competing models to be clearly identified. The association also said that it preferred to be referred to only as 'the country's premier certification and homologation agency'. This was the perfect license that HMI needed and the famous 'Kissa Kursi Ka' (loosely translated as 'The Case of the Seat' but obliquely referring to a controversial Indian film) ad was issued, clearly naming the Maruti WagonR as merely a four-seater as compared to the legally five-seater Santro Xing! As always, HMI managed to raise the hackles of the competition, but I took a clear position in the mass media that the campaign had been understood completely out of context. I pointed out that as a socially responsible corporate entity HMI believed that since the government had pro-actively mandated seatbelts, it too needed to focus on seatbelts and on educating consumers on the safety aspects of seatbelt use, even if the SIAM, because of its own compulsions, remained uninterested and unconcerned about safety. After all, I pointed out to the mass media, a company that said it cared for its consumers ought not to provide cars that did not meet international safety standards; after all, we did not believe that Indian lives were cheaper than lives of other nationalities. Without mincing words, I often exhorted the media to raise safety issues with the competition and SIAM, because 'ultimately the consumer was their only constituency', and asked them to try and remember any instance of either the industry or SIAM proactively doing anything to protect consumer interests. This won the Hyundai brand, broad, if sometimes reluctant, admiration. To spice up matters further, I asked consumers to note that cars in the A2 segment that were being exported to Europe from India then (for all practical purposes, only the Santro in any recognizable number) were the only ones that matched European safety standards. It was a simple way of getting potential consumers to recognize the Santro Xing as the only truly global car in the segment that they could buy in India. This came after a stellar showing in 2004, when domestic sales of the Santro Xing had crossed the 100,000 units mark in a single calendar/model year – the first time ever by any car in the segment.

Though HMI's actions invariably managed to bring unreasonable comment, a lot of negative debate and blatant vilification of the company and me personally in their wake, it never became much of a concern. HMI and I always publicly took ownership for what was said. What was put out in the public domain was invariably based on information and data that could be easily accessed by the public at large, and I believed that this basic honesty in providing information would ultimately be recognized for its sincerity of purpose.

HMI did become a victim, more than once, of the dirty tricks departments of competitors, albeit with the guiding hand invariably well hidden. Strangely, these acts never received the kind of condemnation of the morality brigade of the automotive or advertising fraternity. Probably the worst case came to pass in Hyderabad when a local MUL dealer, Varun Motors, allegedly tampered with the brakes of a Santro and offered it for a comparative test drive to potential WagonR consumers at a dealership location. Interestingly, just a couple of days earlier, a regional review meeting had been held by MUL's top brass in the city, when dealers had allegedly been exhorted to do whatever it took to stall the inexorable march of the Santro towards segment leadership. Given inter-dealer rivalry, it was only a matter of hours before HMI learnt of MUL's internal deliberations, the bravado on display and the basic details of the discussions that followed. But the action that was taken in the wake of that meeting shook us, I must admit, even if only for a day. HMI hit back instantly – but not at MUL.

Though T.M. Kumar strongly believed that a criminal case against the dealer concerned would be a good method to convey a strong enough message to anyone else contemplating such misadventures, at his considered suggestion we decided not to use a sledgehammer on a fly, and ultimately approached the Hyderabad civil court for significant damages. The HMI stance was that MUL's dealer had not just tried to tarnish the reputation of HMI by wilfully manipulating the product, but had actually put the lives of all potential customers who had tried out the vehicle at his premises at grave risk of sustaining or causing bodily harm, or both.

The complaint that was ultimately filed and admitted, and the subsequent arguments managed to get the message communicated sufficiently. The decree, with penalty and costs, in the case OS 239 of 2002 was finally pronounced in 2013. I don't know if the people who often pontificated in public on the need for standards in advertising or other worthies who had much venom to spew against HMI's aggressive advertising posture ever got to know or cared enough, or had the guts or the gumption, to comment on the matter.

Working with the Media

The equally critical third leg supporting the communication strategy of HMI was the unstinted, even if initially cautious and somewhat reluctant, support that it garnered from the Indian media. The 'underdog' tag probably helped HMI get something of the sympathy vote to start with, but sustaining that was a certain freshness in the approach to interacting with the media – an approach based on honesty, transparency and mutual professional respect.

At the very initial stage, during and just after the incorporation process, HMI did work with a well-regarded public-relations firm in Delhi. But I remained unconvinced about the long-term suitability of the approach and repeatedly discussed, with both Y.S. Kim and J.D. Bae, the need for the company to be directly involved with the media. Fortunately, after our first serious sit-down meeting with the firm's very high-profile boss, Y.S. Kim didn't need any further convincing. Much of our first hour was spent listening to a virtual telephone directory of the names of the leading lights of the ruling party and the opposition during the longest name-dropping exercise I have ever encountered in my life. We were then treated to a most banal analysis of the Indian economy along with the 'commitment' that the firm would be giving HMI an insider-view on the happenings in the economy 'from government sources', along with its own analysis to help us 'strategize our communication effort' and 'calibrate our responses in the marketplace' – and, of course, if required, it could help us influence government policy as well, through its 'good offices'. The gentleman was basically offering us the entire world on a platter and repeatedly asking us to trust him and, for some reason, during his eloquent monologue, all I could think of was the serpent Kaa from *The Jungle Book*.

But when the gentleman quoted a fee that was a multiple of the then combined salaries of the entire marketing, sales, service and spare-parts teams at HMI, we were convinced that we were better off not following Alice into blunderland. That was the last time we considered hiring a public relations agency as our voice when speaking with the media. This was probably the first time that an unknown multinational entering the Indian market with such a large investment decided that it ought to interact and speak directly with the media, rather than go through the intermediary layer of a public relations company. It was decided that I would strategize and implement all media communication and relationships with a dedicated in-house team.

I probably started with something of an advantage in dealing with the media because of my wife Meenakshi, one of the earliest among business journalists in the country in the 1980s and 1990s to regularly publish in leading global financial and business publications. Her experiences of speaking with, reporting on and providing analyses of conversations with a wide range of people – from prime ministers, finance ministers and chief ministers of various states to bankers, business leaders, chairmen of banks and leftist trade-union leaders – gave me valuable insight into the way media professionals approached, analysed and projected issues. I learnt from her that handling the media was not an easy task at the best of times. But by taking knowledge-based neutral positions, and willingly stepping back to look at your company, warts and all, from the outside when responding to the media's questions could often prove to be the position of greatest strength that a company spokesperson could take. At the risk of overstating the matter, she would often say the media tends to see the ability of a CEO to acknowledge the company's weaknesses and failures as its greatest intrinsic strength and the best indicator of its future success. She also taught me that once a quote was given, a credible spokesperson could never backtrack and claim being misquoted, unless recorded evidence could be presented, without it further muddying the waters. She also contributed the insight that if I could not say, or was not authorized to say, anything beyond the press release issued or being issued by the company, I ought not to waste the journalist's time.

These insights proved to be just what the doctor ordered when I started interacting with the media on behalf of a then very media-shy TML. Those were the experiences and friendships (many on a first-name basis) that I brought to HMI, but as the pressures of building the distribution network, the marketing organization and the brand steadily peaked, it was clear that getting a full-time media relations team up and running was the need of the hour. During the Auto Expo of 1998, J.H. Kim suggested we consider a young, straight-shooting journalist he had met a couple days earlier to head the media relations team. Journalists would have the additional comfort of being able to speak with 'one of their own' even while they interacted directly with the decision-makers in the company, so this seemed to be a good idea. After Y.S. Kim and I discreetly observed her interaction with J.H. Kim, and a more formal meeting ensued, HMI welcomed Krishnakoli Dutta into the band of pioneers who had set about the task of building the Hyundai brand in the country.

Krishnakoli hit the ground running and after first reaching out to Press Trust of India (PTI) and United News of India (UNI), both

English and Hindi, eventually connected up with over 700 journalists across the country, across newspapers and magazines, across both print and television, and across all languages. She managed to quickly create an unparalleled network of media contacts from Srinagar to Thiruvananthapuram, and from Ahmedabad to Guwahati, who could access her almost 24x7 on the mobile, and whom she kept posted about every little development in the company at the same time as their counterparts or bureaus in the metros. Whenever she felt it was essential, she also made sure I spoke with anyone who wanted to speak with me – which very often was at least four times daily.

Over the next few months, journalists from all corners of the country travelled at HMI's invitation to see the plant taking shape, the prototypes coming to life and the final launch of the car itself. Most importantly, Krishnakoli and I agreed that we would never push any journalist to let us know what had been written after such a trip. This, we believed, was indicative of our intrinsic professional respect for our guests from the media in that we did not measure everything in terms of column centimetres of published news. This marked a major departure not only from the way Hyundai operated globally, but also from the way any intermediary public relations firm, pushed to show 'results' by its client, would normally behave.

I still believe that journalists know best if a story has any meat in it. What perhaps a company can best do is to place its story contextually and in an interesting manner so as to make it appear relevant. If positioned correctly, the media will write about it, as true professionals. No amount of shouting from the rooftops and press conferences on the technological prowess of Hyundai could, for instance, have had as much impact as the simple statement that the company would leapfrog Euro 2 emission standards much before it was mandated by the government that was made on 29 April 1999. Over the next three weeks from that date, and at any time technology was to be discussed, the media listened for HMI's opinion, and of its own accord vaulted the company into a position of technological leadership in the minds of India's consumers.

Over the three years that Krishnakoli and I worked together, we laid down the cornerstones of an approach to the media that I believe played a huge part in the success of the Santro and HMI in India. However much CEOs and CMOs, particularly of successful companies, avoid or deny it, they end up retreating into their boardroom castles for a variety of reasons, but invariably at their own peril. An independent media is probably the closest they would come to learning unvarnished truths of the marketplace. It is always therefore important to directly communicate with the media and treat it as if it were a proxy for the consumer, because when the media seeks answers and obtains them it is on behalf of its constituency, the consumer. This was the underlying rationale for our decision to be constantly involved with non-specialist media. Except during the Auto Expo, auto companies generally seemed content to interact with automotive specialist writers and sometimes, but very seldom, with the financial press. This, we decided, had to change.

The specialist writers undoubtedly served as an excellent technology and performance sounding board, but their impact willy-nilly remained limited by their circulation, the age profile of their readers and typically the language they wrote in – English. It was essential for HMI to first demystify automotive technology and speak in every language in which the consumer spoke in order to get its message across and build both brand recognition and acceptance as it got ready for face-offs in the marketplace with mega-brands TML and MUL. After all, we reasoned, speaking or reading English was not a prerequisite to buying a car!

Perhaps the best reflection of our approach was seen during the 'test drives' that we regularly organized for members of the media, and particularly before a new model was introduced. As a general practice, one member of the top management of the company would be present, and driving, in each of the cars on a test drive. Each drive route was picked to give the participating journalists an idea about the feature that we most wanted to focus on, and reconnoitred with care for road conditions et al twice over the preceding fortnight, along with detailed pit-stop and refuelling schedules, the best places to eat authentic local food en route, and dealer facilities for routine checks and cleaning at night halts. For instance, when the focus was on the Santro Zip Drive's amazing steering response and ease of handling, the route picked was a drive from Bangalore via Hubli and Karwar to Margao. Despite the continuous stream of iron ore-laden dumpers hurtling along continuously, there can scarcely be a better road test for a car's steering and handling than the winding, high-quality tarmac through the jungles and hilly terrain from Hubli to Karwar before the rapid descent near the Karwar Naval Base and port. When we wanted to showcase the comfort and luxury of the Sonata, the test drive involved leaving Bangalore after an early breakfast, having Kolhapur's famous Pandhara Rasa for lunch and reaching Mumbai for dinner – and an 'after-party' – in the days before the Mumbai–Pune Expressway was completed. As a rule, HMI or other work-related matters were never discussed in the evening. It was just the quiet camaraderie of petrol-heads with stories of roads, drives, exhilaration and near-misses. HMI obviously did something right in the way it arranged those test drives and interacted with the media, because even today the journalists who experienced them talk about them with great warmth and affection for the company and its people.

In line with our agreed approach, Krishnakoli ensured that HMI communicated constantly and not just when we wanted to 'pitch' a story because, as we reasoned, journalists instinctively appreciate or understand this. Of course, there is the other, unfortunately more common approach of pushing a public relations agency to work in tandem with an advertising agency to get a specific story published using the space marketing groups in publications, but that can never earn a company the trust or respect of a journalist. It is also crucial to remember that journalists move not only across publications but also across media, and being just as human as a CEO or CMO they could well carry both their goodwill and prejudices with them. I recall that the always-on mode we assumed meant that whenever I travelled to any part of the country, no sooner had I landed than Krishnakoli would call to let me know that she had invited over at least one journalist from that place to meet with me at the local Hyundai office or dealership. At times, she took the liberty of committing to the local press club on my behalf ('conveniently forgetting' to let me know till the day before a trip) that I would be happy to meet with them at their 'adda'. But I instinctively knew she was on the right track and, after much complaining, invariably ended up shuffling my schedule to honour her commitment.

We ensured, additionally, that these interactions were not just to talk about HMI or its products. I recall a very memorable meeting with a group of journalists at the Kochi Press Club when we discussed everything from the land acquisition travails of the then new Kochi International Airport to local politics to what some friends of mine from JNU in the state bureaucracy were doing to what ailed the Kerala State Road Transport Corporation and the state of the 'remittance' economy, without speaking a word about either Hyundai or its products for three hours, over a continuous flow of tea and enveloped in the haze of cigarette smoke. This 'accessible company' image that was consequently built provided the foundation for the exceptional support that brand Hyundai received over the years from media across the country. The openness and accessibility to the media had an interesting side-effect. The general and financial media often called on me, invariably with almost no notice, seeking an opinion on a variety of matters to do with Indian industry and the economy. Most evenings, on my way home, from the rear seat of my car, I gave what could perhaps best have been described as 'tutorials' on evolving future product technology, production trends, financial performance and global market trends in the industry from a practitioner's viewpoint with detailed operating know-how about most aspects of a company's operations. Almost all the journalists I have had the pleasure of knowing have told me how much they valued the time I spent helping them build upon or junk a story idea completely unconnected with HMI, or the help I gave them with a line of inquiry or analysis on some economy-related story while maintaining complete confidentiality about their ideas and their sources. Often, they duly recorded their appreciation with periodic gifts of books that now grace my bookshelf at home. I would like to believe that this helped them see HMI in a more favourable light, and see me as a credible and non-partisan sounding board on matters concerning industry and public policy, which in turn enabled a treatment and projection of HMI with a greater sense of understanding and empathy than a fledgling Korean company could have hoped for anywhere in the world.

It was not as if HMI did not ever get bad or not-so-good press. But we reasoned that getting extra sensitive or hot-under-the-collar about criticism only meant that we hadn't done our job well enough, and had not been able to communicate our achievements, concerns and constraints effectively or convincingly. Blatant misrepresentations following a pattern, particularly when discernibly based on personal prejudices, on the other hand, were approached differently. I recall Krishnakoli, Sanjiv and I going right up the editorial and management ladder at one of the largest and most influential news publishing groups in the country, armed with reams of data and facts to present the HMI point of view on, what appeared to us, the unabated and false negative reporting by one of their journalists. The option was to go with the rash and intemperate suggestion of some of our senior colleagues to ignore the publication at the next company event or block advertising to the publishing group. I believed the latter would at best be counter-productive, and may end up convincing the media at large through the Press Club grapevine that HMI was a churlish, petulant, vindictive and, worst of all, an untruthful company. (I have heard each one of these epithets used by friends in the media while referring to competitors and their top management on more than one occasion.) Sometimes it was difficult to sensitize our Korean colleagues (generally used to a friendly media in a country that then almost literally deified the chaebol) to the fact that the Indian media wanting to know something about the company did not automatically make it intrusive, or it holding a different point of view did not make it adversarial. However uncomfortable the truth was, we reasoned, it was always important to make full disclosure to the media and present the HMI side of the story than to deny off-hand the issue raised by the media – and we ensured that this was done without exception, sometimes to the great discomfort of some of our colleagues.

I believed the truth always has an uncomfortable habit of coming out, particularly when least expected, and if that truth flew in the face of everything we'd been trying to project then the credibility of anything we said in the future would also be open to question. The snide remarks and searching questions about the alleged, and sometimes widely documented business practices of Korean companies in general, and the chaebol in particular, were something that we faced often enough, so giving the media anything but the complete truth would only serve to reinforce the widespread ultra-negative stereotypes. Krishnakoli and I also believed that we ought never to get into angry public confrontations with the media as such an incident would only serve to turn the spotlight unwaveringly on the most minor of our missteps, in the process harming the image we were so carefully trying to create and nurture.

The Indian media responded to HMI with a more than equal measure of trust. Over the years, most new cars bought by journalists and parked on Bahadur Shah Zafar Marg in New Delhi, and similar newspaper-office parking lots across the country, came from the HMI stable, because, I would like to believe, the buyers trusted the company and its management to live up to what they professed, whether in terms of product technology, product quality or after-sales care. That was simply the highest vote of confidence that any company could have hoped for, and HMI received it in ample measure.

7

The Spoils of War

In today's era of e-commerce, when making losses practically the size of sales turnovers and throwing money into extravagant marketing campaigns like it's rapidly going out of fashion is considered the epitome of achievement, I almost feel like I belong to the Jurassic Age when I dare to bring up that ugly six-letter word – profit.

Perhaps due to the extremely strained financial circumstances of HMC and therefore of HMI at the time it came to market, and the reality that there were no venture capital (VC) funds willing to play Santa Claus from one Christmas to the next, ad infinitum, HMI was consistently focused on profitability. Yet, for all the commitment to transparency that HMI practised, the company always remained reticent, even painfully shy, about discussing its financial performance. It was a conscious decision on the part of the company not to focus attention on this aspect, primarily because the dissemination of financial data was not mandatory for unlisted entities but also because the media, with perhaps just one exception – *The Hindu Business Line* newspaper – did not generally show too much interest in the company's financial performance.

The fact that the company had been profitable since the first full year of its operations, was generally known and publicly stated. Since the brands were clearly growing at a decent clip, and moreover since the company wasn't a listed entity in India, its financial performance was not really considered exceptionally newsworthy by the Indian media. In any case, red ink splashed on a company's profit-and-loss statement always makes for a better news story.

Internally, we were all rather chuffed by the fact that HMI was the only manufacturer to have entered the car business after 1995 that was actually consistently in the black. The constant increase both in margins and aggregate profit levels was clear proof of the success and sustainability of our overall marketing strategy. By March 2002, in the third full year of commercial production, Hyundai's profitability and growth trendline was clearly and unalterably established, and only continued to gather momentum thereafter. But I must add a caveat here: the period I refer to essentially covers the period 1997 to 2006, when I was directly associated with the company in an executive role, and does not seek to portray any image of the company's financial operations since then.

HYUNDAI MOTOR INDIA – PROFITABILITY AT A GLANCE
(ALL VALUES ₹ CRORES)

YEAR	EBIDTA	INTEREST	EBDT	DEPRECIATION	TAX	PROFIT AFTER TAX
1998–1999						-50.44
1999–2000	249.65	68.42	181.23	113.60	82.70	59.34
2000–2001	389.60	59.39	330.21	142.25	16.00	171.96
2001–2002	527.66	32.80	494.86	198.16	22.04	274.61
2002–2003	442.05	16.82	425.23	168.02	84.75	164.75
2003–2004	765.38	14.71	750.67	178.55	190.05	378.85
2004–2005	874.33	13.21	861.12	250.01	144.75	406.92
2005–2006	1130.24	3.35	1099.89	295.01	279.78	525.10

While the numbers themselves make for interesting reading, perhaps what was more important was the way the building blocks of profitability had been laid. The most critical of these, to my mind, was the HMI approach to the phased introduction of models. It was decided that in the 'lift-off' stage, the company would enter the volume market and rapidly attain break-even to ensure high utilization of capacity and absorption of overheads. The next stage, firing the 'booster', would be marked by its entry into the mid-size segment to attain profitability, leading thereafter to the 'orbit' stage where HMI would bring in higher-end brands to reinforce the brand image.

Despite the use of such obvious space terminology, there really was no rocket science about the approach. The simple truth of the car business is that as the size of the car grows, prices rise faster than material or manufacturing costs. As part of a future pricing strategy study, I recall doing an industry-wise analysis of the material and manufacturing costs of companies that operated in both the small car (SIAM classification A2) and mid-size car (SIAM classification A3) segments around the end of 2005. From my recollection, and a rough noting which I have been able to retrieve, the index numbers of the costs were as shown in the table below:

ESTIMATED INDEX OF INDUSTRY AVERAGE COST OF A2 & A3 SEGMENT CARS END 2005

Sl. No.	DETAIL	A2 CAR	A3 CAR
1	MATERIAL	100	120
2	LABOUR	100	101
3	EXPENDITURE	100	100
4	DEPRECIATION	100	101
5	TOTAL	100	117

So, if the cost of material was say ₹100 for an A2 segment car, it was ₹120 for an A3 segment car. And because there was little or no difference in the other costs like labour, paint and other consumables, and machine depreciation, in the final analysis, if the total cost of production was ₹100 to roll out the A2 car, it cost only ₹117 to roll out the A3 car, that is, the cost of the A3 car was actually just 17 per cent more than that of the A2 car. A caveat here: Since these averages were derived by comparing informally obtained cost data of three 'manufacturers' that straddled both segments, the figures do run the danger of being broad approximations weighted by sales volumes and also, obviously, remain subject to the speciation of human memory. Moreover, there existed between the three manufacturers, both size and technology differences between their products in the respective segments. Yet, I believe my recollection of the index of cost figures gives a very good idea of the manufacturing economics of the industry. Effectively, therefore, if at the end of 2005 a petrol A2 car cost ₹2 lakh to manufacture, a petrol A3 car would typically have cost less than ₹2.35 lakh to manufacture. (I am deliberately staying away from comparing diesel vehicles of that period, simply because in terms of technology and performance, the HMI offering was generations ahead of what was available in the largest-selling diesel cars in the A2/A3 segments at the time. Any comparison would simply be akin to comparing chalk and cheese.) What do companies typically add on top of this before it reaches the customer? Ask the typical manufacturing guy and this is the answer you will probably get: general administration overheads (the cost of tolerating finance and human resources departments), marketing overheads (the cost of all the fun and games the sales and marketing guys have) and warranty overheads (the cost of all the goof-ups of the design guys and vendors). Though the answer generally remains constant across groups, the 'definition' of each tends to change dramatically.

On top of these overheads, comes the profit margin, and suddenly the ex-factory prices of the A2 and A3 models start looking very different from the relatively small manufacturing cost differential. Add to that the central excise (then payable based on an eyebrow-raising definition of vehicle length and engine displacement) and the state value-added tax (VAT), both levied on an *ad valorem* basis. (The new GST regime effectively continues with that broad definition.) And, it doesn't stop there. After adding logistics costs and dealer margins and then insurance, road tax, registration charges et cetera, the A3 segment car probably ended up costing the final consumer an on-road price that was 70 per cent to 100 per cent higher than that of the A2 segment product. So, there's a lot more to the price differences between products in both segments than justified merely by manufacturing costs.

In a different competitive market environment, the differential may not have been so large. HMI was fortunate to have entered a market where the market leader, MUL, by dint of its near-monopoly position and its exceptional brand pull, could dictate product pricing that enabled, what can be described most charitably as super-normal profits. But then, perhaps, MUL did not believe that anyone could localize to that extent, or create a distribution network and brand salience to take it on. Undoubtedly, matching MUL on the cost structure of the A1 segment cars was near impossible, but the heavy reliance on component imports and the true extent of its localization on both the A2 and A3 segment products and their impact on prices created just the right opening. Through its policies, MUL – even after the huge price reduction on the Maruti Zen after the Santro's entry – had created enough pricing headroom for a highly localized manufacturer to attain at least a break-even pricing in the A2 segment, even at the product launch stage. This is precisely what HMI did. I think it is pertinent to point out that even at the launch stage the pricing of the Santro ensured that the company was not a cash-burn machine, and the profit opportunity created by MUL's pricing policies made the A3 segment decidedly more attractive.

All that HMI needed to do was to penetrate the market and establish visibility and product support across the country with a mass-market A2 segment car, and then rapidly move into the A3 segment with a product boasting globally acceptable technology product to take on the (by then rather dated) MUL product in that category. That it managed to do so despite the entry of TML into the same space at the exact same time is probably more a reflection on TML's product and its marketing strategy than anything else.

In hindsight, I have often wondered how things would have panned out if Ford, GM, Honda or Mitsubishi had followed a similar capital investment and product phasing strategy as HMI did in India. It is not inconceivable that margins both in the A2 and A3 segments would have been significantly constrained right from the start of commercial production, and the consumer in India would have been spoilt for choice and would definitely have got much better value for her money in either segment. As it was, HMI had already raised the technology bar and the products it brought in met global standards of performance and safety. The four biggies named earlier could well have done the same, particularly Ford, which had invested significantly in the creation of a more integrated manufacturing plant than, for instance, the assembly operation of Honda. Similarly, if Mitsubishi had, thanks to its production licensing agreement with HM, focused on bringing the Minica or, even better, the three-box model Y120 into production in India using the manufacturing capabilities of the latter, HMI might definitely not have been able to attain the financial performance that became its hallmark. Then again, would the four global giants have had the knowledge to understand and the humility to treat the Indian consumer as well as HMI had? That to me, ultimately, is the billion-dollar question.

Since my formative years were spent in a company that believed early product-led profitability was a crucial determinant of long-term stable growth, I tried to focus on constantly raising the price bar using product-level interventions in creating the foundation for HMI's consistent profitability. I always recall what Harshad Bhansali, my first boss at TML, and a friend, philosopher and guide, used to say about ensuring a pricing that first created and then reflected brand value: 'Any clown can sell gold at the price of silver. If you're truly smart, show me how to sell gold at Tiffany's prices'. To a great extent, I believe I endeavoured, consciously and unconsciously, to follow this basic principle at HMI too.

The first instance of this approach to pricing was probably witnessed during the introduction of the Santro Euro 2 version in May 1999. Years of dealing with Indian consumers had taught me that consumers tend to consider a company that is able to constantly push its price line higher as reflecting both its own sense of confidence about its product quality and the consumer's acceptance of this perception. This leads to a virtuous cycle of greater consumer acceptance, greater sales, greater profitability, greater investments in product development and quality, and in turn even greater consumer acceptance.

On the other hand, unprincipled discounting can lead to a vicious cycle in exactly the opposite direction. The possibility of the latter being something of a Korean affliction weighed heavily on the retail financial services participants when HMI first approached them for sales support. I recall a long discussion with Dipak Gupta and Gaurang Shah of Kotak Mahindra Bank, during which I sought to assuage their fears that HMI might, like its Korean compatriot, 'do a Cielo' on pricing, leaving them with severely depreciated and consequently non-performing assets on their books. Committing that HMI would most definitely operate a pricing strategy in the mould of TML, I spoke to them at length of how we were committed to constantly refreshing the product to retain consumer interest and keeping the upward pricing stable, thereby ensuring that assets on the books of the retail finance partners would not suffer sudden and unexpected devaluations. But, risking my personal credibility, I did not tell them that all this was really a statement of intent and though we were strategically committed to this approach HMI had not yet finalized clear milestones on product upgrades.

The introduction of the Santro Euro 2 provided me with the first opportunity to show that HMI could walk the talk. Of course, achieving profitability on a per-unit basis at the earliest possible was an imperative that an almost financially stressed operation could never quite forget. When the bill of materials for the upgrade to Euro 2 was compiled, I remember the estimated cost increase for the upgrade being somewhere in the region of ₹1,700 per unit. But I reasoned that pricing it at that level or just above would not give the technology that I was touting as part of an effort to save the planet the kind of cachet it deserved, and therefore the technology itself might not be taken seriously as a differentiator. A significant part of my learning personally came from observing consumer reactions to Intel's famous Pentium chip advertising of that period and I argued internally on the need to price the new technology upgrade appropriately in order to endow it with something of a wow-factor. At this point, we had absolutely no idea just how price sensitive the consumer was, or what she was willing to pay for a technology upgrade that she could not really touch and feel, but I figured on the basis of a quick straw poll among dealers that a 3 per cent increase may just be on par for the course. There was simply not enough time to do any kind of structured market research to establish the pricing fit, because I had already committed in the mass media that the Euro 2 product would be available by 1 June 1999, the day the Supreme Court directives on sales curbs on non-Euro 1 vehicles in Delhi NCR came into effect. Under these circumstances, we just went ahead and put in place a unit sticker price increase of ₹12,000. Of this, an amount of ₹1,000 per unit went towards an increase in the dealer margin because we had promised dealers to up it after having had to go back on our earlier commitments and lowering dealer margins on the day of the Santro's launch. Another ₹4,000 per unit went towards additional excise and sales taxes, leaving the company with a net realization per unit of just over ₹5,000. But, at that price, consumers appeared to be reluctant to switch to environmentally friendly technology. Notwithstanding an enormous amount of coverage in print media combined with high-visibility television debates in which I attempted to reinforce the environmental agenda, the response to the Santro Euro 2 was, at best, lacklustre. It was only after a chance remark on a mass-audience television show where I said that it was not inconceivable that the resale value of non-Euro 2 cars would face a meltdown as their phase-out date came closer, that we began to see some traction in the sales of the new variant.

In Delhi, which seems to be perpetually looking for the next new thing; in Bangalore, which seems to believe that technology is mankind's greatest saviour; and in Calcutta, which has always struck me as a more socially conscious city, the tide was perceptibly shifting. For all the image it portrays of being a modern city, Mumbai trailed far behind in its initial recognition and later acceptance of the new technology. Yet, even among the early adopters, the price hurdle remained a matter of concern. The step up from the normal Euro 1 version was clearly too sharp for the consumers' liking. Conventional logic would have dictated a reduction in the price of the new variant to encourage rapid adoption, but that would have only succeeded in blunting the 'technology' edge that we were hoping would become our big weapon in the fight against MUL. As described earlier, at the dealer showrooms, sales staff were being tutored to bring to the attention of consumers the specific opinions expressed by the Supreme Court about MUL offering higher levels of technology on its exports to Europe than it cared to do in India. By implication, and in sharp contrast, showroom staff pointed out to consumers that HMI did not differentiate between Indian and European consumers and remained firmly committed to moving India out of the dark ages of automotive technology. Then, in one of the first contrarian moves that became a hallmark of HMI, on 21 June 1999 we raised the price of the Euro 1 vehicle models by ₹6,000 – although this was not done across the board. Not wanting to risk a consumer pushback on the more popular variants, the price hike was confined to the lowest variant. Consumers, we thought, would expect a similar hike to follow in the prices of the higher variants and move to the new technology offering.

Much to our relief and amazement, that was precisely what happened. We soon observed that consumers now found the switch to Euro 2 now less daunting in terms of price and sales of the Euro 2 variant suddenly gathered momentum. Needless to say, the effect of this upward shift by consumers on the bottom line of the company was the stuff dreams are made of in the auto industry. In August 1999, HMI became a cash-positive company – a feat yet unequalled by any integrated greenfield automotive manufacturing operation set up without government backing or mandates in a free-market economy anywhere in the world. By January 2000 over 85 per cent of the Santro's sales were of the Euro 2 variant – and the positive effect on the company's financial stability only strengthened us further.

The other example of using product enhancements to drive up prices, and thereby profitability, came in April 2000. HMI tweaked a lower model variant of the Santro by adding on a power steering as a standard fitment at an attractive incremental price. This was made possible by passing on to the consumer a large part of the benefit of the reduced steering component prices that the company got from suppliers due to increased volumes, which in turn enabled localization and a further cost benefit. Simultaneously, some frills on the car were dropped, it was rebranded as the Santro Zip Drive and promoted via a very zippy new commercial. Once again, the sales and profit curves were pushed into even steeper trajectories. Obviously, the larger proportions of what the consumer now forked out accrued to the exchequer and HMI, but as competition and naysayers watched in amazement, power steering – till then considered unnecessary for a 'small' car – became a must-have across all model categories in India.

Continuing with the creeping price-rise approach, HMI very soon found the Cassandras of the financial services sector finally recognizing that the brand would not leave a flood of red ink on their books. Although still quite reluctant, some of the ultra-conservative finance companies of the south too started displaying a semblance of brand neutrality when consumers came to them for auto loans. A critical part of the approach was to closely calibrate wholesale despatches in December with the retail sales at dealerships. The idea was to ensure that dealers ended with negligible or ideally zero stocks of vehicles at the end of every calendar year. Typically, vehicle resale prices are based on the model year – the year of manufacture of the vehicle – and as a result, consumers have generally been averse to buying vehicles manufactured in the latter part of the year – essentially the period of a few weeks after Deepavali to end December, because the fall in resale price would be out of proportion with the use of the car. Conventional sales wisdom therefore seemed to vote in favour of a discount on old model year stocks. I, however, always held the belief that if the consumer was in any case going to benefit from a comparatively higher price on the new model year vehicle at the time of resale, she would not be averse to paying a slightly higher initial price for it, a fact that she needed to be made aware of. In consonance with this, HMI perfected the art of effectively announcing well in advance and then raising prices every January of the new model year cars, thus enabling dealers to clear their previous model year stocks by the end of December every year – thereby automatically ensuring a smooth acceptance of the new, higher price. The first time this happened was in January 2001 – and it set the trend for the rest of industry.

Unfortunately, with some competitors reducing this tactic to the level of the ridiculous by announcing January price increases of merely a few hundred rupees, the efficacy of this approach soon suffered a dilution particularly in the larger markets, with consumers seeing price rise announcements as proverbial cries of 'Wolf!' Yet, given the general inflationary environment in the country, consumers tended to believe that price increases were an inevitable part of existence and, fortunately for the industry, rarely ever did the government or the media subject these claims of cost increases to detailed examination. Estimated indices of four important cost elements: HR (hot rolled) coils, CR (cold rolled) coils, aluminium and the Indian rupee to US dollar exchange rate are presented below. Even in March 2002, when the rupee was at its lowest against the US dollar during the 1998 to 2007 decade, the price of CR coils used for the manufacture of body panels was in rupee terms just 83 per cent of what it was in 1998. Using the exchange rate or material cost increases to justify price hikes was clearly untenable and yet, industry-wide, pre-excise realization probably rose up to 10 per cent during that period. Perhaps there's a lesson hidden in this somewhere – for consumers, the media and the government!

INDICES OF IMPORTANT COST ELEMENTS

YEAR (01/01)	HR COILS	CR COILS	ALU	INR:USD (31/03)
1998	100	100	100	100
1999	97	74	82	108
2000	96	88	113	110
2001	79	76	109	118
2002	69	67	92	124
2003	97	90	93	120
2004	126	119	108	110
2005	190	155	124	110
2006	224	178	160	113
2007	190	155	188	110

Over the years, the auto industry has constantly looked to the government for reductions in levies of all kinds, and various other manner of support whenever faced with market headwinds. Yet, it has on more occasion than one appeared to resort to finely tuned price adjustments just before the Union Budget in order to be able to continue with a higher actual price realization regime, even when excise was lowered, without appearing to defy government attempts to spur demand through tax cuts. HMI generally stayed away from expressing any view in such matters in order not to appear to plough a lonely furrow all the while and make even more frenemies. I recall, for instance, pushing up model year 2001 prices in December 2000, even as the industry was constantly approaching the government to cut excise duties to stimulate consumer demand. This obviously helped bolster the bottom line, particularly with material costs relatively subdued in those days. Much to our relief, there was no official reaction to the move and it appeared that the mandarins of North Block did not take note of the effective cost of CR coils in Indian rupees and its effect on the cost of production, while considering the industry's pleas.

Eventually, if I recall correctly, some other manufacturers followed suit. It soon looked reasonably likely that the excise cuts being sought by the industry would come in the Union Budget, and they did. Industry promptly brought down prices. The price of the largest-selling Santro variant, for instance, fell by almost ₹20,000 in Delhi in the immediate aftermath of the budget as the excise reliefs announced in the budget were passed on to consumers without any delay. But as each industry player tested the waters carefully, the prices unobtrusively crept up again. Within a month or so, HMI first raised prices, initially in the western and southern regions, away from the gaze of Delhi, and another month later in the north too. (Clearly, little has changed. Much the same happened in 2017 after the introduction of the GST. Despite warnings from the government against profiteering, some companies in the industry have done just that!)

I have personally always believed that excise reductions do not create steady growth in the demand for cars; expectations of economic growth and future incomes do. An excise cut has the effect of inducing a certain buyer euphoria as soon as it happens, before sales settle into a long-term trend dictated by economic fundamentals. Contrariwise, an excise hike has an immediate depressing effect on sales primarily because of anticipatory purchases, but even this, eventually smoothens out based on the growth in numbers among the consuming classes, the growth in demand replacement and the simple factor of human greed that calls for a second, third and probably fourth car in the driveway because, ultimately, the excise hike may represent a very small effect in terms of the monthly cost of ownership. If, however, overall economic activity and expectations remain depressed after an excise hike, price corrections will ensure that potential manufacturing sector surpluses get funnelled to the household sector in the form of lower prices, and the parasitical financial services sector too eventually cuts its margins to help bring down the cost of ownership. This would, in turn, act as a marginal demand booster, given the presence of other 'necessary conditions'. The pricing behaviour of the most efficient manufacturer or purveyor of loans would thus have a greater impact on ensuring the attainment of an equilibrium than tinkering with the tax rate would, before economic fundamentals or firm factors move it up or down again. When the government works on the tax levers to spur demand because of the volume of hysteria generated by the least efficient players in an industry, the most efficient end up laughing all the way to the bank. It has always amused me to see that India's auto industry does not quite relish the idea of living by the capitalist credo that only the best ought to survive.

Yet another interesting contrarian move on pricing happened just before the launch of the Santro Xing. By early April 2003 the plant and all the vendor partners were perfectly on schedule to go through with a switch from the earlier variant to the facelift model of the Santro. But the huge dealer stock overhang of the older model was becoming a significant challenge. Conventional wisdom would have meant cutting prices of the existing stock and pushing through a clearance sale in order to clean out the pipeline for the introduction of the facelift version. That, I argued, would have only served to make it more difficult for the price of the new model to be accepted by consumers. Even a consequential two-week bunching up of stocks of the new model at dealerships would have added new grist to the rumours of the consumers' (non)acceptance of the new-look Santro kept constantly churning by the competition. This could then run the danger of becoming a self-fulfilling prophecy because consumers could have got all the wrong signals and actually postponed their purchases or, worse, switched brands. Ultimately, HMI pulled off one more of its famous price feints, and even as it continued to bill out the old model to dealers, it announced that the price of the Santro would be raised by a clearly stated amount on all vehicles to be excised out of the plant from a specific date. The effect was electric. In the days that followed, consumers bought every single one of the old models in stock at dealerships and dealerships sucked up every single unit available in the plant. In the meantime, the switch to the new-look vehicle on the production lines was done exactly on schedule, but excise clearances and despatches of the new-look Santro were obviously held back till we got to the publicly announced date of the price rise.

Throughout an entire fortnight, while the vehicles stood in the stockyard at the plant, HMI's IT systems were completely locked down to prevent file transfers, particularly of JPEG image files, without specific permission. Cameras on mobile phones were fortunately not as ubiquitous and, on the appointed date, with the secrecy befitting a nuclear test, vehicles were loaded onto sealed trucks, scheduled in such a way as to reach every dealership across the country just the night before the launch. The combination of a complete stock out at dealerships for two weeks, the distinct new look of the car by now christened Santro Xing and the advertising push with SRK ensured that the vehicles started selling literally as soon as they were unveiled.

Consumers were clearly taken up with the new look and did not seem to mind the increased price either. On the other hand, consumers who had bought the earlier model just a couple of weeks before were not too peeved at seeing a distinctly different and fresh avatar of the car, because they reasoned that they had after all got what was essentially the same vehicle mechanicals at a much lower price. HMI always managed to ensure consumer acceptance of every single price rise event because it consistently gave consumers the perception of getting a more than proportionately higher value with the higher price, and in that perhaps lay the secret of the success of its pricing strategy in India. In many ways, it was the marketers dream come true. First, the product received a reasonably warm reception at the launch. Then, in just eight months, it was upgraded along with an increase in price and still saw a spurt in volumes. Within the year, it was subject to another upgrade, and despite another price hike witnessed a further boost in sales. Another upgrade and price rise followed within two years, with further strengthening of sales. This set the grounds for a complete makeover, with yet further price hike followed by yet another jump in sales, and so on, for what can only be called a dream run that lasted the best part of a decade. Better-known global brands, often with broadly comparable products, ended up with net price realizations below those attained by HMI, again a distinct first time for Hyundai anywhere in the world.

Operationally speaking, perhaps reflecting its early financial circumstances, HMI always remained focused on ensuring cost-efficiency. In every single area of production, efficiency standards were set, attained and then reset at higher levels. But it was the efforts of the vendor management team that were particularly noteworthy, because they operated in an environment where they had an advisory role at best and no real operational control in practice. So they simply did the best they could. Min Ho Lee and J.B. Lee put together what was essentially a production process upgrading scheme to ensure that vendors met the global cost and quality standards, so critical to HMI's domestic market dominance and planned export push. Under the 100 ppm quality improvement programme, a group of specially trained HMI employees – two Koreans and four Indians – visited every single Tier 1 vendor (who supplied directly to the HMI production line), studied every aspect of their operations and made practical, implementable suggestions ranging from plant layout to production fixture design with the simple objective of reducing rejections to less than 100 ppm produced! By improving production processes, they controlled and often eliminated rejection and rework and thereby lowered the vendors' costs of production. Under the programme, almost half the vendors operated at zero ppm by early 2006 – practically unheard of in India till then – and a significant number attained a level of 50 ppm to 100 ppm. After covering all its 80 Tier 1 vendors under the programme, HMI went on to extend it to over 350 Tier 2 suppliers who were part of the supply chain of the Tier 1 vendors.

These reductions in costs at the vendors', end were largely passed on in terms of lower component prices to HMI, which in turn often passed part of the benefits to consumers, both in the domestic and export markets. The initiatives, for instance, played a crucial role in improving the company's export profitability dramatically.

Focusing on attaining global-quality standards meant that exports from HMI were profitable even as a standalone operation. And this, despite the monopoly pricing of the Chennai Port Trust's wharfage and other fees, which were so high in comparison to similar charges in Japan, Korea or Malaysia that, at times, the port trust earned more on HMI's exports of the Santro to some low-income countries than the company itself did. Of course, the port facilities did not stand comparison with those in any of the countries named. In the initial days of HMI exports, the wharf where cars were loaded was situated so close to the coal jetty that HMI had to move cars from the plant to the port at almost literally the eleventh hour and just in time for the loading to prevent any coal dust from settling on the waxed cars. But the government of India's Incremental Export Promotion Scheme introduced in FY 2004 and the Target Plus Scheme unveiled in the Foreign Trade Policy 2004–2009 came as a welcome boost just at the time when HMI's exports were poised for take-off. One scheme that gave financial benefits equal to 10 per cent of the total incremental exports achieved in FY 2004 over the previous financial year turned out to be an absolute bonanza for HMI, as exports, particularly to Europe, rose sharply. Making things better still was the significant appreciation of the Euro (the currency in which all exports to Europe were initially denominated), against both the Indian rupee (in which the bulk of material, all the manufacturing and labour costs were incurred), and the US dollar (the currency in which imports of some materials were accounted for).

While all these building blocks of profitability came together perfectly, the final icing on the cake was probably provided by the provisions of the memorandum of understanding (MoU) that HMI had signed with the government of Tamil Nadu. The MoU provided that the payment of sales tax collections by the company could be deferred for a period of up to fourteen years, up to a maximum eligibility ceiling defined by the extent of eligible capital investment. For the initial installed capacity of 115,000 cars, 100 per cent of eligible assets, and for the expansion of 115,000 units, 80 per cent of the eligible assets, were considered for defining the deferral amount. By the end of FY 2006, in my recollection, HMI had made fixed asset investments of about ₹2,400 crore after deducting the value of second-hand equipment and preoperative expenses which the MoU did not consider eligible. Against this, thanks to the exceptional showing on the domestic sales front, the company was by then already holding over ₹600 crore of deferred payment tax collections.

Appearing on the balance sheet as unsecured loans, and in spite of the conservative investment practices of HMI, this large cash reserve created a perpetual interest earnings stream, which by the fourteenth year of operations was probably churning out at least ₹200 crore annually as interest earnings. The cumulative interest earnings alone, even by the fiscal year of 2006 had totted up to a tidy sum and in just a few years thence far exceeded the entire original equity investment made in the company by its parent organization, HMC. I have always had an issue with the competitive incentive structures hawked by state bureaucracies to promote investment in their respective states. Beyond encouraging the gold-plating of capex, incentive schemes that are built around the value of capital investments tend to raise capital intensity, sometimes even unjustifiably and, worse still, to my mind, only end up paying for corporate profits and the labour aristocracies of equipment-producing countries, to the detriment of India's poor. I have often wondered whether this is a reflection of the political ideology of the state or the bureaucracy.

But, getting back to the issue of profitability, in the case of HMI it was no accident. HMI had managed to get all the pieces right, starting with the vision to create a foundation based on manufacturing rather than trading and the product strategy that aimed at meeting the needs of a newly emerging class of consumers. The intelligent structuring of state government incentives, the production strategy that constantly innovated in the use of capital equipment to ensure cost efficiency and the vendor strategy that became the perfect amalgam of global technology standards and Indian cost structures came together to ensure a competitive cost of production. And when the company managed to layer on top of this a communication strategy with never-before-seen flourish and a young, focused, well-trained and widespread distribution network, it had put all the necessary elements in place. Then came the pièce de résistance – a pricing strategy that was built on constantly raising the technology bar, thus consistently adding both real and perceived value and creating opportunities to raise product prices consumers willingly accepted. That, ultimately, made HMI the great financial success it became.

8

Staying Stable and Relevant

By early 2004, just over five years after the commencement of commercial production, I believed the foundation of HMI was well and truly in place. It seemed the frenetic pace of life would ease up a bit, and I personally hoped I could move from being a perpetually-in-a-hurry landscape artist to being a less stressed surveyor-of-the-gardens before getting ready for the next burst of explosive growth.

Across the country, masses of technology-oriented, quality-focused, value-seeking consumers looking for convenience of maintenance considered the Hyundai brand their first choice. Without entering the ultimate mass market represented by low-priced products like the Maruti Alto, HMI managed to have in its product line-up a 100,000-units annual volumes grosser. The Santro was clearly an unqualified success. Along with capturing pole position in the domestic market, it went on to become the most exported car from India and a financial blockbuster too. The Accent became a household name both for affordable luxury and for technology leadership, when it became the first mass-market car brand, and only the second car brand in India after MB to offer common-rail diesels.

In fact, with the Accent, Hyundai-branded 'CRDi' practically went on to become a generic name for common rail technology in India – the first, and probably only, such instance in Indian automotive history. The Sonata had succeeded beyond most people's wildest imagination. With looks inspired by the Jaguar, luxurious interiors and American-style soft-ride characteristics, in its first two years it ended up outselling the Honda Accord by a factor of two. Of course, Honda brought its exceptional engine technology to bear on the Indian market, upped its game in the interiors department and successfully wrested back its spot at the top of the pile, only to cede it eventually to the German marquee brand trio of MB, BMW and Audi. The Elantra, a rather accomplished car, ended up a damp squib. I believe this was partially because we chose to listen to consultants and chose to produce a sedan rather than a notchback, partially because of the high-performance 'German technology' promise of the Skoda Octavia, and partially because of a rather uncharacteristic change in pricing strategy pushed by the global-marketing mavens in Korea just ninety minutes before the launch.

We had originally intended a segment-straddling pricing strategy in the hope of drawing interest from potential customers of the Honda City and the Toyota Corolla. Though we had managed in India to significantly narrow the price discount that the Sonata was offered globally in comparison to Honda Accord, in the case of the Elantra, we thought we would reflect the global pricing differentials against Toyota and then start moving it up after six months or so. Unfortunately, however, seeing the Elantra on skid row did not ring as many alarm bells as it ought to have, thanks to continued good showing of the Santro and the Accent.

A few months after that things appeared to start unravelling at HMI. It began with J.I. Kim suddenly being called upon to swap places with B.H. Sung, who appeared not to relish a move from his global marketing role to handling India alone. Of course, India was, after the US, the second-largest individual market for HMC, and probably far more profitable, if not in absolute terms then definitely in terms of ratios.

The change in guard led to the unraveling of a number of strategies and systems that had evolved in response to Indian market realities and the imposition of a somewhat antiquated and antediluvian worldview of strategy. He insisted on implementing it regardless of its impact on both the top line and bottom line of the company. I made my disagreement clear in no uncertain terms, but reluctantly agreed to go along with Sung's approach for at least one quarter. Soon enough, sales were on skid row. Despite a stellar showing in July, sales in both August and September 2004 showed a significant decline over the corresponding months in 2003 and sales in the third quarter of 2004 eventually stayed flat in a year-on-year comparison with the previous year. As stocks in the company's and dealers' storage yard soared to new highs, Sung retreated from his involvement with matters of strategy. But having to get back the lost momentum so close to the end of the year had put us in a rather unenviable position, and that in a market where public perception of constant growth was an imperative in order to ensure it. Then, just as competition had started talking about how the Santro Xing had lost its fizz, we pulled what was probably among the most daring stunts ever in the Indian automotive industry. Using the upcoming festival season as the peg, HMI announced a Harrods-style 'three-day sale' giving customers the chance to buy a Santro at the 1998 introductory price of ₹2.99 lakh. (Very much like the one-week-long 'sale' now given by e-commerce giants, which start at midnight every other month – though with one crucial difference: HMI consistently made profits!)

Though, on the face of it, consumers may well have seen it as HMI having succeeded in turning back the clock on inflation, all that we actually did was to factor in the benefit of the lower rate of excise duty in 2004 as compared to 1998, marginally reduce the pre-excise transaction value by accounting for better overhead absorption, a potential lowering of inventory holding and promotional expenses and tweaking dealer margins. Though the prices of raw material, after going southward continuously from January 1999, had started creeping upwards by mid-2004, the Indian rupee had remained amazingly stable against the US dollar and, but for a spike in 2001 and 2002, had by the end of 2004 essentially gone up to the levels of March 2000. That also gave HMI a substantial cost cushioning and softened the bottom line impact of our lowered price realization.

My experience suggested that Indian consumers, if given a fifteen-day window on an offer, would in any case come to avail of it only on the fifteenth day and in the intervening period would constantly look over their shoulder to see if their neighbours were considering taking up the offer. It's akin to the typical isolation paradox in logic. Of course, by the afternoon of the second day of a long-dated offer there would be a large enough number of busybodies who could be 'persuaded' by the competition to spread a 'pitt gayi' ('It's been thrashed!') verdict about the offer. Even worse, the dealer network typically loses confidence in the scheme and is reluctant to put in the critical extra effort that might just help make the difference between success and failure. Contrariwise, a really small window of opportunity would create, I believed, a sense of urgency and a bringing forward of purchase decisions which might normally have meandered through multiple dealer showroom visits, discussions with family and friends and, unfortunately, been subject to confusion created by finance intermediaries. Taking a cue from the way stock market investors typically rushed with their share purchase applications on the third and last day of an IPO, we decided that the 'special price' offer would be kept open only till midnight of the third day. The element of surprise in the announcement – the time between the decision being taken, the advertisement put out and the opening of the scheme being less than eighteen hours – once again caught the competition flat-footed and, as they scrambled to respond, the trickle of consumers on the first day turned into a veritable flood by the third. By the end of the second day, physical stocks at dealerships had been exhausted and consumers were offered the option of booking their vehicles for delivery at a future date against a token upfront payment and the completion of the finance documentation. In many large cities, showrooms were kept open past midnight on the third day to ensure that every single potential consumer was accounted for. To say the least, the scheme was a stupendous success. Not only did we manage to clear all stocks both at dealerships and at the plant, we had received payments for three months of full production capacity. The huge flood of money into the system enabled us to offer vendors payments before they became due, reaping significant cash discounts in the process. Moreover, interest earned on that amount actively bolstered the 'other income' entry for the year. Thus, 2004 ended on an unprecedented high for HMI. The December sale of the Santro recorded a 140 per cent growth year-on-year, and neither the company nor the dealers were left with a single car in stock.

Yet, even this clawback from the edge of the precipice did not really mend organizational matters and Sung soon resumed second-guessing the overall business strategy and every other aspect of the company's working. Unfortunately, he also appeared to actively contribute to creating strains on the cultural fabric of the organization, and the Indo-Korean cultural balance, built with great effort since the founding of the company, started developing its first cracks. In retrospect, I believe that the trial by fire that the early pioneers, both Indians and Koreans, faced, helped create the microstructure of the alloy that HMI came to represent and endowed it with both strength and sheen. Senior management from among the Korean pioneers had come with substantial global exposure and therefore an appreciation of operating in a different cultural environment. They helped lay down a behavioural pattern for many others who had come directly from Korea and had not been exposed to a genteel culture.

There is no denying that there were intercultural tensions between Indians and Koreans from time to time, and more than a few of the Koreans clearly suffered from delusions about their professional, cultural and racial superiority. They also held unfortunate but sometimes reasonably accurate notions about the poor work ethic of their Indian colleagues, the 'chalta hai' attitude towards timelines and quality of work, and what they perceived as slovenly work habits. Many Indians, on their part, believed that the Koreans, for the most part, were generally simple-minded but devious, boorish, laughingly overrated, over-specialized and unidimensional in their professional knowledge; let alone thinking laterally for solutions, they could barely understand complexities outside their well-circumscribed area of training. Both positions had elements of truth, but for those of us in the middle, both Indians and Koreans, responsible for building and managing the fighting machine, it often meant a tightrope walk and a new-found competence in the art of smoothening out ruffled feathers. But the senior-most Korean leadership among the pioneers comprising people like Y.S. Kim, J.D. Bae, Min Ho Lee, Moon Hee Lee, and others like E.H. Jin, S.J. Hwang, J.B. Lee, S.P. Kwon, Yong Kim, Y.K. Koo, Y.J. Ahn and a few others, had worked closely with Indians in the management and across levels in the organization, and helped ensure a strong dual-culture foundation and an ethos based on mutual self-respect in HMI.

Though I had a little more than a year to complete my second contract term as president of the company, the circumstances had made me rather sceptical about a continued future with Hyundai that could be professionally satisfying. It was then that in a move that was widely rumoured about, but never actually reported, I was invited to lead a leveraged buyout (LBO) team to take over the operations of Fiat in India. Fiat ultimately went ahead and tied up with TML in the hope of scripting a fairy-tale revival, despite the pitifully obvious inherent contradictions. The partnership brought little succour or deliverance for the Italian giant, and ultimately reduced a company with an exceptional range of global best vehicle models to becoming better known for the supply of powertrains to MUL and TML. Reminding me of all the discussions on product, production and market strategy that the LBO discussions entailed is a particularly exquisite gift from Fiat Chrysler's global CEO Sergio Marchionne – a sterling silver, scale replica of a 1902 vintage Fiat model, and an amazing model of the Grand Punto made using ultrasonic consolidation and laminated modelling technologies that his predecessor Herbert Demel had earlier given me. To this day, both continue to occupy pride of place on the mantle in my study.

Sung was recalled to Korea and soon thereafter left the group as well. His replacement, S.S. Yang, came and left India in less time than many expatriates take to unpack the containers of their household belongings and was replaced by H.S. Lheem at the end of 2005.

It had also become clear by then that an 'India listing' of HMI would not happen, since India's bureaucracy appeared more than willing to dilute provisions regarding the listing of the equity of multinationals operating in the country. As far as the Indian bureaucracy was concerned, it seemed that they were quite all right with multinationals taking advantage of subsidies that the Indian taxpayer paid for and profiting immensely from Indian operations, but did not believe it was necessary for those multinationals to share the benefits of their growth with their Indian employees or India's investing public.

It has always amused me to see Indian bureaucrats falling over each other to get multinational investments into their respective states without, I believe, truly understanding or appreciating the cost-benefit ratio of such investments. Multinational investments that flow into national markets are not governed by altruism and move to the location that provides an option for market expansion and a relatively larger profit opportunity. Perhaps a compulsory reading of the theoretical underpinnings of imperialism may at least give India's bureaucrats a more nuanced understanding of the true nature of global capital, even though the class character of the political structure and its approach to shaping India's industrial structure and its ownership or, worse, their own personal ideologies, may continue to define national policy towards foreign direct investment. Topping my personal list of all that we can learn from China is the exceptional monitoring and effective control that the state exercises to ensure the accrual of benefits to the nation in terms of technology and profits, as opposed to those accruing to foreign investors. Though I must add that such superintendence and sharing need not necessarily imply a lack of recognition of intellectual property rights.

The arrival of Lheem signalled clearly to me that, quite in contrast to the globalizing vision of the Chung family and far removed from the likes of B.J. Park or N.M. Kim, or Dr H.S. Lee and others of an earlier period, the entrenched bureaucracy at Hyundai's headquarters appeared to still live in a 'them and us' mindset, and would be more than reluctant to allow a non-Korean, irrespective of his contribution to building the company or de facto position, to take on de jure leadership of the organization too. I must admit, though, that I don't think xenophobia among corporate executives is a particularly Korean affliction. I have often noticed that, with the exception of American corporations and Indian companies, most other multinationals whether of European or Asian origin appear to put nationality ahead of professional competence in deciding leadership positions, whether in the outposts of the empire or at home. I, therefore, often tell youngsters who approach me for advice on joining a company to first check if the language of communication to and at the head office are in English, because only then could they expect to have their performances fairly represented in higher company fora and be appropriately rewarded.

Literally within days, I saw my worst fears on a systematic destruction of the cultural foundations of HMI coming true. With a few exceptions, none of the senior Korean management team in HMI at the time had really seen or experienced the difficulties in building an organization from being an unknown pariah to becoming an accepted leader of the industry. There were clear indications of a general lowering of standards of civility within the organization.

Realizing by early 2006 that working alongside such negatively oriented people, and unfortunately professionally incompetent newcomers, could prove to be rather disagreeable, I clearly indicated my thoughts to two people whom I had come to rely most on – T.M. Kumar and V.D. Bhasin. On 28 March 2006, just days after HMI celebrated the production of its millionth vehicle, I wrote to Chairman M.K. Chung and Vice Chairman Eui Sun Chung (E.S. Chung) thanking them for all the opportunities the company had provided for my professional growth, the faith they had reposed in me and my desire to chase my dreams. The next day I told Lheem that I did not wish to go through with the new contract on offer, met possibly every employee at the plant and the marketing headquarters over the next couple of days, continued with a shoot of a television programme with Siddharth Patankar on NDTV that had commenced a few days earlier, and gave up all my executive responsibilities at HMI at the end of the financial year. Again, I had managed to surprise people – both by my act and its timing. I have always believed it is best to leave when people ask why, rather than when they start asking why not. I did, of course, continue for a short time, an involvement with the Hyundai Trust – a corporate social responsibility initiative that J.I. Kim, T.M. Kumar and I had helped conceptualize and bring to life, till its first disbursal in keeping with its aim to help in the preservation of India's heritage – a contribution towards rebuilding the magnificent, then 127-year-old Senate House of Madras University.

Since then I have had little official contact with HMI, and a purely personal relationship with a few of my Korean and Indian colleagues, including many among the latter group who left the organization to go across the automotive industry, and a few dealer and vendor partners, whom I had in any case known even before my days at HMI. The distance that I maintained, I believe, helped to give me a perspective on the company from the outside.

I have often been asked what helped HMI succeed where many foreign brands have struggled. I think much of the reason for failure often lies at the doorstep of the companies themselves. Many of them have entered India with unfortunate condescension and a baggage of arrogance. I have not hesitated to refer to this publicly on more than one occasion as being indicative of the worst form of cultural imperialism, which has manifested itself in various ways from badly configuring the product, to inappropriate production strategies and investments, to poor communication and an inability, even unwillingness, to build a relationship of equality and mutual respect with the Indian workforce and management personnel.

However, I must add that I can think of only one company that has epitomized many of these characteristics, and yet succeeded even as it treated the Indian consumer with scarcely disguised disdain. Easily identified, it began operations in India in the late 1990s with an assembly plant and equipment which it had scrapped a few years earlier from a nearby country and relocated to India. It then went on to introduce a vehicle which it considered was not good enough for other developing markets but clearly by implication was 'good enough' for Indians, with technology that probably belonged to the early 1980s. It showed little evidence of creating an ecosystem of real industrialization and made a big deal of exporting components and aggregates from India. The global heavyweight continued in that vein when it launched an expensive sedan with probably lower safety standards or quality of interiors for India than the taxis it sold in Dubai, then kept to the same track when it launched a hatchback with interiors and performance that have probably been the worst in class. Finally, it topped it all up with a distribution network that in many parts of the country was often considered a byword for profiteering and anti-consumer behaviour. Yet, its amazing brand power and relevance in India, particularly for the commercial use of one single product in its range, has managed to keep the company growing steadily with exceptional profitability on the back of what in international terms can only be considered enviable pricing power.

HMI never had that kind of brand power, and yet in most of the segments it competed in it has managed to come up a clear winner in terms of product aesthetics, build-quality, product performance, customer support, pricing power and sales volumes, because it has consistently treated India's consumers and their money with the same respect that it treats consumers in the US or China or Europe – and without exception has brought to Indian driveways the same product that it has sold globally.

The other thing that marked out HMI was that, quite unlike many other multinationals, HMI learned to live with constraints imposed by the national business environment and even policy flip-flops, without seeking any change in regulations that impacted either the operations or the products and studiously avoided wasting time trying to influence the environment. When the courts pushed the Indian auto industry, kicking and screaming, to higher levels of emission compliance, HMI's products had already moved well beyond the court-mandated emission norms. When diesel pricing became an advantage for one manufacturer's products, instead of petitioning the government for fuel-pricing parity HMI simply went ahead and brought global standards in diesel technology to the country. When the government substantially increased benefits for exports, HMI redoubled its efforts on the export front, entered Western Europe, and met all its obligations under the Export Promotion Capital Goods (EPCG) license scheme in less than half the number of years mandated by the government and committed by the company. Almost as a matter of policy, HMI preferred to stay away from SIAM's constant advocacy efforts with government and yet consistently supported the majority view that emanated at the association. Even when a group of multinationals led by GM and MB pushed very hard to form a parallel association of 'foreign' manufacturers in 1998, HMI preferred throwing in its lot with the 'Indian' manufacturers because of the complete congruence of interests with the latter that arose from significant capital investments both in-house and through the supply chain. Once HMI indicated its stand, the whole breakaway idea came a cropper.

Only once really did HMI take a stand at complete variance with the rest of the industry. In 2004, as one industry leader after the other congratulated the government on the Indo–Thai Free Trade Agreement (FTA), HMI raised a lone voice of dissent objecting loudly and publicly to the impact it would have on indigenous manufacturing. The FTA seemed almost tailor-made for the Japanese auto majors (and other Japanese companies in consumer electronics and white-goods assembly businesses) and because of what appeared careless construct it would have penalized indigenous manufacturing in India. I recall meeting with Arun Jaitley, then India's union minister for commerce, in his office, without the crutch of SIAM, and explaining to him with detailed financial workings that with the then prevalent tariffs on imported steel raw material and the tariff treatment for steel components proposed under the FTA, it would become more profitable for HMI to divest in India – actually shut down its entire decoiling, blanking, press and some weld lines, a total investment of over US $150 million in those days – get rid of more than 800 workers in India, move those operations to Thailand and import components to meet the vehicle production requirements of the plant in India, and be more profitable in the process. His speed of administrative response fully matched his well-known and documented speed of understanding and recognizing the seriousness of the issue and, literally within days, effectively did away with the perverse tariff regime that penalized value addition in India.

As the components industry also added its voice to the protest, the FTA was recast with significant safeguards. Despite that, subsequent studies have clearly shown just how ill-conceived the Indo–Thai FTA was. I can't say HMI made many friends in Udyog Bhavan due to this very visible and voluble effort in calling for the government's attention. A personal friend in the bureaucracy laughingly called me an 'anarchist in an Armani' for a rather straight-talking interview I had given to the *Business Standard* newspaper to put forward my point of view. A few weeks later, when the minister was in South Korea on an official visit, a scheduled visit to the HMC plant in Ulsan, planned much in advance, was cancelled by ministry officials literally at the very last minute to show their 'displeasure'. In their infinite wisdom, they believed it was more appropriate for the minister to visit GM's Daewoo plant operations in Busan, which they ensured he did. This, despite HMI's investment in India being the largest among Korean companies, the company already being India's largest non-primary manufactured-goods exporter and one of the very few organizations in the country that had met its EPCG obligations much ahead of schedule. Despite its stellar overall performance, productionizing the latest global automotive technology in India and an export performance with no parallels, HMI never got invited by either the heavy industry or the commerce ministry to consult in their perspective-planning exercises. Yet, thanks to India's consumers, the company continued to thrive.

The other interesting thing about HMI that contributed greatly to its performance in those days was the speed of its decision-making. It was perhaps one of the only multinationals where the country head reported, not through a Singapore- or Hong Kong-based regional office with little understanding of and even lesser commitment to India to another head office functionary, but directly to the global CEO. What it ensured was that, if and when an intervention from the apex of the organization was required, it was literally a presentation and phone call away and seldom took more than twenty-four hours. A process of quarterly, half-yearly and annual reviews at Seoul never lost sight of the fact that India was a market of great strategic importance to the company. Every division of the global company – research and development, production engineering, vendor development or finance – provided near-instant support in line with the vision of the chairman.

One particular incident stands out in my memory. In 2002, armed with a carte blanche from Chairman M.K. Chung to pick the most appropriate products being developed at the research and development facilities in Namyang for productionizing in India to further speed up growth, I recall picking the Accent – with a common rail diesel engine – then under development. The drive on the test track, along with four dealers from India who had accompanied Y.S. Kim and me only served to further strengthen my belief in the product. A meeting with the top brass in research and development, to discuss the choice started with a long list of technical reasons on why it could not be done – gummy fuel in India, high sulphur content, rampant adulteration – and then ended inside of two hours with a detailed schedule of activities required to make it possible simply because that was the strategic need of the organization and it had the chairman's nod of approval. It was the success of the Accent CRDi model that contributed largely to convincing world automotive technology behemoth Bosch that India was ripe for higher levels of fuel-injection technology, and the German giant started producing common rail systems in India much before any other OEMs had the guts to move in that direction. (The introduction also made 'CRDi' a generic name for common rail systems in India.) This entrepreneurial touch pervaded all sections of the top management of the company and was clearly communicated down the ranks, thus making for probably the fastest-acting fighting machine in the global automotive world. Its 'need for speed' remained among its most potent weapons.

The other obvious source of HMI's strength lay in the conscious and consistent fostering of a culture of caring for its employees. Almost at the inception, Y.S. Kim had got G.S. Ramesh to work closely with senior Korean and Indian production and administration management members to create a Works Committee structure as a redressal mechanism for workers' concerns, an indirect form of an internal workers' group, though not quite a union. Later, J.I. Kim gave this approach both continuity and further guidance. The seven committee members, elected once every two years from among the shop-floor workforce, were given the responsibility of understanding the needs of the workers and constantly communicating with production management. I still fondly recall the long, sometimes contentious but always positive, discussions with the Works Committee. Even seemingly intractable issues were invariably addressed in a manner that focused on finding a solution. Through a process of training and skills enhancement, Ramesh and his team had ensured that the committee members were trained to understand labour regulation, new productivity processes, read balance sheets and company reports, make presentations and meet with the management on a regular basis to help build a strong foundation of mutual trust based on continuous two-way communication.

In a bid to foster a greater sense of camaraderie, even the senior-most members of the management worked on the shop-floor once a month for a couple of hours at a designated production station, which also changed every couple of months. Though we often joked about the extra cost implications of the exercise, during which units per hour (UPH), the standard productivity measure, invariably fell and incidence of rework (to maintain quality standards) invariably rose, the programme helped foster a far greater sense of belonging across ranks than any other activity that we undertook.

The ensuing transparency and sense of unity brought in its wake the 'Hyundian' spirit and fostered a workplace culture that ensured a long and lasting period of growth in productivity and the workers' incomes, a steady improvement in the quality of the workers' lives – one that remained generally free from strife and discontent. I can't honestly claim there was no friction between Indian and Korean cultures in the organization, but the senior management, albeit with a few glaring exceptions, had generally contributed to the creation of a composite culture. Though HMI was considered rather different from other Korean operations in India, I doubt if even in those days it would have ever placed anywhere in a list of '100 Best Places To Work'. I don't believe any of the Indians in the company were honestly happy with the work-life balance, but the sheer excitement and adrenaline high of continuous growth was a major compensation. HMI served as an exceptional training ground, so much so that even today when 'Hyundians' of those days meet they reminisce fondly of the time they spent in the company in its initial years.

The other major differentiator that helped build HMI was its external face, the face that the consumer invariably saw and interacted with – the dealership network. It managed to instil among its dealer partners a strong sense of commitment to the consumer and consistent ethical dealing by practising with dealer partners the same standards of behaviour and conduct that it preached for them to uphold in their dealings with consumers. I recall an incident in the very early days after the launch of the Santro, when Y.K. Koo, then regional manager and now managing director of HMI, stopped his car on a lonely Delhi street and waited with a car owner whose Santro had burst a tyre till the emergency repair service vehicle from the closest dealership reached the spot and set things right. On that day, HMI won not just the heart of its consumer but also, when the word went around, the respect of every single dealer partner, who then made customer care the abiding religion of their organizations. HMI successfully created and fostered a culture based on complete transparency, ethical dealings, trust and mutual respect for its dealer partners. This, then, provided the foundation for what the company has grown into over the years.

Not all dealers are alike and keeping some of them in line often required a mixture of tact, care and just old-fashioned firmness. One effort still brings a smile. Mildly frustrated about repeated complaints from consumers in Delhi that the front office staff of a particular dealer was less than helpful, we installed a consumer hotline in all Hyundai showrooms in Delhi, with a large sign exhorting customers to just pick up the phone and speak to me if they had any complaints or suggestions. Needless to say, even the act of the customer walking towards the phone, was enough to get the entire dealer organization to be at its attentive best!

Of course, HMI had its share – albeit very small – of unscrupulous dealerships. But swift corrective action taken to rid the network of such elements ensured a near-zero repetition. One particularly galling case involved a dealer using a Euro 2 sticker on a non-Euro 2 car in order to charge consumers a higher price. An attentive customer, who noticed the difference in the sequencing of the vehicle number, sought a clarification on the issue on a Friday afternoon. By the next afternoon, the audit was complete, supplies suspended and accounts frozen. By the third working day thereafter the dealership agreement was terminated. Since that example was set, no other dealership even considered any such deviant behaviour. That was the bedrock of the dealer–principal relationship – complete trust, absolute commitment and resolute action.

Companies are living organisms that constantly attempt to grow and sometimes mutate into a form that can be indistinguishable from the original. But growth and mutation also have the potential to bring in their wake cancerous cells and malignant growth nodes that attack the human elements and relations that the organization is built on – be it with employees or dealer partners – and tend to have an impact on the very foundations of the company that is initially invisible, yet deleterious in the long term. If the organization manages well and institutionalizes the creation of antibodies within itself to tackle such cells and malignant nodes, it can ensure consistent and healthy growth. That process of institutionalizing is essentially the culture that binds the organization.

Even as HMI cranked up its growth after the first million vehicles, it appeared from the outside to be allowing the build-up of more than its fair share of such malignant nodes. Since I had no official interaction with HMI after my departure, much of what I write of the period after April 2006 is not first-hand and is based on what I have learnt from information available in the public domain and, sometimes, but very rarely, from impeccable sources, generally from within the company, more by accident than design. Unfortunately, it appears the first problems started from within what was the one of the most envied parts of the foundation – the relations with employees. The consistent rise in workers' salaries meant that over 60 per cent of HMI's workforce eventually came to own their homes. At a certain stage, technicians' salaries were marginally higher than in MUL, but a combination of a large number of trade apprentices in the workforce and the outsourcing of low-skill and unskilled jobs had helped to keep overall costs production manpower related costs under some semblance of control. The salary levels at HMI had already caused a matching rise in the salary levels in the ancillary units in the vicinity of the plant, and a spread effect was becoming an uncomfortable reality among the older, more established players in the auto component sector in Chennai, who were never really known for their liberal wage structures. Meanwhile, the obvious success of the Hyundai brand in the marketplace, the resultant soaring profitability, and the constant inflow of news on militant trade unionism and HMC's wage settlements in Korea, only served to raise the expectations of HMI's workforce and harden attitudes among a hitherto reasonable and amiable group of people.

It was in this atmosphere that the Hyundai Motor India Employees Union (HMIEU) was formed in 2007 with a claimed membership of over 1,000 workers – an apparent majority of the then official worker count of 1,700 – with an affiliation to Centre of Indian Trade Unions (CITU). It was born with an avowed programme to push for a substantial increase in wage and, as the quality of communication management consistently deteriorated, indulged in intimidating postures and tactics. The management on its part seemed to believe, probably rightly, that a majority of the workers were in favour of a peaceful working environment and that the HMIEU was a minority that was elbowing for greater negotiating power. It argued that the Works Committee, whose representatives were elected by the workers, was competently representing the workers' viewpoint in the wage negotiations. But, given that there was no ballot record to prove the management's contention or otherwise, that stance appeared to lead to something of a flashpoint. Sporadic incidents of indiscipline by young hotheads soon followed, and the generally cordial relations between management and the workforce at HMI saw its first signs of real stress.

The then widely reported and very unfortunate breakdown of communication with the workforce was probably compounded by a widely alleged systematic marginalizing of the Indian plant-level management, deliberately keeping them completely out of the loop on all matters. It led to G.S. Ramesh, who probably could not brook the changes any longer, to leave HMI. Other talented and highly motivated individuals in key management positions in marketing, sales, service, vendor development and production had started leaving the company even earlier. Buoyed by the continuous strong showing of the Hyundai brand in the marketplace, and in the belief that such talent was completely fungible, the company appeared oblivious to the strains on a culture that had been assiduously created and nurtured. When a hasty and precipitate action of dismissing one worker for 'misconduct' was apparently applauded and effusively praised in a meeting in Korea, where it had apparently been presented and perceived as an effort at maintaining workplace discipline, it seemingly ended up as a veritable license for more such ill-conceived action – probably in search of more plaudits. What was probably carefully papered over in reports to the parent company were the existing and emerging fault lines in the cultural foundations of the company.

The company's generally well-regarded culture was eventually restored when Han Woo Park (H.W. Park), a seven-year veteran of HMI, took over in 2009. He represented a non-partisan and truly international mindset in the mould of Y.S. Kim and J.I. Kim, was widely seen to have helped steady the ship and bring back basic equality between Indians and Koreans, which the company was known for in its early years. On Park's watch, attendance went up from an average of 88 per cent to 96 per cent and quality measurements were also included into the calculation of work and incentives. But for a fabric that had constantly suffered attacks of varying intensity, and visibly frayed, even rent asunder, to be brought back to original condition, even at the hands of the most expert darner, is a tough ask. The trend initiated by H.W. Park has appeared broadly to continue since. The process of rebuilding the internal culture of workforce relations, particularly at the HMI production facilities has, according to observers, remained broadly on track.

In that, probably, lies a lesson for other multinationals that are looking to build their businesses in India in the long term. Even if they are convinced that they ought never to hand over leadership of the Indian organization to anyone but one of their own nationality, it would help to ensure that that leadership has a reasonably long grounding in the Indian affiliate organization and an appreciation of the culture in which it operates. Anyone merely parachuting onto the top position of a well-oiled machine, more often than not with a desire to leave their imprint on the organization for future generations to laud, often only ends up creating a mess that can take years to clean up. If the organization and the brand have by then established themselves, and the market continues to display a relatively robust trend line of growth, some of this negative impact of 'paratroopers' can be absorbed by the organization. But with yet-to-be-established brands, this can only lead to a vicious cycle of de-growth and organizational decay.

Worse than constantly air-dropping leadership from the parent organization, can be a constant infusion at the middle and senior levels of Indian executives with debatable professional ability or personal commitment to build on and take forward a culture built on competence and integrity. If such infusions take place in externally facing roles, the long-term damage could be even more serious.

If, for instance, this coincides with a strategic resolve by the company to significantly expand its distribution network, the damage gains a dangerous momentum. Appointments of dealership or authorized service centres, become the starting point of the rot. In a highly competitive and fragmented market, when a new entrant into the dealership business invests at current rates on infrastructure but finds consumer loyalty with the incumbent dealer in the territory unshakeable, the first place to cut corners in order to improve profitability is invariably the workshop. A new entrant then starts by replacing components, even when not required in customers' vehicles that come in for service, or do not change lubricants when due, and so on, thus creating the first elements of customer disaffection for the brand. Unfortunately, with little active superintendence from the company, the scourge spreads and incumbent dealerships' workshops often end up resorting to similar anti-consumer behaviour. (My 82-year-old mother, whose car is probably used for not more than 3,000 kilometres every year, is constantly harassed by the service staff of the dealership she sends her car to, and resultantly ends up getting it serviced, with an oil change too – every six months – just because the dealer employees are constantly pushed to raise service revenues!) When that is still not enough to ensure adequate returns from operations, new entrants are helpfully provided with sales incentives tied to extended periods of soft target achievement at a small fraction of the incumbents' target for the same marketplace. When even such methods are unable to improve the performance of a new entrants to the level that justifies the appointment and so on, other forms of coercion of the incumbents including territory realignments of the original incumbents are resorted to.

In the face of blatantly unethical operating practices, the company may lose incumbent dealers who would have individually contributed more to building the brand than those currently in positions of authority in the company. Worse, the rot may spread like a cancer. Others might explore legal remedies and end up simply dragging the company to court, or getting dragged there for making their views known publicly. Every one of these eventualities will result in a long-term impact on the brand itself, particularly if the matter gets a mention in the media. Obviously, the negative impact of all this can be substantially controlled, and may not affect the company's immediate sales fortunes if it manages to keep its product portfolio fresh and inviting. Expanding product offerings into newer price, size and user segments can keep the profitability pot boiling and the overall sales-volume meter ticking along just fine. The company may even show market-share improvements over a period of time. But with an alienation of the distribution channels, the arrival of a consumer-focused and ethical competitor could lead to a tectonic plate shift of a magnitude that can leave any brand or company, however strong its position, in complete disarray, because every successful brand has a challenger always waiting in the wings to snatch away the leadership position.

The other big area of focus for any company aiming to grow in India should be its absolute commitment to maintaining the highest levels of transparency and ethical conduct on par with what it would claim and practice in the developed markets of the West. Using Indian operations to meet the requirements of the parent company's operations off-the-balance-sheet, for instance, cannot be sustained in the long term as India's standards of corporate financial reporting and official attains the standards of developed Western economies. Cases where multinationals have used their compatriots allegedly linked to trade-union office-bearers at the parent company or even politicians to handle tasks like scrap trading, for instance, at their Indian affiliates have already raised official eyebrows in India, and could impact not just the affiliates' relations with their own employees' union, but also the government's perceptions of the organization as a good corporate citizen. With India's free media and a very alive social media community, that could well become the start of a precipitous slide in the affection of Indian consumers as well.

And yet, since India remains a market with a significant – some may even say 'perpetual' – future potential, global companies will continue to attempt, and strive, to build an Indian business of a respectable size and hopefully profitability. But the challenges they face will be many and multi-hued. India will never be a market for the faint-hearted.

So, is it possible for just anyone to 'do a Santro' all over again? My unequivocal answer to that is: Yes!

Without doubt, the methods of yesterday may not remain relevant tomorrow. But I would hasten to add that the building blocks for success remain unaltered: An organization with the humility to listen; the commitment to treat Indian consumers on par with global consumers in terms of product technology and quality; the long-range vision to invest in creating true capability in India without gold-plating investments; a strong emphasis on ethical conduct with complete transparency towards all stakeholders, be they consumers, dealer partners, vendor partners or the government; a leadership team with both professional and personal credibility – and, of course, a little bit of luck!

It sure worked for the Santro!

Acknowledgements

A large number of people who contributed to making the Santro and, subsequently, HMI into what it eventually became also enabled this book. They deserve more gratitude than words can express.

India's consumers, who provided the unstinting support that enabled the Santro to grow into the proverbial swan.

The first batch of Koreans from Hyundai who came to an alien land with beastly weather, and dedicated themselves to the task at hand with an effort rarely witnessed.

The pioneering Indians who came on board before 1998, when Hyundai was still an unknown entity outside automobile industry circles.

Innumerable early-stage employees at HMI, both Indian and Korean, who came in after the early edifice was in place.

The dealer partners who invested their faith and money to help take the dream forward.

Shah Rukh Khan and Saatchi & Saatchi, who joined forces in the effort to introduce the company to India – and get Indians to love it.

The Indian media – print and electronic, in English and every Indian language – which listened to the heartbeats of a young company, recognized it for its sincerity and amplified it to the world.

Friends in the world of banking whose support at crucial times made the difference between soar and sink…

A few of these wonderful people have been named in the book, but the list is merely indicative and by no means exhaustive or complete; a non-mention is merely a matter of the inadequacy of the story-teller's memory.

A special word of appreciation for Team Hachette India, who worked to bring this book to life, and to those who read the early 'uncensored' version of the book and made so many valuable comments to help get it right.

Most of all, thanks to my family – who gave away so much of what rightfully belonged to them as I focussed my time and energy on my work, and encouraged and supported me as I chased my dreams – and to my parents who taught me to dream in the first place.